AF321669

ETHICS UNDER FIRE

PROFESSOR TOM FRAME joined the Navy in 1979 and after service at sea and ashore for 15 years, he resigned to complete his training for the Anglican priesthood. He was ordained in 1993 and served as Anglican Bishop to the Australian Defence Force from 2001 to 2007. He is presently Director of the Public Leadership Research Group at UNSW Canberra. He is the author or co-author of 35 books on a range of topics including the ethics of armed conflict. His published titles include *HMAS Sydney: Loss and Controversy*; *Stromlo: An Australian Observatory*; *The Life and Death of Harold Holt*; *Evolution in the Antipodes: Charles Darwin and Australia* and *On Ops: Lessons and Challenges for the Australian Army since East Timor* (co-edited with Albert Palazzo).

DOCTOR ALBERT PALAZZO has written extensively on Australian military history and contemporary military history. His major works include *The Australian Army: A History of its Organisation, 1901–2001*; *Moltke to bin Laden: The Relevance of Doctrine in the Contemporary Military Environment* and *The Future of War Debate in Australia*. His recent research has focused on the effects of resource limits and climate change on the future character of war. He is co-editor, with Tom Frame, of *On Ops: Lessons and Challenges for the Australian Army since East Timor*.

ETHICS UNDER FIRE
CHALLENGES FOR THE AUSTRALIAN ARMY

EDITED BY TOM FRAME & ALBERT PALAZZO

UNSW PRESS

A UNSW Press book

Published by
NewSouth Publishing
University of New South Wales Press Ltd
University of New South Wales
Sydney NSW 2052
AUSTRALIA
newsouthpublishing.com

© Tom Frame and Albert Palazzo 2017
First published 2017

10 9 8 7 6 5 4 3 2 1

This book is copyright. While copyright of the work as a whole is vested in Tom Frame and Albert Palazzo, copyright of individual chapters is retained by the chapter authors. Apart from any fair dealing for the purpose of private study, research, criticism or review, as permitted under the *Copyright Act*, no part of this book may be reproduced by any process without written permission. Inquiries should be addressed to the publisher.

National Library of Australia
Cataloguing-in-Publication entry

Title: Ethics Under Fire: Challenges for the Australian Army / editors: Tom Frame; Albert Palazzo.

ISBN: 9781742235493 (paperback)
          9781742242859 (ebook)
          9781742248332 (ePDF)
Series: ACSACS Series ; 5.
Notes: Includes bibliographical references and index.
Subjects: Military ethics–Australia.
          Combat–Moral and ethical aspects–Australia.
          Military discipline–Moral and ethical aspects.
          Australia–Military policy.
Other Creators/Contributors:
          Frame, T. R. (Thomas R.), 1962– editor.
          Palazzo, A.P. (Albert P.), 1957– editor.

Design Josephine Pajor-Markus
Cover image Afghan children run to greet Australian soldiers from the Provincial Reconstruction Team on a visit to the Tarin Kot Prison Facility building site. Photograph by Sergeant Neil Ruskin. Commonwealth of Australia, Defence Image Library.

All reasonable efforts were taken to obtain permission to use copyright material reproduced in this book, but in some cases copyright could not be traced. The editors welcome information in this regard.

CONTENTS

ACSACS SERIES

This book is part of a series produced by the Australian Centre for the Study of Armed Conflict and Society (ACSACS) – a UNSW Canberra Research Centre at the Australian Defence Force Academy (ADFA). ACSACS seeks to become the pre-eminent Australian venue for assessing the past, present and likely future impact of armed conflict on institutions and individuals, with the aim of enhancing public policy and raising community awareness through multi-disciplinary scholarship of the kind this series of books embodies.

Established in 2012, ACSACS utilises the strength of academic research conducted at UNSW Canberra and draws on the university's close and continuing relationship with Defence that began in 1967. In bringing together acknowledged experts in diverse fields of study, the centre hopes to produce creative solutions to a variety of problems, whether questions of history or challenges in policy.

ACSACS also serves as a significant focal point for academic activity prompted by the Centenary of the Great War (2014–18), the 75th anniversary of the Second World War (2014–20), the 50th anniversary of Australia's involvement in the Vietnam Conflict (2015–22) and the 25th anniversary of the first Gulf War (2015–16). ACSACS is well placed to interpret these stories of valour for the thousands of local commemorations being planned across the nation. With its hugely significant database of

1st AIF personnel and computer-assisted analysis of Australian Task Force Vietnam operations, the centre's resources are indispensable tools for those researching Australia's war effort.

The titles published within the ACSACS series will engage both specialist and general audiences with the expectation that individual titles will become standard reference works or textbooks for undergraduate and graduate teaching at UNSW. The subjects reflect the centre's principal areas of interest: the Australian experience of military operations and armed conflict with a particular focus on history, ethics and economics.

The centre's website is: <www.acsacs.unsw.adfa.edu.au> and its staff can be contacted at acsacs@adfa.edu.au.

Previous titles

Moral Injury: Unseen Wounds in an Age of Barbarism, 2015
Anzac Day: Then & Now, 2016
On Ops: Lessons and Challenges for the Australian Army since East Timor, 2016
The Long Road: Australia's Train, Advise and Assist Missions, 2017
Charles Bean: Man, myth, legacy, 2017

CONTRIBUTORS

Dr Deane-Peter Baker came to Canberra from Annapolis, Maryland, where he was an Assistant Professor of Ethics in the Department of Leadership, Ethics and Law at the United States Naval Academy. A specialist in both the ethics of armed conflict and military strategy, Dr Baker's research straddles philosophy, ethics and security studies. He formerly served in the armed forces of Britain and South Africa, and has held visiting fellowships at the Triangle Institute for Security Studies in North Carolina and the Strategic Studies Institute of the US Army War College. Dr Baker created the world's first Massive Open Online Course on the topic of Military Ethics, which launched in February 2016 on the FutureLearn platform.

Dr Matthew Beard is a moral philosopher with a PhD in military ethics. He is currently working at The Ethics Centre in Sydney and is an Adjunct Lecturer at UNSW Canberra. He has published a number of papers and books on a variety of topics including moral injury and post-traumatic stress disorder, cyber-war, torture and medical ethics in journals such as the *Journal of Military Ethics* and the *Journal of Medical Ethics*. He is a noted public philosopher, appearing regularly in print, on radio and TV discussing ethical issues from vampires to anti-vaccination and Ashley Madison, including in the *Guardian*, ABC, *Sydney*

Morning Herald, *The Age* and *Daily Telegraph*. Matt is also a columnist with *The Conversation*.

Adjunct Professor Jamie Cullens served in the Royal Australian Infantry. His military career consisted of command, staff and training postings. He saw operational service in Kashmir with the United Nations and in Panama with United States forces in 1989–90. He commanded NORFORCE in 1994–95. On resigning from the Regular Army in 1996, he spent five years in the resources sector in northern Australia working on native title agreements. He is the former Director of the Centre for Defence Leadership and Ethics and was the Secretary of Defence Scholar in 2008, when he authored a study on military ethics and the ADF requirements for education in this field. In 2015 he was awarded a CDF Commendation for his work at the Australian Defence College. He continues to serve part-time in the Army Reserve.

Professor Charles J Dunlap Jnr joined the Duke University Law School in July 2010, where he is Professor of the Practice of Law and Executive Director of the Center on Law, Ethics and National Security. Dunlap retired from the Air Force in June 2010, having attained the rank of major general during a 34-year career in the Judge Advocate General Corps. In the course of his career, Dunlap has been involved in various high-profile interagency and policy matters, highlighted by his testimony before the United States House of Representatives concerning the *Military Commissions Act* of 2006. Dunlap previously served as staff judge advocate at Headquarters Air Combat Command at Langley Air Force Base in Virginia and at Headquarters Air Education and Training Command at Randolph Air Force Base in Texas, among other leadership posts. He served tours in the United

Kingdom and Korea, and deployed for operations in the Middle East and Africa, including short stints in support of the wars in Afghanistan and Iraq. He also led military-to-military delegations to Colombia, Uruguay, Iraq, and the Czech Republic. Dunlap's commentary on a wide variety of national security topics has been published in leading newspapers and military journals.

BETH EGGLESTON has 15 years of experience in the humanitarian sector and is currently a Director of Humanitarian Advisory Group, which she co-founded in 2012. Beth led the humanitarian advocacy and policy team at Oxfam Australia for five years after returning from three years in Afghanistan with the United Nations Mission (UNAMA) focusing on humanitarian coordination and civil–military interaction. Beth has also worked with a range of NGOs in Tonga, Laos PDR, Afghanistan and Liberia. Among her publications, Beth was involved in the development of *Same Space – Different Mandates: A civil-military guide to stakeholders in international disaster and conflict response.*

BRIGADIER CHRISTOPHER FIELD AM CSC is Commander 3rd Brigade. His service includes postings in Malaysia, East Timor and Solomon Islands; Queensland Reconstruction Authority; the United States Army in Kuwait, Iraq and Afghanistan; and United Nations in Syria and Lebanon. He has completed the ADF Commander Joint Task Force Course and the United States Army Joint Force Land Component Commander Course, and studied at the Centre for Defence and Strategic Studies, the Australian Institute of Company Directors, the United States Marine Corps Command and Staff College's School of Advanced Warfighting, RMC Duntroon and the Australian Defence Force Academy.

Dr Shannon Ford is Lecturer in Intelligence and Security Studies with Charles Sturt University. He is also a Foundation Director for the Asia Pacific Chapter of the International Society for Military Ethics. Before starting his academic career, Shannon spent ten years as a Defence Strategist and Intelligence Analyst. This included working in the Strategic Policy Division, the Defence Intelligence Organisation, and the Information Strategy and Futures Branch. Shannon has completed his doctorate in Politics and International Relations at the National Security College, Australian National University. His dissertation was titled 'Security Institutions, Use of Force and the State: A Moral Framework'.

Professor Tom Frame joined the RAN College as a cadet midshipman in 1979 and served in the Navy for 15 years. He has been a Visiting Fellow in the School of Astronomy and Astrophysics at ANU; Patron of the Armed Forces Federation of Australia; a Councillor of the Australian War Memorial, and judged the inaugural Prime Minister's Prize for Australian History (2007). He served as the Director of the Australian Centre for the Study of Armed Conflict and Society (ACSACS) at UNSW Canberra from 2014 and is the author or editor of 35 books including *Living by the Sword: the Ethics of Armed Intervention* and *Moral Injury: Unseen Wounds in an Age of Barbarism*.

Dr Jai Galliott is attached to the Centre for Cybersecurity at UNSW Canberra and was formerly an Army-funded Research Fellow in Indo-Pacific Defence at UNSW Kensington. He trained as a warfare officer in the Royal Australian Navy before resigning to undertake PhD studies in military affairs and ethics at Macquarie University. He is author of more than two dozen published works on defence strategy and the ethics of emerging military technologies. His most recent books include *Military Robots* (2015), *Super*

Soldiers (2015) and *Ethics and the Future of Spying* (2016). He is lead editor of the Routledge book series on Emerging Technologies, Ethics and International Affairs and an Associate Editor of *IEEE Technology & Society Magazine*. He has spoken at Oxford University and the United Nations, and regularly appears on television and radio.

DR JOHN HARDY is the Director of Security Studies at the Department of Policing, Intelligence and Counter Terrorism (PICT) at Macquarie University. He is also a Fellow with the Research Network for a Secure Australia (RNSA) and the Program Chair for the Safeguarding Australia Organising Committee. John was previously a Post-Doctoral Research Fellow at ANU, a Lecturer of International Studies at the University of Canberra and a Research Associate for the Crawford School of Public Policy and the Lowy Institute for International Policy. He has also taught at the National Security College, the Australian Defence Force Academy, the Australian Graduate School of Policing and Security, and the School of Politics and International Relations, ANU. John's doctoral research was funded by the Department of Defence at ANU's Strategic and Defence Studies Centre, where he was a Sir Arthur Tange Defence Scholar (2010–2013). His research on national security, intelligence and military targeting has involved broad consultation with government and industry and has been published in leading international journals. John has been a security analyst and consultant for public, private and not-for-profit organisations, and works with practitioners from Australian and international organisations on applied research issues.

MAJOR LEE HAYWARD is an Intelligence Corps officer in the Australian Army. In her 13 years in the military she has served in Aceh, Malaysia, Timor-Leste and Afghanistan. Major Hayward is passionate about economic development and gender equality issues, and has taken two periods of leave without pay in the past several years to conduct volunteer work in Africa (Zambia and Senegal). She concentrated on working with under-privileged children, with a focus on female education and health care. Major Hayward has a Bachelor of Economics, a Master of Defence Studies and a Master of Economic Studies. She is currently posted to Army Headquarters as the SO2 Intelligence within the Directorate of Forces Development.

Dr Adam Henschke is a research fellow at the National Security College, Australian National University. His research is in areas of ethics and philosophy as they relate to national security, with specific interests in the ethics of military technologies, cybersecurity, intelligence institutions and just war theory. He is currently working on a book for Cambridge University Press, *Ethics in an Age of Surveillance*, and he co-edited *Binary Bullets: The Ethics of Cyberwarfare* and *The Routledge Handbook of Ethics and War*.

Colonel Ian Langford DSC and 2 Bars graduated from the Royal Military College in 1995 and was posted to 1 RAR. In 1999, he was posted to 4 RAR (Cdo) and deployed to Rifle Company Butterworth and the Solomon Islands. In 2002, he was SO3 Ops – Operations, Headquarters Eight Brigade. This included a deployment to Bougainville as the Deputy Operations Officer with Operation Bel Isi II. He returned to 4 RAR (Cdo) as the Operations Officer in 2004 and was intimately involved with the preparation and deployment of sub-units to Operation Bastille (Iraq). In 2004, Colonel Langford was ADC to the Special Operations Commander and then deployed in 2005 to the United Nations Truce Supervisory Organisation (UNTSO) in Israel, Lebanon and Syria. Throughout 2006–2007, he served as an OC in 4 RAR (Cdo) and deployed his CCG to Timor-Leste, the South-West Pacific (Operation Quickstep), and as the CCG Commander for the Special Operations Task Group, Rotation IV into Afghanistan. For his command and leadership in action, Colonel Langford was awarded the Distinguished Service Cross (DSC) in 2008. Colonel Langford attended the USMC Staff College and the School of Advanced Warfighting in Quantico, USA in 2009–10, returning to Australia as the acting CO of 2 Commando Regt. In 2011, COL Langford served as the Plans Officer at Special Operations HQ and commanded the Special Operations Task Group in Afghanistan 2012–13. For his service, he was awarded a Bar to his DSC. He then worked as SO1 Strategy in the Directorate of Army Research and Analysis before being selected to command the 2nd Commando Regt, including a deployment to Iraq as CO SOTG-Iraq for which he was awarded a Second Bar to his DSC. He is the only Australian to be awarded the DSC three times. Colonel Langford has a degree in Management from Southern Cross University (2001), a Master of Arts from Deakin University (2005), a Master of Defence Studies (2009) and a Master of Strategic Studies (2010) from Marine Corps University.

Lieutenant Colonel Tom McDermott DSO joined the British Army in 2001 before transferring to the Australian Army in 2015. He took part in the 2003 Iraq invasion as a tank commander and has worked in both the United Kingdom Ministry of Defence and the European Union Military Headquarters in Brussels. He attended the Australian Command and Staff College in Canberra in 2011, gained an MA in Strategy and Policy and was awarded the Governor General's Prize as the best student. He has served three tours in Afghanistan, the last as the Reconnaissance Force Commander for the UK's 'Desert Rats', for which he was awarded the Distinguished Service Order (DSO). He holds Fellowships at the Centre for Military Ethics (King's College London) and the Australian Centre for the Study of Armed Conflict and Society (UNSW Canberra). He is presently completing doctoral research into the strategy of Coalition operations in Helmand Province, Afghanistan.

Brigadier Pat McIntosh AM CSC Rtd graduated from Officer Cadet Unit Portsea as an infantry officer in June 1976. He served in the regular Army for 27 years. His command experience included the 2/4 Battalion, The Royal Australian Regiment, the Australian Medical Support Force Rwanda, the Land Warfare Centre and 7 Brigade. He also served overseas with the British Army in Germany, as an exchange instructor at the British Army Command and Staff College and with the United Nations in Rwanda. He was appointed to command the United Nation's Brigade in East Timor in 2001 but could not take up the appointment due to his wife's ill health. On leaving the Army Pat established a financial planning business and is Chairman of RSL Care RDNS Ltd.

Major General Maurie McNarn AO Rtd FAICD retired from the Army as a Major General in 2009 after 33 years in Defence. He commenced as the Chief Operating Officer at the University of Queensland (UQ) in 2009. He has recently retired from UQ after seven years and continues on several boards. Maurie was the Australian National Commander for air, land and maritime forces in the Gulf, Iraq and Afghanistan, for the planning and conduct of the Iraq War 2002–2003. He held appointments as Director Defence Intelligence Organisation, Director General Joint Operations and Plans, Head of Training Command and Chief of Personnel for Army. He was Head of the Royal Military College and commanded at all levels, from Troop to National level. He served in Lebanon,

Syria and Israel with the United Nations. Maurie holds a Master of Business Administration, a Master of Defence (Strategic) Studies, a Graduate Diploma of Telecommunications Systems Management, a Graduate Diploma of Management Studies and a Bachelor of Arts (Honours). He remains an Adjunct Professor at UQ.

DR ALBERT PALAZZO has published widely on the history of the Australian Army and the contemporary character of war. His major works include *The Australian Army: A History of its Organisation, 1901–2001, Moltke to bin Laden: The Relevance of Doctrine in Contemporary Military Environment* and *The Future of War Debate in Australia.* His recent research focused on the effect of resource limits and climate change on the future character of war.

ASSOCIATE PROFESSOR HUGH SMITH AM is a graduate of the London School of Economics and the Australian National University. He joined the Faculty of Military Studies at the Royal Military College, Duntroon as a lecturer in international politics in 1971. In 1986 he transferred to the University College, UNSW at the Australian Defence Force Academy, retiring as an Associate Professor in 2004. He was Convenor of the Australian Study Group on Armed Forces and Society from 1977 to 1985 and Founding Director of the Australian Defence Studies Centre from 1987 to 1991. His publications include *On Clausewitz: A Study of Military and Political Ideas* (2005) and an edited collection entitled *The Strategists* (2001). In 1995 Associate Professor Smith conducted a review of the Ready Reserve with General John Coates. He has also lectured regularly at ADF staff colleges and made submissions to parliamentary committees on topics such as peacekeeping, officer education and service pay. Associate Professor Smith was made a Member of the Order of Australia in 2015 for services to military sociology and the community.

DISCLAIMER

The views expressed by contributors are their own opinions and do not necessarily represent the position of the Commonwealth of Australia, the Australian Defence Force, the University of New South Wales or any organisations with which the contributors were or are now associated. The publication of their chapter in this book does not imply any official agreement or formal concurrence with any opinion, criticism, conclusion or recommendation attributed to them.

INTRODUCTION

TOM FRAME

The publication of this book could not be more timely and the conclusions of its contributors more compelling. It asks questions and raises issues that the Australian Army cannot ignore. Working confidently on the assumption that the Australian Army is committed to its members displaying the highest ethical standards at all times, the contributors identify a number of emerging dilemmas and looming trip-points that should be addressed in the Army's efforts to maintain a culture that affirms moral precepts and the values associated with human decency. But how strong is its commitment?

Most organisations conduct internal reviews in response to external pressures. They are rarely self-initiated. But the Chief of Army, Lieutenant General Angus Campbell, surprised the press and the people when he announced in April 2016 that he had requested an independent investigation of Australia's Special Forces with a particular focus on their conduct during the protracted conflict in Afghanistan. He told Fairfax Media that a 'range of unsubstantiated, third-person, hearsay stories' warranted 'deeper consideration' by the Inspector General of the

Australian Defence Force (ADF).[1] General Campbell wanted the Inspector General to 'consider the range and nature of those stories and to understand the basis of those stories' but did not elaborate on either the circumstances or the conduct prompting the investigation. These stories had come to light during an internal review of the operational culture within Special Operations Command conducted by the Commander, Major General Jeff Sengelman. Subsequent media speculation claimed that 'some within Defence have become concerned that the high-tempo, souped-up intensity of deployments have meant Special Forces regiments have developed their own, closed-off culture forged in the heat of operations'.

The significance of the announcement required no elaboration. The Army's leadership wanted an independent investigation into its own people. The concerns about even the possibility of misconduct among uniformed personnel were sufficiently serious to warrant such action. Clearly, the standing of the Australian Army and its capacity to operate overseas with moral legitimacy was at stake. It did not matter whether Australian Special Forces had acted unethically or unlawfully, the mere circulation of 'stories' was enough to justify this unprecedented action. The professional reputation of both the Special Air Service Regiment and 2 Commando Regiment was in the balance. Had the highly trained members of either regiment violated the ethical standards that are a mark of the professional excellence and exemplary conduct expected of uniformed personnel by the Army and the nation? Could Australia continue to claim that despite ethical breaches by the deployed forces of other Western nations, its personnel have consistently acted in line with the ADF's corporate values and within the laws of armed conflict? Concerns about the organisational culture of the Special Forces were especially troubling because it implied misconduct was not individualised but part of a wider pattern of behaviour that was unethical at best and illegal at worst. If nothing else, the investigation would need to consider the ethical standards to which the Special Forces have been trained and to which they are held to account.

The Chief of Army's announcement highlighted the continuing place and importance of ethics and the necessity of remaining vigilant in inculcating ethical values and promoting an ethical culture across the uniformed community. Members of the Australian Army have a unique place in Australian society: they are the only people mandated to use lethal force in the defence of Australia and its national interests. The Australian Federal Police and the state police services have the authority to use lethal force in situations where their own lives or the lives of others are in peril but they are not empowered to use massive firepower to subdue and defeat an adversary, such as a foreign government, beyond the nation's sovereign territory. Police forces do not operate warships, deploy strike aircraft or use tanks. They are not provided with torpedoes, missiles or high-explosive artillery rounds. The police maintain the peace and uphold the law. Their powers and prerogatives are determined by parliament and their conduct regulated by statutory bodies and, when required, examined by the courts.

The Army's role is very different. To put it bluntly, the Army is in the business of killing people and destroying property. It is deployed for humanitarian assistance and disaster relief missions but its core commission is the application of lethal force. To ensure the Army does not descend into barbarism and its members into brutality, the Army functions within a detailed framework of national laws and international conventions, and operates in accordance with specific mission directives and rules of engagement that reflect practical circumstances and political priorities. Because context largely determines conduct in the management of military operations, the Army's leaders are given substantial discretion in the use of force. Given the consequences of using such force in terms of its effect on people and property, and the potential for military action to cause immediate damage and long-term harm, questions touching on where, when, what and why massive firepower is employed cannot and should not be avoided. The decision to kill people and to destroy their homes demands a compelling and convincing explanation. Taking human life must always and everywhere be justified. The audience for this justification must include those directed to kill others. There are two reasons for their inclusion. They either see their victims and observe the consequences of using force or they are indirectly complicit through the support they offer to those who are directed to kill others. Justifications for the use of force will inevitably involve interpreting and applying the law but, in more telling ways, these justifications will draw directly on ethical principles and the values and virtues undergirding them.

Attitudes towards violence and force, conflict and war are strongly shaped by the implicit assumption or explicit application of values and virtues. These values and virtues are apparent well beyond the experience of Army service. They are foundational to most aspects of human living including parenting – an activity that has seen a considerable shift in attitudes over the past thirty years with respect to the use of force. Some mothers and fathers believe it is wrong to smack children either to punish misbehaviour or to correct poor behaviour because it introduces impressionable children to physical coercion at an early age. If they have force used against them, they will use force against others. Conversely, some parents will argue it is negligent not to smack children when they ignore or injure others because they need to be compelled, forcibly if necessary, to recognise moral norms and respect social customs. If there are no consequences for behaving badly, they will continue to behave badly. In both positions, there are many assumed beliefs about human nature, how personality is shaped and temperament is changed, and who possesses the entitlement to commend good behaviour and to condemn bad.

It is possible to extrapolate one's beliefs about nurturing children within the family to the regulation of an entire nation's behaviour towards its own citizens and its neighbours on the world stage. Those with a positive view of individual and collective human nature will appeal to an inherent sense of reason and fairness in discouraging bad behaviour and in imposing a system of incentives and rewards to encourage positive behaviour. Those with a pessimistic view will argue that nations, like people, are fundamentally selfish and self-centred and that threats or resorts to force are usually necessary to discourage aggression and restrain greed.

The Army's existence embodies a prudent realism about the experience of human affairs and the continuing evolution of human civilisation. As part of the ADF, the Army safeguards the nation's life, including the wellbeing of the people and the security of their property. But it is also used not just to defend the nation's interests but to *advance* them. The Army is not mobilised every time the nation is threatened. Threats are not always military in nature. Frequently the threat is to the nation's financial interests such as the imposition of tariffs or trade restrictions. At other times the threat may not be so acute as to require an armed response. Contrastingly, the Army is sometimes mobilised in response to events that have nothing to do with Australia's national interest but everything to do with the preservation of human dignity. In Rwanda and Somalia where genocide and poverty had unleashed a wave of human suffering, Australia's commitment to human dignity and its ability to alleviate human suffering led to deployments motivated simply by compassion. In addition to providing medical care and distributing food, national compassion was accompanied by the threatened use of force against those who perpetrated genocide and profited from hunger. Although genocidal Rwandans and Somali warlords did not threaten Australian sovereign territory, the assertion of Australian virtues and values was very much on display. But this expression of these national characteristics was not without ethical dimensions. Why did Australia choose to intervene in these places but not in others? Why did Australia agree to rules of engagement that ignored the root causes of the suffering and which were powerless to prevent further violations of human rights?

In addition to ethical critique of the national defence and security objectives the ADF exists to serve, the Army's internal culture has a significant bearing on how it performs in operations and the extent to which it discharges a necessary duty of care to its members. Is the Army an ethical organisation that promotes and practises ethical behaviour at all levels? Are ethical principles taken seriously? Does the Army provide sufficient ethics education and training for its members, especially for those sent to morally confronting places requiring ethically demanding decisions? Is there ethical accountability and how is unethical behaviour treated? Are the ethical standards expected of uniformed personnel also applied to civilian staff, including the ADF's political leaders? And what provision is made for servicemen and women who profess a conscientious objection to performing a specific duty? Will they be accommodated or alienated? These are some of the questions that arise in modern military service.

This book is concerned primarily with the ethical issues and challenges that emerge for the Australian Army from contemporary armed conflict. Each of the chapters reflects the primacy of values and virtues – declared and undeclared – in interpreting and assessing individual and collective human conduct and conflict. Although human beings have always been in conflict with one another, the matters that bring them into conflict and how they are to be resolved have changed. These conflicts involve a collision of values and virtues – ethics – before they become concerns for law. In any event, because something is lawful does not make it ethical, while law can be used to frustrate ethical action. Getting the ethics right usually assists in shaping laws that give principles the right kind of practical expression.

The first thing to consider is: what does being ethical actually mean? An ethicist has some idea, most ADF members don't. They are not sure whether it encompasses actions and attitudes, acts of omission or merely those of commission. And what kind of ethics do they have in mind – Platonic ethics, Aristotelian ethics, rule ethics or virtue ethics? And why are they ethical? Can an institution be ethical or do ethics only apply to individuals? Has this any relationship to morality or connection with spirituality or are they essentially personal and therefore private matters? Is there an objective basis to ethics or is it merely a matter of subjective opinion based on a set of conventions and norms? Who said being ethical is good or desirable anyway and where did they gain this insight? Is being ethical in the natural order of things – part of being human? Can ethics be taught and learned? If so, who will decide the course content and the teaching method employed? What prevents soldiers from being unethical or changing their ethical outlook to one others don't share? How will uniformed people be held ethically accountable? What role does the *Defence Force Discipline Act* (DFDA) have in promoting ethics or is a code of conduct or charter of responsibilities needed? From my observations, I don't think many people know what ethics really is or why they should be ethical in an unethical world. And why should anyone assume the existence of such knowledge?

In my 15 years as a Service officer (1979–1994), there was never any attempt at systematic ethics education, although my intake joined at the impressionable age of sixteen and we were highly susceptible to being moulded morally. From my observation of the programs offered at initial entry training establishments for both officers and other ranks, I am still not convinced that recruits or officer trainees – those most tainted by the confusions of postmodernism – are given an adequate grounding in the whole ethics enterprise in either their initial induction or continuation training as part of their general preparation for adult life and military service. Yes, my class was subjected to character guidance and moral discipline courses during our initial entry training and subsequent lectures on the pathology of leadership and management as part of junior staff training. Each stream touched on ethics but, and this is my point, it was *ad hoc* and the training was not articulated. We never built on firm foundations. Ethics training was always as though the whole subject was new to us. Over the past 30 years the approach to ethics education and training has markedly improved. Ethics is no longer considered a mere compliance matter or part of wider risk-management strategies. Ethics is about promoting personal well-being and operational efficiency and effectiveness. Ethics contributes directly to individual resilience and collective performance.

Ethics education and training has become more urgent because of the rapidly changing environment in which military operations are being conducted. The end of the Cold War in 1990 was followed by a proliferation of intra-state wars and, in contradiction to the 1648 Treaty of Westphalia, by international interference in the affairs of sovereign nations, commencing with the United Nations' operation to protect the Kurds in Northern Iraq during late 1991. Since that time, Australian units have been deployed to Rwanda, Somalia, Namibia, Cambodia,

Bougainville, the Solomon Islands, Timor-Leste and a number of less well-known places. A national concern for human life and the dignity of individuals has propelled the ADF into the forefront of government thinking and acting about this region and beyond. While the use of Australia's armed forces during the Korean War, the Malayan Emergency, the Indonesian Confrontation, the Vietnam Conflict and the 1991 Gulf War was understandable but not strictly mandatory and therefore open to moral critique, the recent deployments have been for purposes that have more to do with altruism and compassion, ethically laudable motivations, and less with bare-faced national self-interest. Yet, those serving in the nation's uniform have never been more wary of the agendas that lie behind many operations.

Whereas a century ago in the South African War of 1899–1902 Australians considered it a great adventure to fight the Boers to enhance the economic interests of the British Empire, to place Boer women and children into concentration camps and even to shoot unarmed Boer prisoners when they could not be easily detained, the expression of conscientious objection has become more common as the operations have become, in my view, less objectionable. While we rightly expect personnel to render their contracted service without question – a difficult thing given they can hardly envisage all of the scenarios within which the Army will be deployed – this principle does not remove the need to formulate and provide an ethical explanation or commentary of an operation. Resorting to force is always a moral issue. Thus, the use of coercive force is something that should always and every-where be explained. It is not surprising then that uniformed men and women are being ethically challenged by their service and that they want the case for its moral validity to be persuasively argued at least by those committing them to the action. While they do not expect complete or perfect answers, they appear to want a forum in which to discuss and debate the ethics of their own Service and the government's policies.

This book will broaden and hopefully enhance discussions already underway. The contributors have drawn on their own experiences, provided many helpful case studies and practical examples, identified areas of priority concern and pointed to the need for either enlarged education and training or deeper consideration of the issues. Part 1 focuses on the contribution that ethics makes to the effective conduct of military missions. Charles Dunlap insists that ethics is not merely about compliance, expediency, and avoiding scandals. The study and practice of ethics promotes excellence. Tom McDermott used his British Army service in the Middle East to highlight the importance of an ethical culture to an army engaging an adversary whose tactics include inciting unethical behaviour. It is easy for a unit to descend into barbarism if its ethical principles are not firmly held and forthrightly asserted.

In part 2, Maurie McNarn and Pat McIntosh reveal some of the challenges they faced as commanders in the context of international coalitions. Australia's friends and allies have different standards for determining ethical conduct. Managing the effects of these differences represents a first-order challenge that requires a clear sense of morality and legality, in addition to courage and integrity. Similarly, Army personnel working with multinational organisations whose own ethical standards might be unclear, confused or inconsistent creates the need for exemplary leadership as there are life and death consequences.

Part 3 highlights the ethical dilemmas faced by deploying personnel when traditional frameworks and conventional approaches to acting ethically do not address the circumstances of modern conflict and the new areas of moral 'grey'. Deane-Peter Baker wonders whether ethics teaching at military institutions is effective in preparing young men and women for the questions they will face once deployed. The same doubt applies to academic research and the ability of philosophers to appreciate the dynamics of countering insurgency, preventing ethnic cleansing and training local forces with poor discipline. Ian Langford explains the emerging need for particular preparation for Special Operations personnel, given the scenarios in which they are usually active. My own chapter calls for a rethink of the way the ADF manages personnel who claim a selective conscientious objection to either the moral justification for a particular deployment or the ethical quality of a specific operation. If ADF personnel are given more extensive ethics education and training it is very likely that uniformed men and women will conclude from time to time that they cannot reconcile a deployment or mission with their conscientious beliefs and will seek alternative service.

In part 4, Beth Eggleston offers a personal reflection from the vantage point of a Non-Government Organisation (NGO) working with the Australian Army in the context of humanitarian assistance and disaster relief missions. She identifies the complexities faced by NGOs, the compromises they are willing to make and those they will not countenance in working collaboratively with uniformed personnel. Notably, the ethical standards observed by the NGO sector have common features with those expected of the military. Lee Hayward, an officer in the Australian Army, describes her experience of working with an NGO and how the cultures of aid agencies and the Australian Army converge and diverge. Plainly, there is some way to go before the NGO sector and the military have a more nuanced grasp of each other's mandate.

Jai Galliott, Matthew Beard and John Hardy focus our attention in part 5 on the ethics of emerging tactics, principally their effect on human wellbeing, human interactions and on the rules that have previously regulated the conduct of armed conflict. It is clear that both the circumstances of conflict and the implementation of new technology have changed the conduct of warfare and the demands placed on individuals. In contrast to the vast industrial scale of the two world wars, modern conflict has highlighted the place and the importance of the individual participant, whether friend or foe. Precision weapons target specific individuals whose combatant status might be contested. In the quest for a competitive edge, the possibility of drugs being developed to enhance individual performance raises a number of ethical questions alongside the continuing debate about targeted assassination.

Part 6 reminds us that the internet has become a weapon of war and that the IT systems that support military communications, intelligence analysis and precision targeting are attractive targets. Shannon Ford notes the use of social media, especially by the Islamic State in Iraq and Syria (ISIS), to recruit fighters, spread propaganda and validate success. He also notes the dangers of Western governments militarising social media and the need to apply just war principles to the conduct of any campaign that exploits its possibilities. Adam Henschke explores the ethics of cyberweapons in the belief that such an exercise tells us something about the existing beliefs we have about the ethics of warfare. He concludes that new technologies like cyberweapons challenge our existing beliefs and reveals some of the particular intuitions we have about moral situations.

In part 7 we are offered three depictions of military ethics. Hugh Smith explains how the teaching of ethics to new entry officers within the Australian Army has evolved over the past 40 years. His chapter outlines his own considerable achievements in raising the profile and quality of academic contributions to the study of ethics. Similarly, Jamie Cullens argues from his two decades of teaching ethics at the Service staff colleges that a more closely articulated approach needs to be taken by every organisation involved in training uniformed personnel for the ADF. He believes there are too many omissions in what is taught and too great a gap between the ethics training given to officers and soldiers during the course of their careers. As an Army formation commander, Chris Field outlines the place of ethics in the units he commands and mentions some of the things he has done to enhance ethical awareness and ethical behaviour. He is conscious that uniformed personnel at all ranks grapple with the circumstances of their service and will always need assistance in coming to terms with might appear to be ethical dilemmas but which could be dissolved with more creative thought.

The questions being asked by personnel at all levels must be taken seriously if conscience is to be respected and Service morale is to remain buoyant. Everyone from the Chief of Army working in Canberra to the newest Army recruit being trained at Kapooka must be given the tools necessary for enlightened engagement in ethical discussion. Not everyone wants or needs the same tools. Each of us lives with our own thoughts and convictions. We approach questions and shape answers in the light of our own life's experiences and make decisions about how we will act according to values and virtues that we have acquired from a range of disparate sources. But we do not think about moral precepts in a vacuum; we do not arrive at ethical principles alone or unaided. Conversation is critical in shaping our vision of the world and discerning our place within it.

What we think we believe is revised and refined by the ideas and insights that we gain from interacting with people who see the world a little differently because their journey in life has taken them in other directions across and over different terrain. What might seem perfectly acceptable to me seems entirely unacceptable to someone else. What I regard as truth or wisdom, another person might consider falsehood or folly. It is, in fact, difficult to 'do ethics' without the company of others. It is in conversation with others about these things that I sometimes discover what I really do think and discern when I am not sure of what I actually think or, perhaps, might be confused about what I ought to do. Others might tell me what they believe but only I can decide what I will believe and what I will do about my belief. As we mature as people and grow in wisdom it is likely that our views will either change or become more consistent and cogent. Our views are never static and many are liable to change very quickly, especially if we are uncertain and particularly when we are thinking about ethics.

The importance of ethical conduct within a community mandated to use lethal force is perhaps self-evident. The consequences of ethical misconduct among people with access to weapons are grave and far-reaching. But creating the conditions in which ethical conduct is instinctive requires continuing education and training, and attentiveness to emerging issues and challenges. A close reading of the following chapters reveals a number of priorities that need to be addressed. I have identified at least ten.

The *first* is the evolution of the historic just war tradition, changing attitudes towards national sovereignty and the status of the nation-state, and the difficulty of applying the just war theory in the context of proliferating intra-state warfare. *Second*, trainers need to focus on the interconnections and conflicts between legal, professional and ethical conduct and the distribution of political and ethical accountability in the profession of arms. *Third*, the relationship between the operation of the DFDA, the statute for the International Criminal Court, the scope of the criminal law, processes for professional performance reporting, and ethical conduct. *Fourth*, the responsibility for whistleblowing on the United Nations and individual national contingents allegedly engaging in corruption or misconduct, mindful of the diplomatic sensitivities in doing so. *Fifth*, the apprehension and prosecution of alleged war criminals, the pursuit of national policies of 'reconciliation' following genocide or widespread human rights abuses, and concepts of justice. *Sixth*, the requirement for chaplains, medical staff and other 'non-combatants' to bear firearms and the consequences of such a policy for professional ethics. *Seventh*, the need to develop the means of differentiating between a conscientious (or ethical) and a political objection to an order or some form of military service. *Eighth*, the legal recognition of conscientious objection (pacifism) and selective conscientious objection (objection to particular wars) in relation to volunteer and obligatory service needs to be clarified. *Ninth*, soldiers need help to differentiate between an illegal order (which must be refused), an unnecessary command (which can be ignored) and a general instruction (which is subject to individual discretion). *Tenth* and finally, the ethical dimensions of the political–military interface, particularly the public disclosure of professional advice rendered to commanders, politicians and bureaucrats.

The Australian Army places a great premium on ethics, especially in the practice of leadership. In a letter addressed to all personnel distributed in September 2016, the Chief of Army, Lieutenant General Angus Campbell, explained that leadership was critical to fulfilling the Army's mission:

> Ethically informed, values-based leadership that inspires,
> resources and enables subordinates to achieve their best
> work is always expected of Army's leaders, at every level. Let
> our values of Courage, Initiative, Respect and Teamwork
> be our guide. The purpose of focusing on our values is that,
> for our unique organisational setting, these are the values

that build integrity in leaders and enable us as individuals and organisations to create relationships of trust. It is never appropriate to regard military incompetence as mitigation for ethical failure.[2]

These words give priority and urgency to this book and its conclusions.

Most of the following chapters began as presentations to a conference jointly hosted in May 2016 by the Australian Centre for the Study of Armed Conflict and Society (ACSACS) at UNSW Canberra and the Australian Army's Modernisation and Strategic Planning (MSP) Division (now known as Land Capability Division). The authors benefited greatly from the vigorous conversations that followed each presentation and, with my co-editor Dr Albert Palazzo, we are personally grateful to the Rector of UNSW Canberra, Professor Michael Frater FTSE, and the Head of the then MSP Division, Major General Gus McLachlan AM, for their goodwill and support. The commitment of UNSW Canberra to ethics education and the Army's investment in ethics training is reflected in the publication of this work, which we hope will prompt discussion and even provoke debate. Without discussion and debate, ethics will remain a dry topic and uniformed people will be largely indifferent to it. We hope the reader will share the energy and enthusiasm that was evident throughout the conference. Certainly, each of the contributors is adamant that they have something that ought to be heard and possibly even heeded.

PART 1: ETHICAL CULTURES AND ETHICAL BEHAVIOUR

ADF personnel attached to the United Nations' peacekeeping mission on patrol in East Timor. *Commonwealth of Australia*

1

WHY ETHICS MATTER

CHARLES J DUNLAP JNR

British war historian Geoffrey Best stated it simply: '[I]t must never be forgotten that the law of war, wherever it began at all, began mainly as a matter of religion and ethics.'[1] Both national and international law hope to achieve a common ethic in warfighting, creating codes and rules of engagement by which national militaries conduct themselves. But when it comes to war in the 21st century, is compliance with the requirements of the law enough? Beyond the law, does adherence to ethical principles pragmatically facilitate battlefield success?

The law of armed conflict (LOAC) 'obliges belligerent nations to keep their armed forces disciplined under responsible command'.[2] Rules of engagement practised by troops in the field, which incorporate both law and policy, are only a small part of battlefield discipline.[3] LOAC sets minimum standards for the conduct of war, with the goal of minimising unnecessary suffering and facilitating the return to peace. Examples of these minimum standards include a distinction between combatants and civilians, a special status for chaplains and medics, and an obligation to treat the sick and wounded humanely.

Unfortunately, even with these rules in place, lapses occur.

Former United States Secretary of Defense Chuck Hagel – a Vietnam veteran himself – highlighted the importance of trust in a memorandum released on the eve of his retirement from office.[4] In this memorandum he emphasised how critical it is for personnel to conduct themselves honourably.[5] Hagel stressed that trust is essential to the military's self-regulated apparatus. General Martin Dempsey, the Chairman of the Joint Chiefs of Staff, speaking at a West Point graduation, likewise underlined this point: 'We trust you [...] We trust you to win our nation's wars, to be leaders of character and competence and consequence [...] We trust you to leave our profession better than you found it'.[6] These two high-ranking officials believe that trust within its ranks – as well as the perception of it to those outside of the armed forces – is integral to military success.

But is a trustworthy military really important to the people it serves? Instances where the implicit trust between the military and civilian population has failed reveal that a positive relationship between these two groups allows national security policies a greater probability of success.[7] The atrocious violations at Abu Ghraib by American military personnel brought into question the United States military's reputation and brought into the public sphere internal lapses in ethical conduct.[8] From a broader view, '[i]t is fair to say that Western societies expect their militaries to unfailingly demonstrate the highest ethical standards regardless of the circumstances'.[9] Policy is more likely to succeed when civil–military trust levels are high, and individual military members who misbehave threaten this institutional trust.

With this at stake, recruiting ethical individuals should be a priority. Based on available polling of Americans and Australians, trust in the military appears to be integral to future recruitment. In the United States, 78 per cent of Americans see 'military officer' as a prestigious occupation[10] and 64 per cent of adults would encourage a child to become a military officer.[11] Further, 18–24-year-olds are more likely than older adults to encourage a child to pursue an officer position.[12] In a Gallup Poll asking American citizens about their confidence in state institutions, the military maintained a consistent positive confidence rating of 73 per cent from 2008 to 2016.[13] These are important statistics when keeping in mind that the United States military is sustained by an all-volunteer core.

In Australia, the Australian Defence Force (ADF) and the Department of Defence recognise that new military technology and the course of modern warfare require specific recruiting. 'As our defence capabilities become more technologically complex, recruiting Australians with the right skills mix for these capabilities will be even more important. It is not enough to have the best equipment – it needs to be operated and supported by the best people'.[14] They see this as a major challenge. Fortunately, public opinion of the Australian military remains high and will likely support recruitment. In a study on the perceptions of corruption and ethical conduct held by the Australian public, confidence was highest in the armed forces (85 per cent).[15] What would be the effect, if any, on the all-volunteer force if public trust eroded because of ethical failings? It is hard to conceive that the best and brightest the armed forces needs would want to join an organisation that has lost public trust.

The implications for ethical failures on the relationship between national militaries and the public they serve are substantial. But moral and ethical fighting behaviour can also affect warfighting capability on the battlefield. We recognise the power of perception today with the 'weaponisation' of ethics by our chief adversaries. Professor William Eckhart observes:

Knowing that our society so respects the rule of law that it demands compliance with it, our enemies carefully attack our military plans as illegal and immoral and our execution of those plans as contrary to the law of war. Our vulnerability here is what philosopher of war Carl von Clausewitz would term our 'center of gravity'.[16]

Armed conflict, particularly when prosecuted by democracies, requires robust public support. In their book *The Laws of War*, W. Michael Reisman and Chris Antoniou suggest '[t]hat support can erode or reverse itself if the public believes that the war is being conducted in an unfair, inhumane or iniquitous manner, regardless of how worthy the political objective':[17]

[Bin Laden's] guerrilla war, with women and children as *collateral damage*, is part of a broader military strategy to ensnare the United States in a larger East-West conflict [...] the September 11 attack [according to an expert] was to be so 'audacious, impudent and massively inhumane' as to ensure a massive, inordinate United States retaliation that would further inflame Muslim opinion against the United States and the Arab regimes allied with Washington. [Emphasis added.][18]

This 'weaponisation' of ethics is strategic in nature, and it bears Clausewitzean features.[19] We can recognise this relationship mentioned above between the military and the public as one element of Clausewitz's 'remarkable trinity'. In the trinity, the Government, the Military and the People make up an interactive set of forces that collectively drive the events of war. Public opinion shapes the government's policy-making, and the government must justify its actions to the public. Public opinion also influences military doctrine, and the military's doctrine may influence public opinion. Finally, military strategies influence policy objectives, and the government influences military resources.

The Western approach to war traditionally seeks to destroy the enemy's capability to wage war through strategies of denial.[20] Today's adversaries are not seeking to militarily defeat the West through purely kinetic force *per se*, but rather to win by separating the People from the Military and the Government. In other words, to erode public 'will'. As a prime example, the torture at Abu Ghraib was rightly deemed an 'ethical implosion' by the journalist Seymour Hersh.[21] General David Petraeus, then-head of the United States Central Command, summed up America's struggle with this unanticipated form of warfare: 'Whenever we have, perhaps, taken expedient measures, they have turned around and bitten us in the backside'. Whenever Americans have used methods that violated the Geneva Conventions or the standards of the International Committee of the Red Cross, he said: 'We end up paying the price for it ultimately. Abu Ghraib and other situations like that are non-biodegradable. They don't go away. The enemy continues to beat you with them like a stick'.[22]

There may be a link between this tragic event and the origins of the continuing strategy of the Islamic State in Iraq and Syria (ISIS). News outlets have reported that Islamic State militants are hiding among civilians, employing them as human shields and then claiming that the United States-led coalition is targeting innocent people during air strikes.[23] In June 2016, ISIS was able to turn back Iraqi forces from Fallujah with the use of human shields. This tactic has also made it extraordinarily difficult for Iraqi Security Forces and coalition air support to root out the ISIS fighters.[24]

Moral and ethical behaviour can substantially affect warfighting capability in coalition operations. 'A perception of poor conduct by a belligerent erodes the just cause of war and undermines its legitimacy because causing unnecessary deaths or damage is seen as counter to international norms and customs. *In modern coalition warfare, attention to the law of war is a strategic imperative*' (emphasis added).[25] As Brian Egan, the legal advisor to the State Department, explained in early 2016:

> It is not enough that we act lawfully or regard ourselves
> as being in the right. It is important that our actions be
> understood as lawful by others both at home and abroad
> in order to show respect for the rule of law and promote
> it more broadly, while also cultivating partnerships and
> building coalitions.[26]

Egan rightly points out that a state at war must now be able to demonstrate to the global community that its 'most consequential national security and foreign policy decisions are guided by a principled understanding and application of international law'.[27]

The German experience in the Second World War demonstrates another outcome of the failure to engage in ethical warfare in compliance with international law. According to British historian Richard Overy, German troops during the war were indoctrinated with the image of a 'bestial enemy' and given licence to fight by any means, criminal or otherwise.[28] As a result, '[t]he criminalisation of warfare produced a growing indiscipline and demoralisation among German forces themselves. The German army shot fifteen thousand of their own number [...] The regime imposed ever more draconian terror on its own forces to keep them fighting'.[29] The perception of moral conduct clearly still matters. Furthermore, a military's enforcement of an ethical culture will likely aid in deterring law-breaking. This was illustrated early in the post-9/11 era when American military lawyers found themselves at odds with their civilian, political-appointee counterparts. Professor Richard Schragger noted:

> Military lawyers seem to conceive of the rule of law differently. Instead of seeing law as a barrier to the exercise of the client's power, *these attorneys understand the law as a prerequisite to the meaningful exercise of power*. Law allows our troops to engage in forceful, violent acts with relatively little hesitation or moral qualms [emphasis added].[30]

Schragger explains that law makes just wars possible. A set of ethics that aligns with international law creates what he calls a 'well-defined legal space' where 'soldiers can act within this space safely and thus more efficiently, without having to resort to their own personal moral codes'.[31] But why should an individual soldier not retain some personal moral code on the battlefield? The United States military has examined this issue, balancing soldiers' private rights with maintaining order and command: 'The order may not, without such a valid military purpose, interfere with private rights or personal affairs. However, the dictates of a person's conscience, religion, or personal philosophy cannot justify or excuse the disobedience of an otherwise lawful order'.[32] In a pluralistic nation with a multitude of personal moral codes, allowing individual soldiers to pick among them as a condition for order obedience would lead to battlefield chaos.

Today's 'millennials' – whose demographic mirrors that of most militaries – have strong views on personal ethics in the workplace. According to the 2016 Deloitte Millennial Survey, personal values have the greatest influence on millennials' decision making.[33] Millennials are by no means a 'benign workforce'.[34] Almost half (49 per cent) have chosen not to undertake a task at work because it went against their personal values or ethics.[35] Clearly, today's troops need to know, and perhaps even be convinced, that what they are doing is legal and ethical. This may help ameliorate moral injury, best defined as the damage to a soldier's moral conscience as a result of a perceived moral transgression and subsequent emotional shame.[36]

Even with this evidence on the importance of ethical warfare, some still question whether ethical and legal restraints in fact inhibit effective warfighting. In reality, most of the constraints on warfighting are not dictated by legal and ethical imperatives, but rather by the strategic judgments of operators. For example, air strike campaigns can cause collateral damage. Effective leaders weigh the benefits of every air strike against this risk. Collateral damage can provide insurgents with a major propaganda victory. Even when justified by law, it works to the insurgents' benefit. But coalition leaders can weigh these risks too heavily. Exceeding what ethics and law require is sometimes counterproductive. Establishing a 'zero tolerance' model for casualities has come back to haunt coalition leaders. Predictably, in 2008 US Air Force Colonel Eric Holdaway, the Director of Intelligence at the USAF's Central Command, revealed, 'some of [the coalition's] enemies have clearly located themselves among civilian populations'.[37] With more conservative policy on air strikes from 2009 to 2010 alone, the number of civilian deaths in Afghanistan rose by 31 per cent.[38] Along similar lines, one of the chief arguments against drone strikes is that they can potentially radicalise civilians in the strike zone. While the American drone campaign is not 'winning hearts and minds', the locals may still agree with the results because 'they viscerally hate the militants and feel betrayed by their own government. [T]he drones were the closest thing to getting your prayers answered'.[39] It may well be counterproductive to go beyond what international law requires regarding collateral damage.

Constraints are typically based on military judgments, not ethical or legal mandates. Do such constraints, ironically, engender just war issues? General John Michael Loh, the former Commander of the United States Air Combat Command, believes:

> the current policies regarding rules of engagement, non-combatant casualties, and emphasis on body count in the war against the Islamic State overly constrain the air campaign, will cause an endless duration to the conflict, misread the Geneva Conventions and violate accepted principles of a morally justifiable war. These excessive restrictions prevent winning.[40]

Harking back to John Stuart Mills, a person may cause evil not only by his actions, but also by his inactions. Furthermore, inaction could create a 'moral hazard'.[41] If not expertly crafted, Rules of Engagement (ROE) can carry with them a moral hazard of sorts when they operate to prevent a strike that is actually permissible under international humanitarian law. Restrictive ROE can operate to shift risk from militaries, which can then avoid being criticised for causing some civilian casualties if they were to strike, to what might be a much larger number of civilians trapped under ISIS.

> Increasingly, liberal democracies will impose policy constraints – rules of engagement – that exceed the level required by law. [...] Such policies limit civilian casualties that may result from attacking terrorists, but allow the certainty of civilians being slaughtered at the hands of those same terrorists if they are not eliminated. That is self-defeating at best, and counterproductive at worst. To be sure, it is immoral.[42]

Policies, not ethics or law, are often the true source of concern among warfighters. Certainly the law or ethics can be wrongly blamed when things go wrong. Consider the ethics and laws at the root of the famous incident chronicled in the memoir *Lone Survivor* by Hospital Corpsman First Class (HM1) Marcus Luttrell. As he and his colleagues contemplated killing a group of goat herders on an Afghani mountainside who had observed their presence and were likely to report their position to the Taliban, and one of them argued strongly in favour of killing them, Luttrell began to think: 'If this came to a vote, [I] was going to recommend the execution […] And in my soul I knew [my colleague] was right. […] But my trouble is, I have another soul. My Christian soul'.[43] Luttrell seems to think that sparing the lives of the goat herders brought on an attack by Taliban fighters that later led to the deaths of his colleagues. Ultimately, the decision not to kill them, however, reveals a different motive. 'Look at me, helpless, tortured, shot, blown up, my best buddies all dead, and all because we were afraid of the liberals back home, afraid to do what was necessary to save our own lives. *Afraid of American civilian lawyers*'.[44] Others on the scene have questioned Luttrell's story. Mohammad Gulab, a witness who helped save Luttrell, insists that the Navy SEALs did not die because the goat herders informed the Taliban. Instead they were tracked, outmanoeuvred, and outgunned even before they let the goat herders go free.[45]

Given the importance of ethical warfare, the question remains of whether today's combatants can agree on a single international code. Or instead, are we destined to live in a world of ethical asymmetries? In the Western world, we start from a universalist ethic based on the idea of human rights.[46] In some of the battlefields today, there is an opposing ethic. This ethic comes from a view that defines the tribe, the nation, or the ethnic group as the limit of legitimate moral concern.[47] A Bedouin saying goes: 'Me against my brothers, me and my brothers against my cousins, me and my cousins against the Stranger'.[48] ISIS created its own rules relating to war and the conditions under which enemy combatants may be targeted, tortured or killed.[49] Thus it can claim its combatants are acting lawfully according to their own rules, despite the fact that ISIS fighters habitually violate binding international humanitarian law.[50]

Differences in culture thus become a second source of conflict. The very idea that there could be a 'universal' agreement on ethical behaviour is a Western one, some would argue.[51] This was essentially the argument of Colonel Wang Xiangsui of the Chinese Air Force in the late 1990s. He suggested that non-Western nations are not bound by the so-called 'international law' expressed in armed conflict conventions.[52] There are, however, real conceptual asymmetries. Consider the remarks of Peter Maurer of the International Committee of the Red Cross: 'You treat detainees humanely, because you know the other side will also treat detainees humanely'.[53] But the Islamic State's conduct has not aligned with what Maurer has deemed universal conduct.[54] While reciprocity was once the major sanction underlying the laws of war, it has broken down with respect to non-state actors who are indifferent to accepted legal restraints.[55] Obligation without reciprocity risks the warfare strategy breaking down. Particularly when one side feels bound to protect the civilians of both sides, and the other side deliberately does not. This has been termed a 'humanitarian double standard'.[56]

Should militaries yield to expedience if they want to defeat today's adversaries? If militaries were to do so they would create a global political environment where LOAC violations become rampant. So can ethics do what reciprocity once did? 'Law is the judgment of the community at large, but the impetus for ethical conduct among warriors must come from among other warriors.'[57] The challenge for commanders is to teach their troops the scope of international law while also instilling in them the 'ethos of the professional warrior'.[58] It is not enough for soldiers to know the rules and follow them. Without deep reserves of character and moral strength, troops in today's high-stress battlefield situations may not be able to withstand the psychological toll and may give in to undisciplined impulses. 'Honor, not law, is the key to battlefield discipline.'[59]

Acknowledgment: The author thanks Ms Amy Richardson, JD and LLM candidate, Duke University School of Law, for her indispensable work on this chapter.

AVOIDING THE DESCENT INTO BARBARISM

TOM McDERMOTT

barbarism
ˈbaːbərɪz(ə)m/
noun
1. absence of culture and civilisation.
2. extreme cruelty or brutality.

On Saturday 16 March 1968 at 8 a.m., around a hundred American soldiers from Charlie Company, First Battalion, Twentieth Infantry Brigade stepped off helicopters into a small village in South Vietnam. With almost half a million American troops in the country, such a landing was commonplace; one of tens of thousands that took place during the Vietnam War. The actions that followed were anything but normal. Over the next four hours the American soldiers literally cleansed the village of life. With a level of violence that even the soldiers who took part would later proclaim was 'just like [Hitler's] gas chambers', Charlie Company systematically killed every living man, woman, child, infant and animal present. Sources placed the death toll at 504. Babies were killed in their mothers' arms, young women were raped before they were murdered, and the old killed in their beds. While M16s were the most common murder weapon, many of the victims were hanged.[1] By the time this orgy of violence was over, the village of Son My, known to the Americans as My Lai, had ceased to exist: cleansed by bullets, hate, fire and revenge. By the very definition above, the soldiers had brought barbarism to Son My.

Every Western soldier needs to be interested in incidents like the now-infamous My Lai Massacre. The actions of the American soldiers in Son My represent the almost perfect case study of a descent into barbarism; a four-hour nightmare that sums up everything that can go wrong with leadership, situational pressure, group culture and individual behaviour. The central question we should ask is 'how did this happen?' Around two-thirds of the members of Charlie Company took part in the massacre. They had only been in Vietnam for about three months. What was it that turned these American kids, in just 99-odd days, from normal people into mass murderers? Were they all, deep down, psychopaths? Were they just following the orders of their leaders, Company Commander Captain Ernest Medina and Platoon Commander Lieutenant William Calley? Or, in a manner akin to William Golding's *Lord of the Flies*, had the very horror of the situation in Vietnam driven them into a temporary, collective madness?

This chapter is designed to help military officers and soldiers to think about how atrocities like Son My happen. It will examine what shapes the behaviour of soldiers in war, what drives soldiers into barbaric acts, and what you can do about it, whether as an individual or as a leader. I will offer no concrete answers; to do so would be normative and thus dangerous. As anyone who has fought in war will tell you, every situation is different and there are no preordained solutions. Only *you* can work out what you should do in any given situation. But one thing remains true: no matter what you choose, you will live with the consequences. This is but one of the responsibilities borne by professional soldiers.

Three experiences of war and a reflection on ethics

My interest in military ethics comes from reflections on my own actions in war. I joined the British Army in January 2001, and watched the terrorist attacks on 11 September 2001 unfold via a television in the Academy café. Ironically we were supposed to be in a lecture entitled 'The Causes of War', but the seasoned historian told us to go and watch the live footage instead. He said it would be 'instructive' to those of us just joining the Army. He was right. Over the next 15 years most of my cohort would serve in Iraq and Afghanistan as part of the Global War on Terror. Three moments from my own experience stand out as prominent in my views on military ethics. It is worth outlining them briefly as context.

The first was the invasion of Iraq in 2003. Some 555 days after watching the Twin Towers collapse in New York I crossed the border into Iraq as part of a British Armoured Division. This was a military action that is rare in modern times: the deliberate, conventional invasion of another sovereign nation. Those who invaded Iraq saw the stark transition between peace and war, delineated by just a line on a map and an executive order to invade. In retrospect, it was the very starkness of this transition that made it ethically remarkable. At one moment all societal controls on the power to legally kill were constrained. As we sat in neat lines in Kuwait, poised to invade, we had no more right to apply violence than the average man at home. However the moment we crossed the border these controls were left behind. Those who invaded were suddenly immersed in the full experience of war, like a leap into ice water. We all suddenly learned how we would behave, often with dramatic effect.

The second was the conduct of deliberate 'kinetic strike' operations in Afghanistan. Here was a very different sort of war. Western forces had been conducting operations in the country for nearly a decade, and had built up an unparalleled network of sensors with which to track and target the enemy. Hundreds of drones criss-crossed the sky, offering an ever-present if opaque window into Afghan society. Here we fought war through a screen, watching insurgents for days, sometimes weeks, before striking with missiles from the air. The physical risk to us was low. This was a war of ethical disassociation. There were no visceral emotions: no rage, anger, terror or desire for revenge. Equally there was little sense of the effect of violent action. With such low risk and apparent military efficacy, this style of war was highly attractive, but what were the consequences for our sense of morality?

The final formative experience involved the conduct of ground operations in Afghanistan over a protracted period. Here I learned how the nature of war is to seek to corrupt those who are immersed within it, particularly over time. I discovered how the sheer *otherness* of combat, like a magnet next to a compass, seeks to draw your moral reference point away from its true course. I discovered *dehumanisation*: the capacity to start to believe that the lives of your enemy are somehow without worth. I learned how such corruption can take place slowly over time and under pressure. Along with my colleagues I learned about the power of the *group*; its capacity to influence those within it for good or ill, and its power to be a gateway to, and a defence against, atrocious behaviour.

The morality of the wars in Iraq and Afghanistan can, and will, be debated for many years to come. For me the key point of reflection is that most of us who fought there were unaware of the effect war might have on our behaviours. We were unprepared, both as individuals and commanders, for the ethical shock of combat. While we cannot change the wars of the past, we can better prepare ourselves and our soldiers for the conflicts of the future. We can think better, and fight better. This starts with a simple model to help us understand behaviour in war.

The individual, the situation and the group

I believe that three factors influence behaviour in war: an individual's predilections, the power of the situation of war, and the influence of the group. These are shown in the simple diagram below:

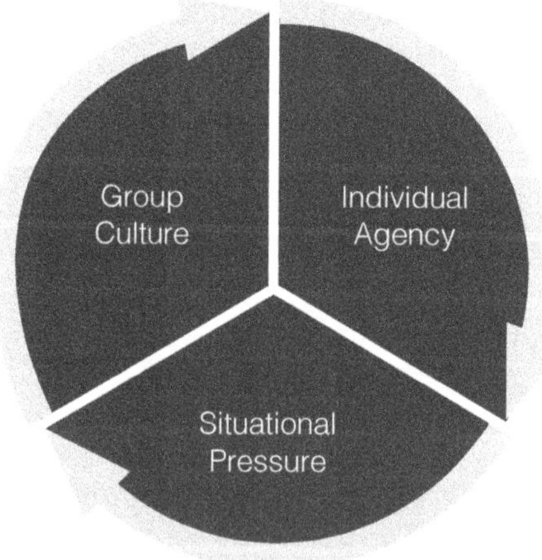

Figure 1: The three influence model[2]

I do not intend to go into depth on individual predilections here. We could barely scratch the surface of the formative psychology that makes up each soldier. A commander needs to remember that by the time a soldier falls under their influence they will have had (on average) a minimum of eighteen years of 'life experience' that will guide their individual choices. Socio-economic background, parenting, schooling and the stability of their upbringing will all have contributed to their developing an understanding of ethics and morality; what is viewed as 'right' and what is viewed as 'wrong'. This will guide action and re-action. Underpinning this 'moral compass' (as you might call it) are a set of inherent traits like aggression, passion, compassion and empathy and each manifest in different ways. The 'moral compass' and the inherent traits are the baseline for individual action. They must be understood and leveraged for each soldier.

What militaries must keep at the forefront is that there are some people who, due to their predilections, are temperamentally unsuited to the stresses of combat, and who should not be given the right to apply legal violence on behalf of the state. Private First Class (PFC) Stephen Green of the United States Army, who raped and murdered 14-year-old Abeer Qasim Hamza al-Janabi in Iraq in 2006, was one such character. An unstable man with a long history of criminal convictions, Green was diagnosed after the murder as a psychopath and sociopath.[3] Corporal Clayton Matchee of the Canadian Airborne Regiment was another; a man whose predispositions to violence contributed to him beating to death Somalian teenager Shidane Arone during the 1993 Somali famine relief mission.[4] Were there warning signs before these murders? Should they have prompted intervention? Could some sort of testing have identified the potential for brutality in these individuals in advance? The answer is: possibly.

The question is how to do this. Large-scale psychometric testing has proved broadly ineffective in the past; the United States military experimented with the Rorschach Test in 1944 but soon discarded it as unreliable.[5] With no useable method, most militaries turn to the only real evidence of behavioural tendencies that they have – previous conduct. Almost every defence force uses criminal convictions as a filter for suitability for service. Technically, the United States military precludes those who have been convicted of felonies from service.[6] After enlistment this remains the practice, and the commission of a violent crime usually leads to immediate discharge.

It is, however, at times of greatest operational pressure that these standards are often threatened. During the Global War on Terror, the urgent need for troops forced the United States military to take what might be seen as desperate action. In 2006, 34 476 recruits were granted what are known as 'moral waivers' from the usual criminal threshold. This was 19.6 per cent of enlistments, and a marked increase from 7.8 per cent a decade earlier. In the United States Marines, 54.3 per cent of enlistees in 2006 had previous convictions waived, a remarkable five-fold increase from 1997.[7] Stephen Green was in receipt of one of these waivers.[8] The effect of this decision on the 'moral foundation' of a force is almost impossible to track in causal terms. That it will have an effect should be accepted. Militaries must hold a constantly critical eye to the moral standard of the individuals they attest into service.

The second factor in the model is the influence of the situation of war. In 1971 Professor Phillip Zimbardo conducted the famous Stanford Prison Experiment, an examination into the power of situational forces on individual and group behaviour.[9] Some 33 years later, Zimbardo was asked to give evidence as an expert witness at the trial of Ivan (Chip) Frederick, a United

States Army Staff Sergeant. Frederick had been the Night Shift Commander of Tier 1A of the Abu Ghraib detention centre, where he dealt out systematic and brutal abuse to Iraqi prisoners. Along with the now-infamous Charles Graner and Lynndie England, Frederick punched and stomped on detainees, piled them naked in pyramids for photos, and forced prisoners to masturbate in front of each other.[10] Most soldiers would argue that, as the non-commissioned officer in charge, he bears even greater responsibility than Graner and England for what happened at Abu Ghraib.

In his expert evidence, Zimbardo argued that it was principally the corrupting power of the situation at Abu Ghraib that led to Frederick acting as he did. Frederick was not an inherently violent man. Extensive psychoanalysis concluded that, perhaps unlike PFC Green or Corporal Matchee, he had no predispositions to abusive or sadistic behaviour. It did, however, conclude that he was an 'obliging, docile and placating' character who was experiencing 'extreme exhaustion' at the time of the incidents.[11] Zimbardo argued that, like in his prison in Stanford, the particular cocktail of violence, fear, pressure and stress of the Abu Ghraib environment had overwhelmed Frederick's limited resilience. His natural response had been primeval, and violent. While Frederick must bear the responsibility for his actions, Zimbardo suggested that this responsibility should be diminished. The court martial did not agree, and jailed Frederick for eight years.[12] It is perhaps of note that, after the court martial dismissed Zimbardo's evidence, an independent panel that reviewed Department of Defense detention operations in 2004 leaned heavily on his work in explaining the causality behind detainee abuse.[13]

My experience of war leads me to agree with Zimbardo. Indeed I would take his assertion further. In his seminal work *On War*, the 19th-century German military theorist Carl von

Clausewitz argues that war is an entity of enduring nature; a 'total phenomenon' that is to be 'regarded as a blind natural force'. I believe the 'primordial violence, hatred and enmity' that Clausewitz describes as part of this nature has an enduring effect on those fighting within it.[14] General William Tecumseh Sherman recognised that 'war is hell' but what can be added is that its effect is to corrupt.[15] This effect can be sudden or gradual, but I would suggest it tends to deepen over time. I believe war's corrupting effect expresses itself in three ways: through the provision of the power to apply violence, through the removal of social constraint, and through the stirring of visceral emotions such as fear, rage, hatred and disgust. Herein lies a corrupting triad to which we are all vulnerable.

The power to apply violence is central to this corruption. This is not a familiar space for most Westerners. From the mass industrialisation of the slaughterhouse, to the blessed stability of a secure society, we have steadily sanitised violence from our lives. We do not have to physically defend our possessions. We do not have to fight for a mate. We are no longer even required to kill our food. As the British military historian John Keegan writes in *The Face of Battle*, 'direct, face-to-face, knock-down and drag-out violence is something which modern, middle-class Western man rarely if at all encounters in his everyday life'.[16] Blood and death are strangers to almost all of us. Centuries of development in theological, legal, philosophical, political and social theory have created a society epitomised by social constraint; a mostly unspoken social contract of non-violence.[17] In return for this contract we are able to live our lives in relative comfort, free of existential fear.

We felt this keenly in the invasion of Iraq. For the soldiers waiting in Kuwait for the war to begin the normal social contract remained firmly in place. We had no greater authority to kill than the average man. We had no exposure to the more

visceral emotions of terror or disgust, bar the natural excitement
and nervousness of waiting. Laws and customs explicitly bound
our behaviour. The moment we crossed the border, however, this
situation changed. Rules of Engagement were released, and provided a gateway for the application of violence. Social constraint
started to degrade. The strength of visceral emotion, both positive and negative, began to build. It was actually surprisingly
difficult to get someone to fire the first tank round; but once the
barrier was broken the concept of social constraint changed dramatically. It was not just that we were *able* to threaten or use violence; it was the very reason we were there. For each soldier, this
new paradigm of social constraint tested the resilience of their
moral compass. I vividly remember one of my soldiers, in passing, saying to me, 'You know, we could just kill any one of these
people on the street, and no one would know about it'. He was
right. To their credit, and the credit of their preparation, most
soldiers managed to maintain a coherent line despite the twisted
environment. Others did not.

The best way to think about the power of war to corrupt
is in terms of ethical risk. All war carries it. The level of this
risk is, however, not a constant. Different scenarios carry different risks. The invasion of Iraq was a conventional war and one
for which we had trained extensively. In that sense, the maintenance of some form of societal control was perhaps simpler. The
enemy was broadly identifiable by their uniform and equipment.
Victory, in the form of the capture of Basra and Baghdad, was
definable. These factors reduced the ethical risk. However as the
war dragged on, and as the character of the conflict changed, I
believe new ethical risk factors came into play. The Iraqi people
became steadily dehumanised in the eyes of the coalition soldiers as the insurgency grew. The lines between combatant and
civilian blurred. A growing body count and the proliferation of

Improvised Explosive Devices (IEDs) led to a persistent fear of death. Repeated tours compounded fatigue. Victory was undefinable. Hatred and disgust for the Iraqi people became common. In *Black Hearts*, the journalist Jim Frederick captures a vivid picture of the capacity the 'long war' in Iraq had to corrupt personal values. His story of individual and group barbarity in Baghdad's Triangle of Death in 2006, and the murders that resulted, should be required reading for all young officers and non-commissioned officers. Dehumanisation, a faceless enemy, persistent fear of death, visceral emotions: these are all factors that increase the ethical risk of the situation of war. It is up to the commander to understand, and then seek to mitigate, this risk.

The final factor in my model is the influence of the group. Almost all Western militaries are based around hierarchical structures. From corps and divisions, through brigades and battlegroups, and right down to platoons and sections, soldiers identify themselves as members of groups. My experience is that these groups are far better defined than those in civilian life. Military groups are labelled with the deeply historic military iconography of cap badges, corps insignia and uniforms. Explicit systems of rank and seniority exist, with both legal and customary authority. Soldiers and officers often live together in enclosed bases, binding the group geographically. Our identification within these groups goes deep into our military psyche. Often we consciously and unconsciously reflect stereotypes: the suave cavalryman, the gritty infantryman, the aggressive paratrooper, the logical engineer. These shape not only our beliefs and attitudes, but also our behaviours.

The influence of military groups, and particularly small military groups, runs deep because they are what are known in social psychology as *primary groups*. These are defined as 'particularly close small social groups whose members share close, personal, enduring relationships'.[18] Primary groups are most commonly found in families, and for many soldiers this is exactly how they consider their comrades. Such close cohesion among soldiers, and particularly combat soldiers, is wholly desirable for the military. It fosters the loyalty, reliance, courage and determination that pulls people through hardship, and leads to acts of valour. Basic training is designed to initiate and inculcate recruits into the military *primary group*, and most of our regimental iconography is there to deepen and reinforce it. The influence of such groups on behaviour is great. In *Obedience to Authority*, Stanley Milgram used a theatrical electric shock experiment to prove people's susceptibility to those in authority.[19] Fewer will know about Solomon Asch who, ten years before Milgram, proved that people are also highly susceptible to group decisions, even when the group goes against their individual instinct.[20] These studies are fascinating, and worthy of deeper investigation by military professionals.

When you examine military groups deeply, however, you realise there is danger as well as benefit. The problem is that groups are not inherently moral; they are actually agnostic. They will apply their collectivising influence equally whether the actions of the group are virtuous or evil. As such, they can drive soldiers to great valour, or quite exceptional evil. In Son My, two-thirds of the soldiers in Charlie Company took part in the massacre. I would suggest much of this is because the group did it together. Individual responsibility for actions was diffused. Pressure from the peer group came into play. Visceral emotions of hatred and disgust were fed and magnified by the collective. The soldiers from Charlie Company of 1-502nd Infantry Regiment in *Black Hearts* are another good example, where a group that became deviant and brutal worked to twist the behaviours of others within it. The power of the group, and its ability to influence behaviour for good or ill under stress, must not be underestimated.

Individual predilection, the situation of war and the influence of the group: these three factors drive behaviour in war, for good or for ill. Everyone will have their own view on which of the three is pre-eminent. What seems clear is that the right cocktail of individual weakness, a dire situation and a corrupt group can twist the ethical reference points of all of us. Barbarity can be the outcome. We must do all we can to defend ourselves against these influences, and this is where we now turn.

The virtue ethic and behaviour

It is perhaps of no surprise that the best tool we have for controlling behaviour in war (bar not going there) is also one of the greatest threats: the group. Commanders can use tools of leadership and social engineering to construct a group that helps individuals withstand the corrupting power of the situation of war. I believe this can be done through a very old concept in moral philosophy: the development of a virtue ethic.

Virtue ethics reaches as far back as Plato and Aristotle, and is one of the oldest forms of normative ethics. Instead of delving deeply into existential questions over 'right' and 'wrong', it instead places an emphasis on virtues and moral character as the guides for decision making. Virtue ethics argues that if you can hold to certain cardinal virtues, and remain rational under pressure, then your conduct should remain virtuous. It offers a 'whole of life' approach, espousing virtues such as prudence, justice, fortitude and temperance as guides.[21] The idea of a virtue ethic has long resounded with soldiers in the form of *stoicism*, from Marcus Aurelius through to modern proponents like Vice Admiral James Stockdale, an American naval aviator who was a prisoner of war for seven years during the Vietnam conflict.[22]

Much of the investment professional militaries put into leadership, command climate and culture today is actually focused on the construction of a virtue ethic within primary groups. There are a number of tools militaries are able to lean on to do this. One is history. For the Australian Army, the virtues demonstrated by the Australian Imperial Force at Gallipoli form the bedrock for the modern Army's collective virtue ethic.[23] These virtues, modernised and contemporised, are then verbalised and expressed in policy. For most militaries, a set of military values are central to this verbalising. Choosing these words is a more complex problem than perhaps first imagined.

Over the page is a selection of military value sets from various armies, ranging from the Australian Army through to China's People's Liberation Army (PLA). There are some continuities. 'Loyalty' features heavily in the Chinese inventory as does 'discipline'. 'Courage', understandably in war, is nearly universal. There are also key differences. Only some of these words are what you might describe as 'laden with ethical value'; designed to prevent soldiers from drifting towards barbarity. In the absence of these value-laden words, it is much easier to leverage the resulting virtue ethic towards evil acts. An example is Reserve Police Battalion 101 of the Wehrmacht in the Second World War. This 500-strong unit were among the most prolific and most brutal killing machines of the Holocaust, murdering over 87 000 Jews. In 1941, during Operation Reinhardt, they shot over 43 000 people in two days. No constructed sanitisation of the gas chambers for Battalion 101; each victim was executed at close range.[24] Like any military group, Battalion 101 had a virtue ethic (either written or unwritten). They used this to motivate soldiers to do a job of unimaginable horror, and to keep doing it without descending into madness. 'Loyalty' to the Reich would certainly have been part of it. 'Courage' would likely have been there.

Australian Army:	United States Army:	British Army:
Courage	Loyalty	Courage
Initiative	Duty	Integrity
Respect	Respect	Discipline
Teamwork	Selfless Service	Respect for Others
	Honor	Loyalty
	Integrity	Selfless Commitment
	Personal Courage	

Singaporean Air Force:	Chinese PLA:
Loyalty to Country	Loyalty
Leadership	Honour and Heroism
Discipline	Discipline
Professionalism	Strength of Will
Fighting Spirit	Unity of Purpose
Ethics	Professional Qualities
Care for Soldiers	
Safety	

Figure 2: Comparison of national army values[25]

'Discipline' would have been central. All are common terms in modern military values.

Conspicuously absent would have been words like 'compassion, 'integrity', 'empathy' or 'ethics'. These words are different from subjective terms like 'loyalty' in that they are intrinsically linked to a higher concept: the idea that human life has value, and that taking it comes with cost. These are the words that link values to those espoused by International Humanitarian Laws; the assertion of equal rights to life and liberty, and the codification of the just war principles.[26] If you go back and look at the military value sets listed above, it is now relatively easy to pick out those words that are laden with ethical value. Their removal fundamentally changes the foundation of the value set, allowing far more scope for interpretation in terms of what is 'right' and 'wrong'. Take, for example, the Australian Army's 'Contract with Australia'.[27] The removal of the single word 'compassion' allows it to be easily translated into an imaginary value set for *Daesh* or the *Islamic State* group operating in Syria and Iraq.

The Islamic State Contract:

I am an Islamic State soldier who is an expert in close combat

أنا جندي من الدولة الإسلامية ومتختصص في القتال عن قرب

I am physically and mentally tough and courageous

أنا قوي جسديًا وشجاع عقليًا

I lead by example, I strive to take the initiative

دائمًا أكون القدوة الحسنة، وأجاهد لأخذ المبادرة

I am committed to learning and working for the team

أنا ملتزم بتعلمي وعملي من أجل الفريق

I believe in trust and respect for my Country, my mates and my Army

أنا مؤمن بتقديم الإحترام والثقة من أجل وطني، أصدقائي و جيشي

the Quran is my badge of honour

القرآن هو وسام شرفي

I am an Islamic State soldier, always.

أنا جندي الدولة الإسلامية، دائمًا وإلى الأبد

Figure 3: The Islamic State contract; no need for compassion?

Figure 4: Iconography: the 'Taliban Hunting Club' and 'Expect No Mercy'[28]

Military value sets are only one part of constructing a virtue ethic, but I would argue they are one of the fundamentals. They provide the foundations which provide a consistent guide for both the group and the individual. For commanders, the devil is then in the detail of making this ethic a lived reality within the *primary group*. Professor Richard Holmes, the renowned British historian, once described military doctrine as 'not just what is taught, or what is published, but what is believed'.[29] The same rings true for a virtue ethic. It must be espoused in every action, every directive and every plan. It must be particularly reflected in the behaviour of leaders, whose actions have a catalytic effect on others (given the power of their trappings of authority so well exposed by Stanley Milgram in 1961). As the former Chief of the Australian Army, Lieutenant General David Morrison, once said: 'the standard you walk past is the standard you set'.[30]

The iconography used by military groups is a good example of where detail is important. I would suggest that the creeping proliferation of emblems like the 'Taliban Hunting Club', shown above, and the somewhat surprising 'Expect No Mercy' motto of the 1–101st Aviation Regiment of the United States Army, both stand in stark opposition to a desirable virtue ethic. Liberal democratic armies should not encourage a culture that glorifies the animalistic hunting of other men. Such dehumanisation is a gateway to atrocity. Nor should we give directives to our soldiers to be 'merciless'.

The virtue ethic and leadership

The nature of a group virtue ethic is deeply reliant on a key input: leadership. Over time, any group will develop an ethic. Strong, ethical leadership is almost always required to steer this in a positive direction, and give it resilience against the corrupting nature of war. Toxic or non-existent leadership hastens the descent into barbarity, often acting as the final gateway to the atrocity taking place. This can take place through an active input, in the delivery of barbaric orders. At Son My, Lieutenant William Calley explicitly ordered his soldiers to shoot civilians, and then reinforced these orders with his own actions. This clearly played a major role in both commencing and sustaining the massacre.[31]

More worryingly though, the leadership gateway to atrocity is more often passive; the result of not giving direction, or giving orders that are vague enough to indirectly legitimise actions. The only command boundary given to Clayton Matchee in dealing with detainees was 'just don't kill them', thus legitimising all and every action up to beating detainees to death.[32] In his examination of Abu Ghraib, Phillip Zimbardo concluded that a lack of leadership interest and oversight meant that 'a general norm of permissiveness prevailed that created a sense that the guards could do pretty much whatever they felt like doing'. Ken Davis, one of the Military Policemen at Abu Ghraib, stated that the direction given to them regarding detainees was 'use your imagination. Break them. We want them broken by the time we come back'.[33] Commanders at all levels must remember that silence can sometimes be the greatest crime that a leader can commit.

War is hell and part of its enduring nature is the power to corrupt. Medal of Honour winner Sergeant Sammy L Davis rightly observed that 'war is always an assault on the humanity of every individual caught up in its destructive path'.[34] Having seen war in a number of different forms over the past 15 years, I have concluded that it is hubris of the most dangerous kind to believe you can immerse yourself in conflict without moral risk. This is not something we can ignore. The West professes to use force to sustain freedom and justice; when we torture and brutalise, we fundamentally undermine the moral justification of our actions.[35] Abu Ghraib is perhaps the best recent example as to how, for the West, moral failure equals strategic failure. The actions of American soldiers in that hellish pit of a prison have damaged the moral authority of the United States to use force for years to come.

Understanding the nature of war, and how to resist its corrupting power, is vital for those who aspire to be masters of the profession of arms. It must be seen as a central part of leadership; no matter which leadership model you aspire to adopt. The process of resistance starts with understanding. We need to spend time analysing the ethical risk of the character of conflict we face in a given scenario. Understanding the effect of war on individual and group psychology is essential; the effects of dehumanisation, enduring fear of death, faceless enemies, isolation and visceral emotions like hatred and disgust are all doorways to barbarism. Recognising and acknowledging them is the first step to defending against them.

Once we understand ethical risk, we then need to dedicate ourselves to deliberately defining and constructing a virtue ethic that helps us overcome it. There are myriad tools to do this, but I would suggest that military values are central. The words we use cannot be selected hastily, nor is this a simple task. It must be remembered that the Schutzstaffel or SS's motto was 'Meine Ehre heißt Treue' or 'My Honour is Loyalty'.[36] Forces that aspire to fight just wars must move beyond subjective terms like 'loyalty' and 'honour', and espouse alongside them values that are intrinsically linked to concepts of life and liberty. These are the foundations of a virtue ethic that helps prevent the unconscious drifting of moral reference points in war; a guiding light in the darkness.

The final responsibility, as with so many things, rests on the shoulders of leaders. A virtue ethic is a conscious choice, and one that can only really be made by those invested with legal and cultural authority. Leaders must remember that nature abhors the void. If they don't set an ethic for the group, it is almost guaranteed that it will set one itself. In the worst case, war, with all its corrupting power, will set the ethic for them. At that stage disaster, and barbarism, is almost an inevitability.

Acknowledgment: This chapter is a personal reflection on collaborative work undertaken in 2015 with Lieutenant Colonel Steve Hart RM and Dr David Whetham (Kings College London). People like Steve and David safeguard our souls in war, and I am ever thankful for their leadership and tutoring.

PART 2: OPERATING ETHICALLY IN THE JOINT ENVIRONMENT

An Australian soldier in Rwanda as part of the United Nations' mission that followed ethnic cleansing in 1994. *Commonwealth of Australia*

3

ETHICS AND INSTITUTIONAL CONFLICT

MAURIE McNARN

For uniformed personnel, conflicts and contradictions are worthy of close attention because they are the source of moral challenges and ethical compromises. Ethical decisions are rarely simple or clean cut; compromises are made, contradictions abound and constraints bind us. Yet, for all the systemic and personal complexities they present we cannot afford to ignore or step back from ethical issues. Why are ethics important? Because individuals make decisions and outcomes are influenced by those individuals. Each individual's decisions are influenced by personal views, values, attitudes, experience, prejudices and views of morality – whether we consciously acknowledge it or not. This caveat has direct operational consequences on everything from planning to the conduct of operations, as well as circumstances when combat operations cease. So I ask the question: can you actually have ethics in war or is the proposition inherently contradictory? Is it a contradiction that contemporary, primarily Western nations need to justify ethically or morally a political decision that leads to killing? Arguably, it is easier to justify operations for peacekeeping or humanitarian operations, rather than conventional war, even if a war is 'good' or 'just' from the legal, media and public perspective.

Political considerations and legal constraints aside, however, I believe it is ethics that distinguish actions in warfare from barbarism and perhaps allow uniformed personnel to live with their decisions. I suspect there is a degree of contradiction and hypocrisy in what militaries say and teach versus what militaries practise when on operations. Yet, I would still argue that ethics remain a matter of absolute importance.

What experience informs my views?

Many of my remarks on the strategic-national level are informed by my time as a Colonel Operations in Joint Operations and Plans for the first Timor operation, my time at Strategic Command as Director General Joint Operations and Plans for the Australian Defence Force (ADF) during operations including Anaconda in Afghanistan, the Commonwealth Heads of Government Meeting in Brisbane and cleaning up after the 'children overboard' issue, as National Commander in the Middle East 2002–2003 and as Director of the Defence Intelligence Organisation through, for example, Iraq, Afghanistan, Second Timor, a rising China and North Korean nuclear tests.

What has influenced my ethical outlook?

Throughout my military career, I was fortunate to have great mentors. As Colonel Operations I served under Major General Michael Keating and then Major General Peter Cosgrove during the Timor operation. I observed leaders such as Air Vice Marshal Alan Titheridge and worked directly to Generals Cosgrove and Ken Gillespie as National Commander. In Iraq, I had a very insightful Chief of Staff, Colonel Ross Boyd, who was a great sounding board for my thoughts. Personal ethics, leadership example and professional mentoring are the keys to shaping ethical behaviour. I also learnt the value of people with whom you can debate issues and wargame. Ethics or values lists are only words. It is interpreting them and giving them form that matters and sometimes there is no easy or good decision. As a commander it is sometimes about the 'art of the possible' and the least unethical decision. Values will not provide answers. Values are a guide only. Ultimately, subjective decisions will need to be made.

Discussion, training, example and mentors were therefore important, but so was understanding that it is you who makes the call and you who is held accountable. Experience reinforced that ethics are highly personal. What one person may think is reasonable and central to their values may be anathema to another. I have worked with people who claimed they were 'doing God's work' in the Middle East. I hasten to add they were both Christian *and* Muslim in different situations. This was quite disturbing to me but perfectly reasonable to others. This tension is not theoretical. It can affect decisions. I also discovered some people found it easier to be ethical, at times righteously indignant, if it did not directly affect them. It is always different with 'skin in the game', where you are accountable or responsible for a decision.

So do you have a role in the ethics of an operation or war?

Traditional just war theory provides a framework with sets of principles, satisfying what is necessary and sufficient for a war to be permissible. As a commander, the six typical principles that were most useful to me were:

- Just cause: the war is an attempt to avert the wrong kind of injury.
- Legitimate authority: the war is fought by an entity that has the authority to fight such wars.
- Right intention: that entity intends to achieve the just cause, rather than using it as an excuse to achieve some wrongful end.
- Reasonable prospects of success: the war is sufficiently likely to achieve its aims.
- Proportionality: the morally weighted 'goods' achieved by the war outweigh the morally weighted 'bads' that it will cause.
- Last resort (necessity): there is no other less harmful way to achieve the just cause.

These points will always be an issue for debate – and were before, during and after the Iraq War. There will be polarised ethical positions and polarised political debate and there can be quite different debates for different operations. We might contrast Timor with Iraq ('good' versus 'bad' wars), or characterise Iraq and Afghanistan in terms of the morality or 'justness' of these commitments. Yet even at the theatre level I saw limited scope for discussions about the 'just war' or the rights and wrongs of a particular conflict. You might have some influence in the information provided to decision makers, but it will not be your decision. I noted the six principles above simply because they offer a framework. Circumstances may also dictate how a commander operates, the degree to which the commander has freedom in decision making, the level of political and senior officer interference, resource considerations, the prevailing rules of engagement, the community's reaction to a deployment and the media's depiction of an operation, and how the commander explains the point and purpose of a mission to their troops. These are a few of the many factors arising from circumstances.

As a commander I saw little scope or point to getting into the ethics or morality of the war. Once the decision is made it is more about the ethical or moral behaviour of your troops and your decision making in the conduct of the operation. There is still a need, however, to present a positive rationale to your community, the media and the troops going into harm's way. There is, then, an inconsistency at times between political decision making, senior military advice, planning and operational security versus the public message. It may also manifest in contradictory written and verbal orders that can raise interesting ethical and career choices. Consequently, the practicalities are in how the operation is conducted and the role of ethical behaviour. The second part of 'a just war' is where reality and ethics tended to intersect.

Ethics – more useful in the conduct of the operation?

Of use to me where ethical decision making met reality were the principles of:

- *Discrimination*: distinguishing between military objectives and civilians, and intentionally attacking only military objectives.
- *Proportionality*: damage must be proportionate to the military benefit achieved.
- *Necessity*: the least harmful means feasible must be used.

These three points all matter to the ethics of war and I found them directly relevant to my decision making, however other essential factors beyond ethics are in play and affect decision making and ethics.

Other elements that affect decision making

Ethics do not exist in a vacuum and they are not always absolute. On operations there will, of necessity, be compromise. There are a number of elements that shape decisions and ethics. The influence of each element can vary. Therefore, in what follows they are not presented in any specific order of priority other than to note where ethics confronts reality. But first perhaps is politics because a nation usually goes to war or conducts military operations for political reasons. Those reasons will influence the ethical boundaries of the operation from forces and firepower deployed to rules of engagement and political intervention.

Politics is pervasive at the theatre and national level and only the most naive commander would expect otherwise. Politics comes in many guises and not all are parliamentary-based. *Government* politics can be local, national or international in practice. It is about alliances and relationships and seeking advantage not directly related to the specific conflict and tends to reflect parliamentary or government policy objectives. *Institutional* politics involves the different services (Navy, Army and Air Force), or Branches/Corps/Professional groupings that seek advantage in force structure, advancing competing options for government, and securing command appointments. *Bureaucratic* politics is the remit of public service departments, civilian and uniformed bureaucrats, personalities within departments seeking control, influence, rivalries, ambitions, individual political views, and what stakeholders consider the national interest or information to be given to politicians. *Personality* politics can lead to command elements being bypassed or marginalised in an operation.

There is a necessary political element of a 'sales pitch' to the community. It may be correct, it may skirt around the truth or only be partially be correct; it may introduce elements that are unrealistic into the mission that a commander and troops need to work around; this can produce practical and ethical challenges. There may be the politics of our elected officials with perhaps different collective and individual motivations in both government and opposition. There may be the politics of the different departments; for example, Defence and the Department of Foreign Affairs and Trade may have different desired outcomes. With allies this might manifest in splits that lead to quite different reporting to Australia and to government. Finally, there can also be issues of personal power between senior bureaucrats and, on occasion, their personal political views. These factors shape decisions and flow down to the troops, for example, shaping the circumstances where the rules of engagement are applied, resourcing, the support available to the commander and troops on the ground or limitations placed on the commander and the troops, all of which can ultimately affect decisions and ethics in the conduct of the operation.

Legal issues are critical in making operational decisions. You need to ensure your intended action is legally defensible. But meeting a legal requirement does not necessarily make an action ethical. While something may fit within the rules of engagement it must also still be necessary. There will also be a degree of subjectivity about how proportional and necessary an action may be. The same might also be the case with discrimination. Very capable legal advisors have been key in my appointments. In Iraq I had two outstanding lawyers. Considerable time was invested in defining and discussing Rules of Engagement with combat forces in preparation for operations in Iraq. Component commanders, unit commanders and lawyers set the context, wargamed situations and set the culture, both legal and ethical; for example it was acceptable to not fire or drop your bombs if you had reservations about the target. There is a definite cultural element to such decisions.

When on an operation, culture is pervasive and it will vary incredibly depending on location. Ethics do not always translate between individuals, religions, organisations or countries. We should not assume that we are always dealing with ethical people or with people who hold the same ethics. We need to understand the ethics or lack thereof of in the opposition – will they use human shields, locate in hospitals or schools, or murder prisoners, and how will your force deal with that? For example, a relatively minor matter that we might consider unacceptable could be perfectly acceptable to others in the Western Coalition multinational headquarters in Kabul. We had Australians working 24/7 and they were making decisions that could mean life or death for someone. All Australian personnel were prohibited from consuming alcohol. This was not the case for some of the other nationalities, whose personnel consumed significant quantities of alcohol and used the operational IT system to access pornography while on duty. Australians might consider such behaviour to be an ethical issue as well as operationally wrong.

Other nationalities did not. For troops on the ground it might be confronting social practices that are abhorrent to us such as abuse of children, but accepted in the culture of that country and outside our mandate.

We might also consider if culture can be influenced by your role and responsibilities and the extent of casualties. While not for a moment downplaying the effect of every Australian casualty, it is the United States that had the lead role on operations and which suffered the most casualties. Australia did not have primary responsibility for prosecuting the wars in the Middle East and actively avoided managing a province. We have been able to be relatively selective in where we deployed and what we did, for reduced risk and maximum alliance benefit. In Iraq, success or failure was really down to the United States. This reality can influence culture, risk, aggressiveness and the interplay of various elements with ethics and perceptions of ethics. In Timor we did lead and led well. It was difficult and challenging involving differing cultures in the coalition. But it was not conventional war, nor was it on the scale of the conflict in the Middle East with its ethical challenges.

Media is another significant factor. With modern communications, the internet, mobile phones and even helmet cameras on troops, the media cannot be avoided. It is useful, therefore, to consider if the media is an ethical actor. Is the media required to deal ethically with the military or military with the media? We might consider whether the media is simply a business to be managed. Does the military have an ethical obligation to provide information to the public via the media? How much is it advisable to tell the media and when is it reasonable to mislead? Do you present the party line even if you know something is untrue? You need to have considered whether lying to the media is unethical or simply dangerous. There might even be instances when telling the truth is dangerous if continuing operations could be imperilled. Is omission of information or selective provision of information ethical? The media is complex and in Iraq it was treated as a significant line of operations.

In truth, there are many very professional, committed, ethical people in the media, as in any profession, but also a few that are not, and you need to understand the difference and engage them on that basis. The media may also hold an ethical mirror up to you and your operations and decisions, and they may ask you difficult questions, but remember they will influence your community, politicians and the people you deal with in Canberra. They are a critical element in your consideration of culture, ethics and community expectations, particularly how our operational behaviour may be viewed in Australia.

Community expectations are inextricably linked to media and politics. My view in Iraq – going back to the first six principles of 'just war' – is that the decision to commit forces is political and if people object there is a political process. Your subsequent actions on operations will, however, be judged by the community – your ethics and outcomes. For me, a shorthand approach in my decision making was the question: will this decision pass the front page of the *Australian* or the *Sydney Morning Herald* test? A decision may be legal but would it meet the community's expectations of our military and the image or standards we publicly promote? Community expectations are also complex and can easily change, which makes the ethical positions taken by politicians, senior officers and media quite important.

Personal attributes and professional ambition are other operative factors. Ambitions including yours and those of subordinates, senior officers, public servants, politicians and institutions (corps, services) affect ethics and culture. People are flawed. Some need to be liked, some want to be seen as 'tough', some have no concept of operations or violence (people who use movies as a point of reference as if they are in some way a window to understanding Defence operations are a concern), some are self-righteous. Others just want power and promotion. It all affects ethics, culture and decisions both positively and negatively.

In sum, all the elements described above affect ethics and decision making. Where, then, do we compromise? This question brings me back to discrimination, proportionality and necessity. First, let's look at the discrimination criterion. We have had, at times, the luxury of agreed targets, particularly air targets. Targets could be carefully selected for minimal risk of danger to civilians or of our aircraft being shot down. However, a material percentage of 'smart bombs' have technical failures, pilot error can occur or intelligence can be faulty. Target selection is thus made knowing that errors occur. Commanders sometimes cannot avoid a trade-off between risk and ethics in achieving the mission. On the other hand it was critical that we had a culture where pilots felt empowered to make a decision to not drop ordnance, a decision our pilots were prepared to make. What of the ethics of destroying infrastructure? Do you blow up bridges that will be needed post-conflict or do you stop an armoured division from possibly moving? Risk cannot always be clearly quantified and decisions will be made on imperfect information. What happens, for example, to hospitals if you damage electricity infrastructure for good operational reasons? What are the ethical compromises when reality intrudes?

Proportionality is an equally vexed consideration. There were several occasions when I played the 'red card' in Iraq on the grounds of proportionality. In this context, the 'red card' is a serious objection that cannot be dismissed or over-ruled. In one case unsuitable air weapons were planned to support entry to Baghdad contrary to the United States Air Force's own operational analysis. My question led to public yelling, personal abuse and some pretty unpleasant behaviour by a senior officer. In fairness, he took issue with the temerity of an army officer questioning a senior United States Air Force officer on air-delivered ordnance. But there was also the ominous pronouncement: 'If this costs one American soldier his life you will be personally responsible'. This was ethically interesting in terms of discrimination. Were American lives to be valued above Iraqi civilian lives?

The decision ultimately went in my favour with the support of Commander Central Command. But what would be the consequences if General Cosgrove, General Gillespie or ultimately Prime Minister Howard had not backed my decision? What if they were Australian battalions going into Baghdad facing possible urban warfare and heavy casualties? Would my decision have been different or wrong? Personally I have no doubt the American officer was incorrect. It turned out that he had not read the detail of his operational order that said several weapons were unsuitable for urban strikes. The answer was to use different weapons systems, some of which were ground-based. After a very frosty and at times quite unpleasant 24 hours, the American commander, after having checked the facts, said that our assessment and concerns were correct. No one wanted a trip to the Hague. So proportionality and the element of judgment come into play. Is it ethics, just legally wrong or simply a dumb decision? Do we have a moral responsibility if we sign up to an operation, even if it is not our forces that will use the weapons or conduct the action? What will we risk personally?

Finally, there is the consideration of necessity. On another occasion a plan was put forward to use the 'mother of all bombs' ('MOAB') and other ordnance on Iraqi divisions that could be judged to no longer be a direct threat. You could also build a case to justify a strike. Here the United States 3rd Army, Marines and

7th Fleet stepped in and backed me on the question of 'Why strike this target?' The response was 'Well, the Air Force [USAF] might as well pack up and go home'. It was suggested that was not a bad outcome if it meant we had won and now needed to think about the post-war phase.

So where does that leave you ethically?

Ethics can be personal and situational. In practice it can be about compromise and the best of several bad options. Different wars are fought for different purposes and call for different military operations to carry out those plans. Ultimately, war is won by killing the enemy. This reality is unlikely to change. However, the way in which an army goes about killing the enemy will constantly change due to politics, civilian casualties ethics, new technology, legal issues and community expectations. Also liable to change is how closely we skirt ethical principles and legal lines to achieve success in a mission. Consequently, I am very cautious of those who package up neat answers, lists or adopt an absolute position in the discussion of ethics.

Ethics is subjective and can be situational. It does not translate consistently in our own culture, let alone across cultures. Your allies and enemies may not share your particular view of ethics. Personal values and experience will play a role, as do the particular circumstances and people's ability to rationalise behaviour. There is not always a clean, ethical answer to questions of right and wrong and this is what makes ethics a challenge. My last two points relate to context and consequences.

The distortion effect

What I might term the 'distortion effect' can challenge ethical behaviour. My experience in Lebanon as a junior officer was where the abnormal becomes the normal, people start to behave unethically. Under pressure, the strength people find from basic decency and social structure may weaken, allowing psychopaths and sociopaths greater opportunity to act without constraint, and seemingly balanced people or units to go rogue. How do you avoid getting drawn into this descent into barbarism? I would argue that if you spend too long in a relatively unfettered environment you can lose perspective.

In Iraq a massive complex military machine was deployed, on a scale experienced by few Australians, and incorporating different cultures, both regionally and amongst allies. In this environment, for example, aggression is needed, speed of decision making and reaction can be critical, multiple players are involved, rules can be fluid, serious damage and casualties occur, ethics vary and you have a licence and power to kill and destroy. People can be drawn into this culture and circumstance where right and wrong, ethics and values are drowned by a capacity to rationalise or hide actions. It is a dangerous mental and physical space for any force to occupy. In passing, I would mention in relation to 'distortion' weaponry developments, for example, the ethics of drone warfare. Does it become too easy and removed from risk when the use of drones and missiles or a raid are being watched on a screen? Do our ethical values change or become distorted? There may be considerable scope for further examination of ethics and decision making in this space. This is where training, discipline, culture, rotation policies and ethics are critical to avoid the 'distortion effect'.

The ethics we can afford?

There is some discomfort in questioning our commitment to ethics – but I have occasionally wondered how much that commitment has been tested. Are ethics really tested if you have not suffered substantial hurt? When major damage occurs will we see how ethics survive or will it be the ethics we can afford? Individual soldiers have made great personal sacrifices but has Australia or the ADF really been tested yet at a national level and what will we do if it happens?

A comment made to me some years ago occasionally comes to mind. I will paraphrase the point with less eloquence. President Abraham Lincoln was a great statesman and a wartime leader. Although a politician accustomed to compromise, he was also a man of strong moral principles shaped by clear ethical precepts. In simple terms, we might argue the strategy of both sides of the American Civil War in 1861 was to send an army that would meet in battle. The contested issues might be resolved. This way of thinking was quite reasonable at the time. But what if you were to tell Lincoln and his cabinet in 1861 that this was not a viable strategy? What if you had outlined the need to mobilise manpower en masse into the military, harness the industrial might of the North to crush the South, suspend *habeas corpus*, set up prisoner of war facilities akin to concentration camps, blockade the South, then attack the economic, political, legal, social and civilian structure of the Confederacy? Then, once you had achieved military victory there, would you be required to suspend the democratic and economic rights of Americans in the South? In 1861, someone giving such strategic advice might have been deemed not just unethical but probably mad. A few years later, when immense hurt had been inflicted on each side, this is what happened.

Again, while not in any way to make light of significant costs paid by individual soldiers and their families, and ethically the support we should be providing them, it could be argued that Australia and the ADF has not faced a serious threat to our national security (we have not had our own '9/11') nor casualties on the scale of some of our allies for several generations. One could question whether the bulk of our Defence Force is as tested and 'battle hardened' as some might argue – and so, have our ethics really been 'stress tested'. Strategically, we have largely been able to be selective in our commitments, operational areas and risk. We operate with complete air superiority and without loss of ships or aircraft. It would be fascinating to observe the level of our tolerance and the ethical and cultural effect if Australia suffered significant national damage or heavy casualties. It might well challenge our ethical position. We might also ask if ethical positions during previous conflicts over the past century would be different to discussions today; ethics are situational and change over time. The positive thing is that currently we tend to get it right most of the time, we do care about ethics and we have some very experienced people. This is a good baseline.

*

If you are lucky, your legal position on a decision may be clear and even ethical. But ethics will remain personal and situational. I was fortunate to have had some great mentors and examples in ethical decision making. I have also experienced less ethical behaviours. These experiences serve to broaden and deepen a personal perspective. I experienced good commanders at crucial times in critical appointments. Although I am perhaps a touch sceptical and even cynical at times, I continue to have considerable confidence in the decision making of current commanders in the field. This was the assessment I offered in an interview with the *Australian* in 2015. My views have not changed. There is also a personal effect on both those making the decisions and those executing the decisions. The best I can offer is to ensure that first your decision is legal and second that you can live with your decision or action because you do have to accept the consequences of your decisions and actions.

4

ETHICAL DILEMMAS IN MULTINATIONAL PEACEKEEPING

PAT McINTOSH

As the commander of the first contingent of the Australian Medical Support Force in Rwanda in 1994, I have first-hand experience of the ethical dilemmas that sometimes arise from multinational peacekeeping. While I will relate my observations to that operation, I will try to do so in a way that allows my insights to be extrapolated to other multinational peacekeeping operations. I will reflect on the ethical dilemmas we faced in Rwanda from the perspective of the following three areas: first, dealings with a United Nation's (UN) force headquarters, in our case the UN's Assistance Mission in Rwanda Headquarters (UNAMIR HQ); second, dealings with non-government organisations (NGOs); and third, task-specific issues, which in our case were medical ethical issues.

Dealings with UNAMIR HQ

I will concentrate on the ethical dilemmas of dealing with UNAMIR HQ and avoid the everyday frustrations that also affected our work. The main dilemma concerned Chapter VI of the UN Charter. Chapter VI provides for the 'Pacific Settlement of Disputes' including 'negotiation, enquiry, mediation, conciliation, arbitration, judicial settlement, resort to regional agencies or arrangements, or other peaceful means of their own choice'. The UN authorities used the mission's Chapter VI mandate as an excuse to avoid any confrontation with the feeble Rwandan Government or the more powerful Rwandan Patriotic Army (RPA). Because UNAMIR II (which was established in May 1994 – after the genocide) was authorised under Chapter VI of the UN Charter the general belief was that we could not interfere with the actions of the host government, which effectively was the RPA. We were deployed under Chapter VI because UNAMIR I (which was established in late 1993 and continued until the genocide began in April 1994) was a Chapter VI mission, and this was continued when the UN was invited back into the country by the national unity government. Despite being a Chapter VI mission, our mandate was robust and our rules of engagement were likewise robust, despite what people may think. The Australian Government had negotiated an appropriate Status of Forces Agreement (SOFA) and we had the freedom of movement necessary for us to fulfil our mandate of protecting anyone under threat. The bottom line is that the UN does not need an excuse for inactivity. It is best to limit Chapter VI operations to observer missions. If armed forces are to be deployed with a mandate to protect, it should be done under Chapter VII, which allows the UN Security Council to 'determine the existence of any threat to the peace, breach of the peace, or act of aggression' and to take military and nonmilitary action to 'restore international peace and security'.

A further complicating issue was an inadequate understanding of the conflict's history and the effects of this ignorance on the overall operation. Paul Kagame, the head of the RPA, had formed a government of national unity after a three-year, ethnically driven civil war. Power-sharing was a key plank in the Arusha Accord that the UN and the Organisation of African Unity had brokered in August 1993. Despite the Accord, Kagame and the RPA effectively controlled the country. The new government had a Hutu President and Prime Minister and Paul Kagame was the Defence Minister and Deputy President. The RPA detested the UN because UNAMIR I withdrew in the face of the genocide. It was clear that the UN was only allowed back in to the country to provide the new government with legitimacy that would free up access to international aid and support. The RPA, however, had no intention of allowing the UN freedom of movement or action. Consequently, the RPA used roadblocks to control or block the movement of UN elements or to deny access to certain locations. While the rest of the UN complied with the restrictions imposed by the RPA, the Australian contingent did not. This decision resulted in significant tensions and some very serious incidents. UNAMIR HQ invariably took the view that we should have avoided the incidents rather than recognise that we were performing assigned tasks and operating under agreed rules. The ethical dilemma was clear: do you take the easy path and not do your job, or place your troops in harm's way and be labelled a troublemaker? While inactivity is a moral wrong, the uncomfortable truth is that if you take the latter approach and lose people you may find yourself without support.

A good example of the belief held by UNAMIR HQ that we did not have the power to interfere was when the RPA announced that they intended to forcibly close all of the internally displaced persons (IDP) camps. The RPA had previously closed camps by firing into them. We know because we had to sift through the bodies to treat those who had survived. When the Colonel Operations made the announcement at the force commander's morning briefing there was acceptance of what the RPA planned to do, I challenged the Force Commander and explained that we knew that the outcome would be a massacre and that we had an obligation to ensure that the camps were closed in a way that was acceptable to the international community. I was told that we could not intervene because it was a decision of the Rwandan Government and as UNAMIR II operated under Chapter VI, the UN force had no ability to act. I spent the day trying to convince the Colonel Operations that Chapter VI was irrelevant and that our mandate to protect anyone under threat meant that we had an obligation to act. In the end, I threatened to recommend to Australia that we withdraw the Australian Medical Support Force rather than be party to a massacre. The next day the Force Commander and a Special Representative of the Secretary General visited the President and told him that the UN would not allow the camps to be closed in the way that the RPA intended. Operation Retour, a co-operative operation between the UN, RPA and NGOs to manage the camp closures was then planned. It did not prevent the massacre but managed to delay it by a couple of months.

Another ethical dilemma was whether to disobey directions from superiors when being asked to do the wrong thing. On more than one occasion, commanders on the ground were ordered by superior officers to give up control of UN personnel to the RPA Gendarme so as to avoid a potential conflict with the RPA. This was against the SOFA, as the Gendarme had no power of arrest over the UN personnel. An example was when a section commander took a UN sergeant into protective custody as he was being detained by the RPA after a vehicle accident the RPA had deliberately caused. The RPA repeatedly drove at UN vehicles coming in the opposite direction, forcing them off the road. On this occasion, a UN vehicle being driven by a Zambian sergeant was forced off the road in Butare. Unfortunately, RPA soldiers happened to be on the side of the road. The vehicle struck the soldiers, pinning one under a wheel. Two Australian vehicles with medics and an infantry section happened by and stopped to help care for the RPA soldiers. In doing so they observed the Zambian sergeant being detained by the RPA Gendarme. The section commander informed the gendarme that they had no power of arrest and that the matter would be investigated by the UN military police. As the RPA had no intention of giving up the sergeant, the section commander took the sergeant into protective custody and withdrew back to the UNAMIR Tactical Headquarters in Butare. The RPA followed and surrounded the headquarters building. The colonel commanding the headquarters ordered the corporal to release the sergeant. Despite being significantly outnumbered, the section commander refused, resulting in another standoff that the UNAMIR HQ had to defuse.

A significant example of the unknown consequences that can result from taking the easy path occurred when Belgian troops were ordered to hand over their weapons to the Interahamwa-Rwanda Government Forces (RGF) in UNAMIR I. The strategy of those behind the genocide was to kill President Habyarimana and blame the Tutsis and the UNAMIR I force. The reference to the Tutsis was to incite the Hutus to initiate reprisal killings, causing the Tutsis to congregate in places of protection. While this was happening the RGF would slaughter the educated class, regardless of their tribe, because they would not condone genocide. The reference to UNAMIR's role in the killing of the

President was to force the withdrawal of the UN without a fight, as the RGF knew that they could not defeat the UNAMIR forces. The means to the desired end was for the RGF to target the most capable element of the UNAMIR force, the Belgian battalion.

Deeply embarrassed, the Belgians would withdraw, opening the way for the RGF to lobby the UN to remove the remainder of its forces. The RGF had concluded from the United States' withdrawal from Somalia that national embarrassment could be an effective tactic. The Hutus challenged the Belgian soldiers who were assigned to protect the Deputy Prime Minister, who was also pregnant. The Belgian soldiers were told to give up their weapons, which they did after being advised to do so by their superiors. Unarmed, they were subsequently slaughtered. Within a few days the Belgian battalion had departed and the lobbying for the UN to withdraw commenced. UNAMIR I withdrew in the midst of an unfolding genocide. We can only speculate on what would have happened if the Belgian soldiers had refused to surrender their weapons and used force to protect the Deputy Prime Minister. They might well still have died but their sacrifice might have led to a very different result.

A significant ethical dilemma was UNAMIR's unwillingness to fund the provision of humanitarian support. Australia would not fund it either, even though the government gave its contingent a secondary mission to provide humanitarian support within the limits of capacity. The failure of the UN to fund humanitarian support would have been acceptable except for the fact that UNAMIR HQ agreed to provide medical support to Rwandan VIPs. This service for the privileged was provided while the maimed bodies of ordinary Rwandans were dumped on the Australian contingent's front step. There was spare capacity because most of the UN force allowed themselves to be constrained by the RPA thus resulting in few injuries or casualties. The workaround with UNAMIR HQ was convoluted but effective. Pressure was put on UNAMIR HQ to permit UN employees to be placed on our dependency list. This allowed us to manipulate the patient list to record patients as UN employees, to use the Australian Government emergency card to buy pharmaceuticals in Nairobi and to seek supplies from *Pharmaciens Sans Frontières* (PSF).

A challenge for contemporary conflicts where the UN has little control over the timing of the deployment of force elements relates to mission creep. It is very easy to allow yourself to be sucked into tasks that are outside your mission. The Australians provided the quick reaction force for Kigali for the first couple of months. We also trained UN troops to operate M113 Armed Personnel Carriers. We trained and worked with the RPA to clear mines and booby traps from public areas. We were asked to join with the Canadians to provide security in the south-west sector until another force element arrived. These tasks had to be carefully considered and justified. While we should do what is in our power to make the mission a success, commanders must be able to justify and defend putting their troops in harm's way when doing something that is not a core task. A good way to determine what you should accept is to think about how you would justify the decision at the subsequent inquiry should someone under your command be killed. And importantly, you should always share the risk with your superior headquarters.

It is now more than twenty years since the Rwandan Genocide. In the space of a few months in 1994, perhaps a million Rwandans were killed. The UNAMIR HQ made many mistakes on the ground, the most serious being the narrowness of its interpretation of Chapter VI, which resulted in mass slaughter. Narrow procedural rules were followed, even when it was clear that many lives would be lost. Too often, adherence to process was put ahead of adherence to sound ethical behaviour. Perhaps

Rwanda

that is the most important lesson to take away from my brief recollections.

One of the significant dilemmas international peacekeepers face is working to a force headquarters that does not have all the staff functions needed to do the job. And where they do have a relevant staff function the person does not have the essential skill sets or language skills needed to perform effectively. In Rwanda, UNAMIR HQ did not have an intelligence staff function, a psychological operations (psyops) capability or a legal staff. In an environment where most of the fleeing RGF and Interahamwe (a Hutu paramilitary organisation supported by the Hutu-led government) escaped around or through Lake Kivu to what was then Zaire (now the Democratic Republic of the Congo) or were contained in Internally Displaced Persons (IDP) camps in the south-west sector, the security situation was precarious. Also, the RPA were thwarted by French efforts to allow the perpetrators of the genocide to flee or to hide in large IDP camps in order to avoid justice.

The early efforts to clear the IDP camps were frustrated by the false belief that it was unsafe for IDPs to return to their home communes and/or that an invasion by RGF forces out of Zaire was imminent. The lack of an intelligence and 'psyops' capability meant that the UN could not make an informed assessment of the security situation in Rwanda or neighbouring countries, was powerless to counter propaganda and unable to get the message to the IDPs and to refugees in neighbouring countries that it was safe to go home. Of course, the failure of the UN to ensure a secure environment in the home communes did not help. There was also the potential risk of a coup by the RPA that would have been monitored very closely by intelligence staff, if they had existed. Paul Kagame had to tread a tight rope between showing a display of national unity and controlling the RPA. Thankfully, he was successful.

When the Force Commander was reporting to the media that an attack from Zaire was imminent, the ABC's Africa correspondent approached me for comment. He knew that the Australian assessment was that an invasion was unlikely. By this time, I had been gagged by the UN and was only allowed to comment on matters relating to my unit. The journalist tried to pressure me into making an 'on the record' comment, threatening that if he reported an imminent invasion that our families would be distressed. I told him that we had direct communication with our families. If he wanted to report that an invasion was imminent when there was no supporting evidence, it would not harm us.

He went against the herd and without any comment from me reported that there was no evidence of an invasion. It can be a source of ethical dilemma when the force headquarters is making claims that you know to be false yet you are unable to comment or counter those claims.

A matter of particular significance in Rwanda was the lack of a legal function within UNAMIR HQ. In an environment where the force was deployed under Chapter VI of the Charter, the rules of engagement were robust, the RPA wanted to control the movement of the UN and deny access when necessary, and the RPA were performing a range of public functions, the need for competent legal advice was ever present. In most cases, when a breach of the SOFA occurred it was the perpetrators who led the investigation. A legal staff would have allowed for the conduct of proper and effective investigations.

Dealing with NGOs

The second area ripe for ethical dilemmas was interacting with NGOs. We were providing medical support to the UN in a country where the health system had been destroyed and there were few options for the treatment of genocide casualties. Also, we had a dual mission to provide humanitarian support within the limits of our spare capacity. We were never going to not help those who were delivered to our door, but our ultimate humanitarian objective was to re-establish the Central Hospital Kigali (CHK) as a referral hospital and re-establish the regional health clinics. This meant that we had to deal extensively with NGOs.

Dealing with NGOs will invariably challenge your ethics. There were more than 300 NGOs in Rwanda. Due to the carnage that was reported in the world media, it became apparent that most NGOs had decided that they needed Rwanda emblazoned on their banners. There were also Australian NGOs, such as Care Australia, who we felt compelled to support. It took some time for us to understand the psyche of NGOs. We labelled NGOs using a '3 M' classification: mercenary, missionary or misfit. We found these classifications to be mutually exclusive. As with most things, there are the good, the bad and the normal. I will cite some examples to provide an insight. These are a snapshot in time and I would expect that NGOs have improved during the past twenty years.

The good

One of the best NGOs was PSF. PSF provides supplies to NGOs delivering primary healthcare. A major part of our key humanitarian objective was to re-establish the regional health clinics but we could not get an NGO to do it. Also, we could not obtain pharmaceutical supplies because neither the UN nor Australia would pay. We approached PSF and they agreed to provide the necessary supplies, provided we only delivered primary healthcare and did not use any of the supplies in the UN hospital. It is a rare event for an NGO to support a military unit, even a medical one. Another worthy NGO was *Médecins Sans Frontières*. They stayed during the genocide, working out of King Faisal Hospital with very limited support. Our doctors and surgeons helped them when they could and the contingent members donated blood in emergencies. Red Cross was also one of the stalwarts. They too stayed during the genocide.

The bad

An example of the bad was an aid organisation that appeared to make profile-raising their priority ahead of a government delegation's visit. As the organisation was publicly funded, they quickly established a clinic, flew in a doctor and sought patients from other health care facilities. After the organisation's 'contribution' was officially noted, the 'pop up' clinic soon closed.

It was the interference of NGOs that led to the failure of Operation Retour. As mentioned earlier, Operation Retour was a co-operative operation between the UN, RPA and willing NGOs for the purpose of closing the IDP camps. The operation took weeks to plan, given the size of some of the camps. The RPA's part was to provide an outer cordon around the camp to prevent any IDPs from fleeing and returning later. UNAMIR's task was to have a security presence in the camp and the communes and to provide logistic support such as medical screening, transport and communications. The NGOs' role was to ensure that there was no food, water or medical stores in the camp on the day it was to be closed as the IDPs would not leave a camp with supplies and go to a commune where there might not be any. When it came to closing Kibeho, the largest of the IDP camps, some NGOs brought extra stores into the camp and told the IDPs that it was not safe in their home communes. As a consequence, the people refused to leave. Two months later the Kibeho massacre occurred when the RPA forcibly closed the camp. No-one was ever held accountable. NGO employees who we knew suggested to us that the likely reason for the NGO action was that the NGOs would have been employed on a contract to service the camp.

Exacerbating the failure of Operation Retour was UNAMIR's inability to comprehend the reason for the subsequent build-up of RPA forces around Kibeho. Lacking an intelligence staff, imbued with an unwillingness to confront the RPA and an inability to recall recent history, the UN yet again let down the people we were there to protect, allowing a small detail of UN troops to be witnesses to a massacre they were powerless to prevent while the bulk of the 5500-person force was nowhere near

Kibeho. The High Commission in London sent me UNAMIR situation reports when I was an exchange instructor at the British Army Staff College. From these reports, the RPA intent was clear. Yet, there was no assessment at the time for the reason for the build-up.

The normal

Representing normal NGO behaviour was our frustrating efforts to get NGOs working at CHK to co-operate with each other, with us and with the hospital administrator in order to re-establish the facility. When we arrived in Rwanda we analysed the local health system and assessed its condition. Essentially, it operated on a hub and spoke system with CHK as the hub and the regional clinics as the spokes. CHK was a referral hospital while the clinics administered primary healthcare. I knew that to make a real difference CHK needed to be re-established as a referral hospital. To that end, we called a meeting with the NGOs operating in the hospital and briefed them on the capability we possessed. I offered to share our capability with them if they agreed to work co-operatively with us and each other to re-establish CHK as a referral hospital. We advised that we would assist the hospital administrator, who was not a health expert, to develop the plan. It came to nought as the NGOs refused to co-operate with us, each other or the administrator.

I have drawn a rather bleak conclusion about NGOs from my experience with them in Rwanda. Hopefully, things have changed. However, when dealing with NGOs it would be wise to know that: NGOs often seek out publicity; NGOs tend to consume lots of resources and look after themselves first; NGOs will not necessarily co-operate with each other or any military force, including the UN, even if they say they will; and NGOs usually are unable to act strategically. When funding dries up they typically leave. But there are exceptions. If you do find an NGO which you can work with, do so. But always remain vigilant because mutual interests will not necessarily align for the duration of the mission.

Medical ethics

When we were deployed to Rwanda in the immediate aftermath of the genocide the demand for humanitarian support was extreme, including wounds that had not received treatment, continuing reprisal attacks, mine injuries and outbreaks of disease. I made an early decision that our main humanitarian effort would be to re-establish CHK as a referral hospital and re-establish the regional health clinics. Success would mean an enduring improvement in people's health treatment and outcomes. Treating the wounded and suffering in an environment where there was little scope for ongoing care or follow-up after discharge had a feel-good factor but would not make a long-term difference in people's lives. Therefore, the biggest ethical issue was whether we should be providing humanitarian support outside of our stated objective, especially as there were more than 300 NGOs in Rwanda offering humanitarian support but none had an intention of re-establishing a referral hospital or a regional clinic.

We did not set out to compete with NGOs but we soon learned that co-operation between them was lacking and that there was little co-ordination of the humanitarian effort. Therefore, we found ourselves providing support in regional areas where the NGOs would not operate. In Kigali, our focus was on the more complex cases that the NGOs could not manage, or aiding people delivered to our facilities at night or on weekends.

Therefore, we found ourselves in a situation where we were working 24/7 when we were only staffed for continuous operations on a surge basis. We had to cross-train our staff and manage our resources very carefully. UNAMIR HQ provided strict limitations on how many beds could be occupied by Rwandans and specified the minimum reserves of medical supplies and gases, while doing nothing to help us procure such items. While the members of our contingent were not given a choice about whether to provide medical care, I hope that the majority would have agreed that we did the right thing. The moral wrong that would have resulted had we looked away would have haunted us for the rest of our lives. The important thing is that we never let the humanitarian effort compromise our mission and we never lost sight of the primary humanitarian objective.

I should emphasise that the restrictions imposed on us by the UN did not apply when we were called out to treat survivors of mass killings when the RPA forcibly closed camps or when the Interahamwe raided communes. As the Interahamwe relied on the IDP camps for sanctuary, they could not allow the IDPs to return home, so they raided communes at night to send a message to those in the camps not to leave.

Another significant ethical dilemma was that we needed to be selective about whom we would try to save. As we could not get funding for humanitarian support and the UN imposed strict reserves on medical supplies, we had no choice but to decide who we would treat based on the probability of survival, informed by the availability of gases, beds and pharmaceutical supplies. Triage was performed outside the hospital and those who could be treated by NGOs were directed to the relevant NGO. For the remaining serious cases, we had to determine how much capacity we had, with the main limitations being the extent of the post-operative care needed and the availability of medical stores.

If we did not have the resources, or if there was little prospect of survival, the person was not admitted to our facility.

A further ethical challenge was the need for our doctors and surgeons to undertake procedures for which they were not qualified or experienced enough to perform because there was no alternative. We supported the surgeons where we could by doing things such as sending digitised imagery to hospitals in Australia to get guidance on complex procedures, but working outside of one's comfort zone was a cause of extra stress.

Another ethical dilemma was the need to provide a different standard of care for UN dependants and others because of the restrictions imposed on us. We did what we could to minimise this, but it was hard to justify, morally or ethically, the need to turn off medical gases for a patient because the gas reserves were critical due to a lack of funding.

*

The Rwandan genocide was a humanitarian catastrophe in every sense. One million people were slaughtered over the course of a few months. Too little was done too late; and what was done lacked consistency and urgency. There were numerous contributing factors to the tragedy that befell Rwanda in 1994–95. Perhaps the most significant was UNAMIR's consistent and narrow interpretation of what it was allowed to do under Article VI. While this judgment is speculation on my part, a more active and aggressive posture by the UN would almost certainly have lessened the death toll. Instead, adhering to formal processes was prioritised. This might not have been unethical conduct in a strict sense but it was certainly far from being ethical behaviour, if responding to dire human need is the foremost criterion for action.

PART 3: THE ETHICAL SOLDIER – EXPECTATIONS AND REALITIES

An Australian soldier near a food distribution post in Rwanda, 1994–95.
Commonwealth of Australia

5

CONNECTING RESEARCH, EDUCATION AND TRAINING

DEANE-PETER BAKER

In the introduction to his 2011 book *Ethics and Public Policy: A Philosophical Inquiry*, the distinguished philosopher and ethicist Jonathan Wolff describes an uncomfortable situation he faced when he was invited to serve as a member of the United Kingdom's Nuffield Council on Bioethics Working Party. Required to give a report to the committee, which entailed outlining the main views expressed in the philosophical literature on the ethics of research involving animals, Wolff ran into an unexpected problem:

> Now, I was perfectly happy to report disagreement, just as the scientists reported disagreement about such things as the feasibility of replacing some current experiments with computer modeling, or the degree to which fish feel pain. However I was far less comfortable reporting the views giving rise to these disagreements. For on the whole, philosophers seemed to defend views that were so far from current practice as to seem, to the non-philosopher, quite

outrageous. The idea that society could adopt any of the views put forward seemed almost laughable. To put it mildly, from the point of view of public policy the views were unreasonable and unacceptable.[1]

This confronting situation forced Wolff to reconsider the widely held view – to which he had also until then subscribed – that the appropriate response to ethical challenges in public policymaking is to approach them in the general way philosophers typically approach all of the intellectual challenges they seek to solve. Wolff realised instead that:

> this common view […] overlooks one crucial point.
> Moral and political philosophy are, after all, branches
> of philosophy. And, it seems, in contrast to some other
> disciplines, the way in which philosophy has developed
> makes it fit rather badly with public policy needs. In science
> and in social science a researcher makes his or her name
> by presenting a view that others find attractive or useful
> and build on. By and large the situation in philosophy is
> the reverse. A philosopher becomes famous by arguing for
> a view that is highly surprising, even to the point of being
> irritating, but is also resistant to easy refutation. The more
> paradoxical, or further from common sense, the better.
> Philosophy thrives on disagreement, and there is no pressure
> to come to an agreement. Indeed agreement is unhelpful as
> it cuts discussion short. At a conference or seminar no one
> takes minutes of the meeting in order to provide a common
> statement representing the views of the group. A seminar
> group can have as many different views as it has members.
> Indeed, to recycle an old joke, it will often have more views
> than members. In public policy, however, a report must

be written, or a recommendation made, or a law or policy
drafted, just as in science and social science a practical
outcome is sought. A need to agree on a practical outcome
creates pressure towards convergence. Philosophy, under
no such pressure, thrives on what Freud in another context
called the 'narcissism of minor difference'.[2]

Wolff's analysis of the problem, it seems to me, is exactly right.
Unfortunately, it is an issue that also raises its head in the field
of military ethics. For better or worse, the majority of researchers who contribute to the scholarly literature related to military
actions and military use of force are, like me, philosophers by
background and training. As a consequence, a significant proportion of the work produced under the 'military ethics' moniker is
afflicted with exactly the sort of problems that Wolff confronted.
The editors of the excellent *Journal of Military Ethics* (a beacon
of real-world relevance in the field) articulate the issue in terms
of professional relevance: 'We are often put in circumstances of
hearing philosophical talks. Often these are wonderfully logically
developed, conceptually clear, rigorously argued – and in the end
professionally irrelevant'.[3]

In raising this problem I do not intend to diminish the
important and valuable contributions that have been made by
scholars working on ethical issues related to the use of military
force over recent decades, particularly since the publication of
Michael Walzer's seminal volume *Just and Unjust Wars* in 1977.[4]
We have come a long way in that time, and the very existence of
this book, and the conference from which it has emerged, provides evidence of that fact. But still, we have a problem, and it is
not one we can afford to shrug off. The problem is experienced by
scholars like me in the awkwardness that arises in trying to communicate to military personnel what other scholars are saying

about 'military ethics'. Much more importantly, the problem arises when military practitioners are confronted by real-world ethical challenges that either have not been critically analysed at all, or have been addressed by scholars in a way that fails to provide the practitioner with any useful guidance.

The challenge, then, is to work out how to get beyond the less than ideal situation in which, currently, the majority of scholars in this field are writing 'papers in which philosophers argue with the positions of other philosophers'[5] (as Martin Cook and Henrik Syse, the editors of the *Journal of Military Ethics* aptly put it) rather than writing papers which engage usefully with the ethical challenges faced by members of the military profession.

Part of the answer unquestionably lies with those of us who work as researchers and scholars on topics in military ethics. It is incumbent on us to resist the lure of soaring philosophical arguments, complex thought experiments, and novel claims and topics, and instead be willing to get our hands dirty wrestling with the often more mundane and sometimes philosophically less interesting challenges that military professionals must deal with. In short, we need to rethink our conception of success. It is, perhaps, at this point worth (mis)quoting the words of the great 17th-century philosopher John Locke – 'It is ambition enough to be employed as an under-labourer in clearing the ground a little, and removing some of the rubbish that lies in the way to knowledge'.[6]

Beyond that *mea culpa* on behalf of my colleagues and me, it seems to me that there is also a *structural* problem that needs to be addressed. A significant reason why so much of what is written in this field consists of 'papers in which philosophers argue with the positions of other philosophers' is that the work of other philosophers is often the only real data we have available to us to work on. Sometimes, of course, we can (and do) gain some understanding of the ethical challenges facing military professionals through biographies and media coverage – and even the occasional movie – but then, unless the scholar concerned happens to have had recent and relevant military experience, the contextual understanding needed to fully grasp the issue is often missing. This came home to me forcefully when, not too long ago, I was involved in a public panel discussion on the ethics of military strikes using unmanned aerial vehicles (UAV). The panel involved a number of scholars, one of whom was a retired military officer. After the panel I asked a serving military officer who had been in attendance what he had thought of the discussion. He responded that while the discussion was interesting at some level, it did not at all reflect actual practice in the use of UAVs as he had experienced it during a recent deployment to the Middle East.

What is needed, then, is for ethicists and the military to find a way to 'close the circle' between the real ethical challenges faced by military professionals and the research that addresses the field of military ethics. I offer one way of doing that through an approach that connects the circle through both education and military training.

Ethicists in the field

Prior to moving to Australia to teach at UNSW Canberra I spent two and a half years on the faculty of the Department of Leadership, Ethics and Law at the United States Naval Academy (USNA). It was a fascinating experience, not least because of the approximately 50–50 mix of civilian and military personnel who were together engaged in the task of shaping future officers of the United States Navy and Marine Corps team. I worked and taught side by side with officers whose primary identity was as submariners, helicopter pilots, Marine Corps and Navy fast jet pilots, surface warfare officers, and SEALs. I even had a colleague who was a CIA analyst on secondment. I learned a great deal about the realities of contemporary military life from interacting with these colleagues. One conversation in particular from that time stands out, even though it was just a brief interaction in passing. For obvious reasons, a significant proportion of the teaching faculty in the Department of Leadership, Ethics and Law were Navy and Marine Corps Judge Advocates ('JAGs'). One of my JAG colleagues was coming to the end of his posting to USNA and mentioned in passing that his next assignment was to the United States Special Operations Command. He added that before reporting for duty at his new posting in Little Creek, Virginia he was first required to complete 'Jump School' (military parachute training). When I expressed my puzzlement as to why a Navy lawyer would need to be jump qualified, he explained by giving me 'a hypothetical'. He asked me to imagine a situation in which (say) a team of SEALs on board an American naval vessel were preparing to use sniper fire to engage Somali pirates who had taken hostages on another vessel. What if there were a need for legal advice before the mission could be given the green light, and what if the only way to get a lawyer on scene in time were to paradrop him into the ocean adjacent to the Navy ship?

In the aftermath of that conversation my overheated imagination concocted all sorts of fantastical situations in which the military might require a military ethicist to be parachuted in to provide ethical advice. Such imaginings – apart from ignoring the fact that the likelihood of me voluntarily throwing myself out of a perfectly good aircraft is essentially nil – are of course silly. But the fact that such a thought is so unlikely served to highlight to me how detached those of us who work in the field of military ethics usually are from the realities of military operations. But that need not be so, nor should it be the case. If it is possible to embed journalists with military forces conducting exercises, and even on operations, there seems no reason in principle why the same could not be done with military ethicists. Indeed, the crucial first step to 'closing the circle' in military ethics must be for the military to open the door to allow ethicists to accompany soldiers into the field, to observe the planning process for an air-strike mission, to stand on the bridge as a fly-away team boards a non-compliant vessel, and so on.

Clearly it is no small thing to ask of the military for them to welcome strangers – civilians – into intimate contact with the world of military operations. This is particularly so when these are strangers who are there to seek out areas in which the military force in question might be acting in a way that is not ethically optimal, with the ultimate goal of publishing their findings! For this to happen, a strong bond of trust between the ethicist and his or her military host must be developed. It will be vital that both parties view the relationship as a mutually beneficial part-nership. The ethicist will need to commit himself or herself to respectfully and, where appropriate, confidentially sharing his or her observations with the parties directly involved in the first instance. The ethicist must also commit to withholding publica-tion of any findings until such time as the military host has had a reasonable opportunity – working in partnership with the eth-icist as necessary – to put in place measures to address the issues of ethical concern, with these measures to be included in any published account of the issue.

On its side, the military will need to commit to not using the ethicists' findings as a justification for punitive action against those personnel who have been under observation, except in extreme cases where such punitive actions are mandated under law. Instead, commanders who are tasked to embed military ethicists in their teams should be encouraged to see this as a positive opportunity to identify and address potential vulnerabilities. In general it will be essential that the military host sees this as a capability-enhancing partnership, and that the military ethicist be assured that she or he will not be prevented from respectfully and appropriately exercising her or his academic freedom. Building the necessary framework for collaboration may well be successful on an *ad hoc* basis; however, consideration should be given to developing a semi-formal framework of understanding that incorporates the key perspectives of both parties involved.

From the field to the classroom

In an earlier paper 'Making good better: A proposal for teaching ethics at the service academies', one of the few papers I have ever produced that directly addresses the methodology of teaching military ethics, I acknowledged that, for good reason, historical case studies are strongly favoured as a vehicle for educating officers and trainee officers about the principles of military ethics.[7] This is because, as Kenneth Pimple puts it (referring to the context of teaching research ethics), historical case studies are 'real, not made up, and students cannot [easily] dismiss them'.[8] In the paper I also pointed out that there are a number of dangers inherent in this practice. For one, young officer cadets and midshipmen may well consider these historical cases to be 'old news', and not really relevant to contemporary operations. It is not only young trainee officers who feel this – I have had several conversations with experienced soldiers who expressed their frustration at being 'dragged through the My Lai case again' (although not by me) during workshops on ethics.

A second danger of relying heavily on historical case studies is that these almost always focus on cases of ethical failure. As I previously contended:

> Arguably the biggest challenge inherent in the use of historical case studies is that those that are usually studied in ethics courses are predominantly negative – that is, they are more often than not cases of ethical *wrongdoing*. While it is obviously useful to illustrate to students how things can go wrong, and for them to consider why things might have gone wrong, an overall focus on negative cases can shape a course in an unhelpful direction by majoring on what *not* to do while not giving students sufficient opportunity to consider and practice what they *should* do. This problem is exacerbated by the well-documented phenomenon of 'hindsight bias'. [...] For midshipmen and officer cadets learning military ethics through the medium of historical case studies, hindsight bias combined with the fact that they are analyzing decisions made by others rather than making decisions of their own, can lead to an unhelpful complacency and overconfidence – 'I would never do that.'[9]

I do not, in making this point, propose an end to the use of historical case studies. To the contrary, in 'Making good better' I outline an approach to using them that I argue holds the potential to negate these drawbacks substantially. Nonetheless it seems clear to me that current pedagogical practice in teaching military ethics could be considerably enhanced by the inclusion, alongside historical case studies, of research findings developed out of direct experience of recent and relevant military practice. Officer cadets and midshipmen, in particular, are eager to catch a glimpse of the world into which they will soon enter, so the question of relevance does not arise. Such field-based research is also not limited to cases of significant ethical failure, as historical case studies tend to be, and so offers more utility in helping students think through what ought to be done, rather than only what ought not to be done. Finally, as any experienced lecturer knows, the effectiveness of classroom teaching depends to a considerable degree on students' subjective assessments of the credibility of the lecturer. For the lecturer to have 'been there and done that' (or at least 'been there and seen that') rather than having 'sat here and thought about that' is a considerable boost in that regard.

From education to training

In 2009 Professor Wilbur Scott of the United States Air Force Academy (USAFA) attended a conference on 'Small Unit Excellence'. United States Marine Corps General James Mattis, presently United States Defense Secretary, opened the conference. At the time he was the commander of United States Joint Forces Command. Mattis centered his remarks on the trial of the Marines who had been charged for the killing of some 24 Iraqi civilians in the town of Haditha in 2005. The central thrust of Mattis' speech was that he believed strongly that these Marines had been 'let down' by not having been provided with training that would enable them to navigate the circumstances encountered that day appropriately.

In response Scott, along with two colleagues at USAFA (Damian McCabe and David R McCone), added additional elements to the teaching program at USAFA, elements designed to improve students' decision making skills and better their understanding of the challenges of irregular warfare. Included

in this effort was designing a 'tribal engagement field simulation'
designed to assess students' abilities to make 'morally grounded
decisions', as part of a capstone course, 'Sociology of Violence
and War'. As described in a paper by Scott, McCabe and McCone:

> Readings in the course were selected to introduce the cadets
> to theories of violence [...], irregular warfare [...], cross-
> cultural competencies [...], naturalistic decision-making
> [...], and applications to the Air Force [...]. Late in the
> semester, cadets then took part in a field exercise at a mock
> Afghan village – designated by us, *Villagistan* – located at a
> nearby military installation.[10]

The Haditha case played a central part in the course, and students were asked, among other things, 'to formally identify the
decision points, specify each decision made and its associated
rationale, and weigh each of those against the outcome that followed. The question to the class then was: if we were to run the
scenario over again, exactly as described, what different decisions
could a leader make that might produce more desirable results?'[11]

The final field exercise in 'Villagistan' was conducted at an
impressive facility:

> *Villagistan* has about 30 buildings, to include a mosque,
> marketplace, police station, town hall, and homes for
> villagers. Veterans of the wars in Iraq and Afghanistan have
> suggested improvements to make it increasingly realistic. A
> roster of local actors and role players is available to populate
> the village for selected exercises (at a fee). The village has
> available an impressive array of costumes and props. It also
> is wired for sound and smell, and a wide assortment of these
> can be pre-selected. For example, calls to prayer from the

mosque and other sounds, as well as the smells of rotting
garbage, open sewers, and the like, are offered. Finally, more
than one hundred cameras in the village make video/audio
recordings of what takes place, both in the streets and in
specific rooms within houses. The action can be interrupted
at most any time and playbacks used to review and critique
what took place.[12]

The paper offers an in-depth assessment of the students' performance in this simulation, which makes for fascinating reading. For the purposes of this chapter, however, we need only note the main outcome. Despite considerable classroom preparation and discussion, *the students generally performed poorly in making sound decisions during the field exercise.* At first glance this suggests that the entire endeavour was an exercise in futility. Scott and his colleagues show from the data they gathered that a better explanation for this could be expressed in the terms set out by 'conscious competence learning theory'. Following this model, what occurred in this case is that the students moved from 'unconscious incompetence' to 'conscious incompetence'.[13] This is a vital first step, a necessary precondition to moving on to 'conscious competence' and then ultimately 'unconscious competence' (in which the learner selects the correct course of action as a matter of 'second nature').

What is necessary to complete the transition from 'unconscious incompetence' to 'unconscious competence' is, as Scott and his colleagues point out, training – or more specifically *dilemma training*:

> the purpose of this training is for participants to develop
> mental constructs which then serve as prototypes to
> be recalled and enacted in subsequent, similar-looking

situations. We know that the scenarios must be robustly true-to-life if they are to fulfil our intended purpose. To serve decision-makers well, these prototypes must adequately match the situations in which they will be applied and be sufficiently detailed to allow nuanced application.[14]

What seems clear from all of this is that, in order to produce soldiers, sailors and airmen who are ethically competent requires more than (though certainly not *less* than) education in military ethics. What is also needed is for that education to be deliberately and coherently linked to ethics *training*. This need not be 'ethics-only' training. Indeed, as the experiment carried out by Scott and his colleagues suggests, setting up training activities specifically for this purpose could be prohibitively expensive.

A better option, it seems to me, is to integrate ethical dilemma training into the existing training activities and exercises that military forces already undertake to prepare their personnel for operations. Ethical challenges for military personnel are seldom, if ever, 'free standing' – they arise in the context of practical, operational decision making. Ensuring that the ethics training embedded in existing training activities and exercises is sound will, once again, require a degree of involvement and access by military ethicists, with all the trust implications mentioned earlier. Indeed, in some respects this engagement will also represent the beginnings of new research, as the research–education–training cycle begins again.

*

In sum, my argument is that in order to equip the next generation of military personnel to face the challenge of 'ethics under fire' with confidence and competence, both military ethicists and the military forces they serve must commit themselves to the following set of actions. First, those of us who are ethicists must consciously and conscientiously resist the temptation to expend our efforts on writing 'papers in which philosophers argue with the positions of other philosophers'.[15] Instead, we should commit ourselves to engaging with the real-world issues faced by military personnel even where those issues lack the academic 'glamour' of complex philosophical discourse. Second, to enable ethicists to research the ethical challenges faced by military personnel, the military will need to find ways to give ethicists meaningful access to the profession of arms. This will require a delicate but important partnership of trust between ethicists and their military hosts. The research developed through this partnership will inform and enrich ethics education delivered by ethicists to military personnel. Third, to finally 'close the circle', the research-driven principles, concepts and models taught in the classroom must be coherently integrated, in the form of context-appropriate dilemma training, into the cycle of training activities and exercises carried out by the military, which will again require the close involvement of ethicists.

I am aware that my proposals ask a great deal. To put them into action will require time and resources. It will involve developing and negotiating relationships of trust. It will oblige ethicists – and, perhaps more importantly, the universities that employ them – to be willing to pursue a different conception of 'success' from that which is traditional in academia. It is a lot to ask. But if we are genuinely committed to equipping the men and women who serve our nation to be able to face the complex ethical challenges inherent in contemporary military service, so that our nation can retain legitimacy and our soldiers, sailors and airmen can come home with their heads held high, then it seems to me that it is not too much to ask.

6

ETHICS IN SPECIAL OPERATIONS

IAN LANGFORD

Many professional groups such as doctors, lawyers, engineers and teachers have codes of ethical conduct that provide them with a construct by which to apply their skills within their profession. These codes protect the integrity of these vocations, and provide for a comparative standard in the assessment of what each particular profession sees as important in terms of value and ethos. Throughout the past decade, Australia's military professionals at various service academies have shown increasing interest in the study of ethics. Most Australian Defence Force (ADF) schools now include some form of instruction on professional ethics, through which students are encouraged to think about ethical problem solving.

The study of ethics is particularly relevant to the Special Operations community, whose members have faced ethical challenges in a myriad of circumstances since the terrorist attacks on the United States on 11 September 2001. Australia's Special Operations are often regarded by the public and the government almost exclusively as 'man-hunting operations'. What such observers do not realise is that the targeting of high-value individuals is just one type of task among a much broader range of options. For example, Special Operations are well suited for operations that come with high risk, including the conduct of highly sensitive missions in complex terrain at very short notice. Such operations are often focused on collecting sensitive intelligence, carrying out clandestine operations in isolated locations and targeting individuals in high-intensity combat. With high risk comes high levels of responsibility. Special Forces personnel are specially selected and trained individuals who are expected to possess decision making abilities appropriate for tasks involving strategic risk. In order to be effective, personnel serving in Special Operations must have a strong ethical framework that empowers them to undertake ethically challenging missions without compromising their own moral and ethical standards.

The changing international operating environment

Human society continues to undergo extraordinary social and economic change. New strategic partnerships are being formed and long-established relationships are coming under pressure. These trends are all symptoms of a rapidly evolving global order. Nation-states, non-government actors and private citizens increasingly have the means to affect the international system. A more dynamic world order with an increasing number and type of change seekers makes the ability to accurately forecast likely events as part of national security contingency planning a difficult and highly problematic activity. Continuing conflict in the Ukraine, the rise of Islamic State, the Sunni/Shia proxy war in Yemen, the increase in tension in the South China Sea, the potential for 'cyber-conflict', demographic pressure on the environment and the pressure of resource scarcity all influence

Australia's security; several of these crises were nearly impossible to forecast and thus serve to remind all military planners of the unpredictability of the global system.

The conduct of military forces, once committed to conflict, is guided by rules articulated in directions often known as 'rules of engagement'.[1] These rules provide military forces with the lawful authority to employ lethal force as well as to use specific weapon systems in prescribed circumstances. Whereas morals are codified by religious, legal and historical interpretations, ethics are shaped by sociological, secular and personal perspectives. Thus, ethics tend to be highly subjective. They are not universal and are largely temporal in their application. This presents challenges for the military where, for example, in one circumstance it could be ethically appropriate to lie to the enemy (perhaps in order to confuse or deny them information), yet on the other hand, it would be morally wrong to lie to a military commander or court of inquiry. Ethical decision making has its own obligations, each motivated by rules, goals and situations. For Special Operations, an understanding of the origins of these rules, goals and situations is essential to ensuring that personnel are prepared to make the *right* decision, regardless of the circumstances.

Rule-oriented ethics

Rules most often provide the critical criteria for ethics and ethical judgments.[2] The questions 'What ought I to do?' and 'What is right for me to do?' reflect not only a sense of obligation, they acknowledge that a standard exists for establishing what is obligatory and what is right. From a historical perspective, these were religious questions referring to the will of God, albeit often interpreted differently and sometimes with ill intent.

Rule-oriented schema have a long history in monotheistic religions. Those of the Hebrew faith lived under an elaborate code of conditioned and unconditional laws by the beginning of the Christian era. The covenantal requirements of Mosaic Law amounted to 613 injunctions: 365 'thou shalt not' prohibitions and 248 'thou shalt' obligations. Far from being burdensome, these laws clearly defined divine commands and injunctions, providing a secure moral framework for life. Christian moral law was defined as living in an obedient relationship with God, defined by the words and works of Jesus, the incarnate Son of God. Formal teaching such as the Sermon on the Mount, apostolic traditions and practices, the early Church's creeds and catechism, the theological writings of St Augustine and the doctrinal prescriptions of St Thomas Aquinas have provided Christians with a holistic conception of morality. Jesus warned his followers against conforming to the standards of this world by focusing on selfless love and working towards the coming of God's Kingdom of charity and compassion. The followers of Islam, noting their varying degrees of observance, can be more rigid than both Jews and Christians in their understanding of morality, which is depicted as strict obedience to a set code or to religious leadership. *Islam* means 'to submit' and a *Muslim* is 'one who has submitted'. The Quran, the recited teachings of Muhammad,[3] the Prophet of Islam, defines the essential duties decreed by Allah and binds Muslims to loyal subjection. Religiously based, rule-oriented approaches to ethical theory therefore establish the standards and criteria for determining right and wrong.

Goal-oriented ethics

Goal-oriented ethics ask 'What is good?' and 'What goal should I seek?' The criteria for determining right and wrong are no longer historical standards (as guided by a rule-oriented approach), but instead consider future consequences as a primary focus. The 'good' decision is measured by its ability to attain a desired goal. Aristotle defined the good all men seek as 'happiness'.[4] The philosopher Jeremy Bentham elaborated on this 'happiness' principle, describing it as the principle of utility, 'that principle which states the greatest happiness of all those whose interest is in question, as being the right, proper, and only right and proper and universally desirable, end of human action'.[5] For John Stuart Mill, the greatest happiness principle was expanded to include the 'general good': 'the happiness which forms the utilitarian standard of what is right in conduct, is not the agent's own happiness, but that of all concerned'.[6] This goal is commonly known as 'the greatest good for the greatest number'.

For Special Forces personnel, goal-oriented aspirations are reflected in the development of military strategies, plans, and operations. This also involves more immediate objectives such as accomplishing missions or tasks as a function of developing military capability. The same general approach is taken to military deterrence, training personnel and maintaining weapons systems as a part of military capability and readiness.

Situation-oriented ethics

In the early 1960s a pattern was developed to explain moral decisions that came to be known as 'situation ethics'. The two leading proponents at that time, Joseph Fletcher and John AT Robinson, asked 'What is appropriate to the situation?' or 'What is fitting?' In situation ethics, the particular circumstances of a situation provide the criteria for determining right and wrong. Situations were seen as unique and without precedent. Judgments were therefore relative to the circumstances; according to Robinson and Fletcher, the circumstance itself should determine what actions should be taken. Of rule-oriented judgments, Fletcher said, 'Situation ethics keep principles sternly in their place, in their role of advisers without veto power'.[7]

A major limitation of situation ethics is its focus on the unusual, once-in-a-lifetime circumstance. It is not geared to day-by-day living; it provides no plan. Any realistic person knows that under certain conditions people must act according to the situation to ensure their safety and survival. If a Special Forces person was isolated behind enemy lines, we know they would lie or steal to survive and return to friendly forces. In this context or situation, such behaviour is ethically acceptable. This fact does not mean, however, that ethical theory should tolerate lying or stealing in other situations or circumstances. Situation ethics resist systematisation; they must not become normative. They are an exception rather than a rule. Without appropriate checks and balances, situation ethics could lead to ethical drift and from there into unethical anarchy.

Yet some caution is required when applying rules, goals or situation ethics to the challenges that soldiers may face in the conduct of operations. All three approaches can lead to moral aberration: exclusive attention to rules can result in legalism; rigid adherence to utilitarian goals that provide the greatest good for the greatest number can promote a tyranny of the majority; and pre-eminent attention to situations without context can result in ethical and moral chaos.

Ethics in Special Operations

The ethical framework that exists in Australian Special Operations consists of a combination of rules, goals, and situation-oriented ethics.[8] When considering these ethics, the lack of a universal theory of employment, coupled with the nature of Special Operations (which typically occur in high-risk situations where an individual's moral and ethical framework is likely to be an essential factor in operational success) make the conduct of Special Forces personnel a vital area of study, given the tactical nature of these operations and their likely strategic consequence.

Rule-oriented ethics in Special Operations fall under Rules of Engagement which are enshrined in Australian law and subject Special Forces personnel to a legislative framework that requires their conduct and operations to be consistent with Australian statutes. The decision to conduct Special Operations and the capability inputs that sustain them are subject to the same constraints that affect the ADF as a whole. International laws of armed conflict, the *Defence Act* and the just war tradition apply as much to Special Forces as they do to the rest of the ADF. Every Special Forces action must be justified in legal, moral and ethical terms. These 'rules' are immutable.

Goal-oriented ethics in Special Operations are defined by military strategy, orders and plans that provide soldiers with guidance on and resources for the conduct of a mission. It is critical that all members of the Special Forces team intuitively understand the aims and objectives of their missions, as well as the nature of the strategic circumstances in which they operate. Through joint planning, unambiguous guidance and unified mission goals and objectives are provided to those tasked with the conduct of a mission. These 'goals' must nest with strategy and orders. All personnel assigned to the mission must understand them as well.

Situation-oriented ethics in Special Operations is absolutely critical to mission success. Much depends on Special Forces personnel being able to make informed decisions that are guided by rules and goal-oriented ethics, yet are not always bound to them, according to the situation or context at hand. Examples of an application of situation-oriented ethics are: the use of 'cover stories' (false narratives often employed by personnel to provide force protection to themselves during missions where they are at high risk of compromise or capture); deception (lying to mask location or as a means to protect force elements and future operations); and time-critical decision making (where a 'balance of probability' threshold is used rather than a 'beyond reasonable doubt' test in order to ensure the action or decision is timely). This methodology comes with elevated risk which, for Special Forces, would require additional scrutiny as part of the risk mitigation review.

The use of situation-oriented ethics is arguably the area of greatest risk in terms of ethical 'drift' in Special Operations. Its effective application is critical to mission success. The perspective of 'situation' and 'context' as ethical determinants have time-constrained aspects to them. As mentioned previously, in some instances, it is permissable to lie, steal and cheat, but outside of such situations and contexts, lying, stealing and cheating breach both rules and goal-oriented ethics and are therefore unacceptable.

The 'Remarkable Trinity'

In order to control the degree in which situation-oriented ethics can be limited to the appropriate context, Special Forces personnel must develop an appropriate model that acts as a guide. It will not replace good decision-making but it offers a framework in which good decision making can prosper. Situation-oriented ethics is influenced by three key unique characteristics: Context, Heuristics, and Belief Systems (see Figure 1).[9]

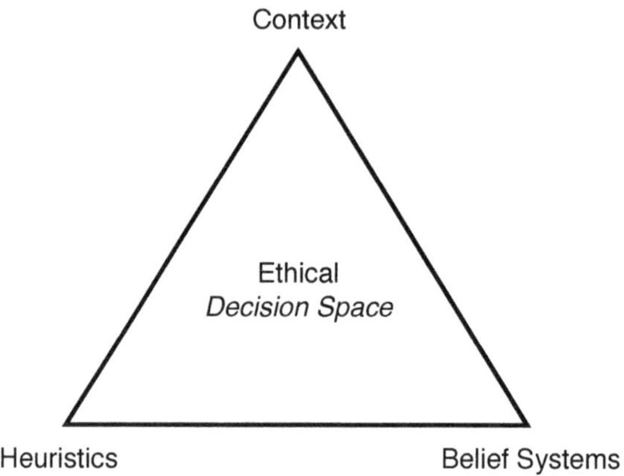

Figure 1: 'A Remarkable Trinity'

Context

Context describes the set of circumstances or facts that surround a particular event or situation. The context, or *situation*, recognises the effects of a multiplicity of facts and influences that affect problems and their solutions. In Australian Special Operations, this context is typified by strategically important phases of military operations, such as its missions in Iraq in 2003, and counter-terrorism missions against government-directed criminal activity such as the North Korean drug ship *Pong-Su*, which was boarded off the New South Wales coast in 2004.[10]

'Fog' and 'Friction', which describe the confusion and dynamic nature of military operations, add complexity to the evolving situation that typically occurs when Special Forces conduct an operation.[11] The operating situation, combat fatigue, time of day and the disruptive nature of Special Operations all affect the ability of soldiers to make ethical judgments important to mission success. Additionally, other contextual human factors such as trust, the routine of continuous operations, high readiness demands, training and readiness standards, tribalism and division of responsibilities amongst personnel all collectively contribute to making each situation unique.

Heuristics

Heuristics are simple and effective tools in the form of rules that people often use to rapidly form judgments and make decisions. They are effectively 'mental shortcuts' and usually involve concentrating on one aspect of a complex problem while ignoring others. Common heuristics include such things as the 'rule of thumb', 'common sense', perceived causation, correlation, and coincidences. In the military, and in the Special Forces in particular, heuristics take the form of various decision support mechanisms that include dynamic targeting tools, standard operating procedures (SOPs), and tactics, techniques, and procedures. Heuristics usually govern automatic, intuitive judgments which are necessary in Special Operations, however they can also be used as deliberate mental strategies when working from limited information.

Heuristics work well under most circumstances, but they can encourage systematic deviations from logic, probability or rational choice theory. This 'normalisation' error occurs when the heuristic overrides an understanding of the situation. The deviation between the heuristic and the reality threatens the ability of the commander to make the best decision. The resulting errors are called 'cognitive biases' and are shown to affect people's choices in military situations including target selection, application of the rules of engagement, or decisions on mission-critical elements of an operation.

Heuristics form part of ethical decision making, particularly in Special Operations. In order to ensure that Special Operations plans and decision making are informed by the constantly changing operating environment (which will require the use of situational ethics), Special Forces personnel must intuitively understand the opportunities and limitations of heuristics and how they affect decision making. Decision makers could be effectively 'de-biased' through training and by being offered various heuristic tools to aid problem solving. For example, personnel can be trained to make very accurate decisions when decision making entails recognising patterns and applying appropriate responses for actions such as direct action missions. Special Forces personnel must have the ability to recognise the underlying 'deep structure' of problems in different formats and domains. This is particularly so in ethical decision making, where (as demonstrated in the 'Trinity'), every situation has its own context whose perspective will be informed by the belief systems (world view) of the decision maker, as well as the *decision tool* (heuristic) being used to solve the problem at hand. The type of decision tool employed will affect the solution, and it is vital that the commander understands this and mitigates its effects to ensure that they are able to accurately understand the problem without bias and design a solution, free of as much 'heuristic influence' as possible.[12]

Belief Systems

Belief is the state of mind in which a person thinks something to be the case, with or without there being empirical evidence to prove that it is with factual certainty. As previously discussed, rules, goals and situation-based ethical frameworks are affected by experience and interest. Awareness of this is important, and thus the discipline of epistemology is concerned with delineating the boundary between justified belief and subjective opinion. Below is a representation of the interplay between the truth (situation), and Belief Systems which derive knowledge that, in turn, informs decisions.

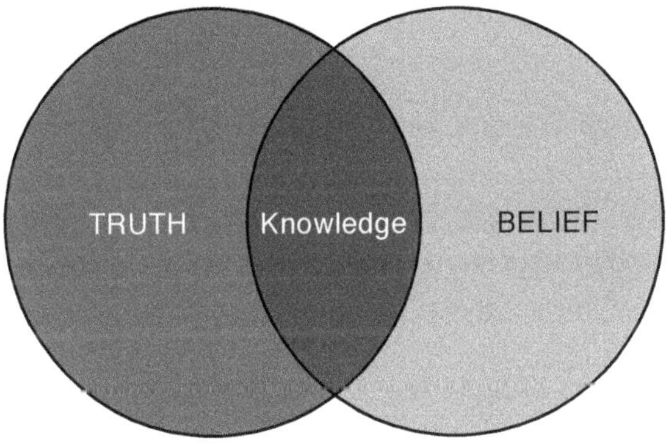

Figure 2: Belief Systems and their effect on decision making: the Venn/Euler diagram[13]

The influence that Belief Systems have on our perception of knowledge (with truth) is significant; as operations throughout this past decade have shown, Special Forces personnel rely heavily on their personal views as part of their ethical decision making; as a collective system, religious, philosophical and ideological tenets affect beliefs, and when combined with experience, rules, goals and the prevailing situation, all play a role in influencing ethical frameworks.[14]

Application of the 'Remarkable Trinity'

When combined, Context, Heuristics, and Belief Systems form an 'Ethical Decision Space' (see Figure 1). What is essential in Special Operations is the capacity for personnel to have a level of self-awareness and education that recognises the importance of *rule-* and *goal-*oriented ethics as normative principles of behaviour, but that there will be circumstances where *situation-*oriented ethics are necessary. In these circumstances, personnel must understand their *ethical decision space*; they see that the conditions in which they operate will be affected by the context, their own belief systems, and the heuristic being used.

Strong and virtuous leadership as a core driver

A strong ethical culture requires a leadership framework that promotes moral and ethical behaviour as an essential capability in Special Operations. Given the strategic nature of these operations, where ambiguity is common and the context is complicated, an effective leadership framework must emphasise openness, nuance, agility, integration and teamwork.[15] When Special Forces personnel find themselves in circumstances where regulations and mission objectives fail to provide sufficient guidelines, the aptitude for innovative leadership is an absolute virtue. This kind of leadership is essential in situation-specific environments, where leadership decisions are required that potentially contrast rules and goal-oriented leadership, but are necessary given the problem at hand. In these instances, an appropriate level of awareness, informed by the education and experience of the leadership team, should prevent the risk of an ethical 'drift' which might normalise situation-specific ethics as acceptable.

Future challenges

Special Forces are often the nation's first responders to emerging national security crises. The nature and complexity of their tasks generally require the employment of the latest military, scientific and technological advances. Special Forces personnel are often on the edge of the unknown and the need for adaptable and agile solutions to complex military problems underpins their ability to generate effective solutions. Australian Special Forces require an ethical framework that is able to absorb new technology and new ideas of warfighting without compromising itself.

By way of example, the American theological ethicist Daniel M Bell addressed emerging ethical issues in the use of drones and unmanned systems during the 2012 Fort Leavenworth Ethics Symposium. Over the past decade these technologies have become synonymous with Special Forces.[16] He expressed concern that use of drones dehumanises the enemy in the minds of Special Forces personnel by creating what he termed 'a PlayStation mentality'.[17] Bell thought that the use of drones might convey an impression of cowardice to those sympathising with the enemy.[18] If killing becomes no more than a video game, Special Forces could find themselves in an ethical decline.[19] Bell explored the enduring 'character and the profession of arms'[20] and concluded that by using drones, Western militaries are in danger of 'technology replacing character'.[21] Technology is only as good as the people employing it, he observed,[22] and remarked that Special

Forces could be in danger of becoming mere 'button pushers'.[23] Bell feared that as drones become ubiquitous they will create 'less room for professional judgment and influence of virtues of professional soldiers on operations'.[24]

Another emerging technological area of concern for the Special Forces is 'human performance factors'. These are 'medical or biological interventions to the body designed to improve performance and capability'.[25] An example is the introduction of medications designed to change the neural functioning of the brain in order to enhance its operating capacity. Advantages in this area could lead to improvements in focus and decision-making; however, any attempt at human enhancement must be taken cautiously because the underlying presumption is that emotions are pathological in nature and therefore a distraction to decision making. Emotions should, however, be understood as inseparable from the way that humans evaluate events, and as such, any efforts to dull or repress them would not *enhance* decision making, but rather detract from it. Repressing emotions *may* restrict unethical behaviour, but it could also potentially undermine ethical behaviour typically motivated by appropriate emotions. As an example, an 'enhanced' person whose impulse for aggression was enhanced may be less likely to move in defence of a people deemed as *hors de combat*. As such, Special Forces will need to work closely with scientists and other experts to determine precisely what role emotions have in ethical behaviour.[26]

*

Australian Special Forces are increasingly concerned with ethics – their evolution and application. Ethical behaviour is not only expected, it is critical for mission success. Only through an understanding of a person's background, their understanding of rules, goals and situations, as well as a perspective on their training, beliefs and education, can ethics be promoted in a manner that ensures they are a capability multiplier rather than a mission risk. Ethical frameworks such as the 'Remarkable Trinity' provide an opportunity for Special Forces personnel to pursue not only military-specific objectives but ethical goals. These support mechanisms may help to increase adherence to the ethical principles that govern armed conflict, noting that ethical challenges will always be an important component that Special Forces commanders must consider when assigning personnel to missions, roles and tasks.

7

MORAL OBJECTION AND POLITICAL DISSENT

TOM FRAME

A nation's decision to commit its resources to an armed conflict and to mandate the use of lethal force will always be controversial. For uniformed men and women, disagreement over when force is used and how it will be delivered has an intensely personal dimension because it touches on their moral integrity and physical safety. Although Service people remain citizens of the Commonwealth and participate in its common life, they are obliged to obey lawful direction from the government and to fulfill the tasks they are legally assigned. But they also overhear the party debates, observe the public protests and come to their own opinions about a conflict and its conduct. Being apolitical in the performance of one's professional work does not require political docility in one's personal outlook. The potential for dissonance is high and the possibility for angst is real.

Service people have rarely been properly prepared to handle the range of highly complex political and legal, ethical and moral issues arising from the operations to which they are frequently committed. Foremost is a perennial failure to help them distinguish accurately between legitimate moral objections and what I will refer to as 'routine political dissent'. This lack of clarity has complicated conversations and conclusions about when and where and why uniformed personnel might be justified in deciding to refuse service. A poor working grasp of the just war tradition in both its classical and contemporary forms is largely to blame for confused conceptions about the moral status of an operation, a judgment that also applies to many parliamentarians and most pundits.

The central challenge is moving from a focus on legal responsibilities and institutional regulations, which have centred on obligations and duties, to developing a capacity to reflect and an ability to reason so that soldiers can, *first*, differentiate between moral conviction and political dissent, *second*, articulate and explain their position, and *third*, canvass options and negotiate alternatives to actually refusing service. This movement needs to be accompanied by four things. First, general acceptance that most deployments involve some controversy, whether it is moral or political. Second, broad acknowledgement that contemporary soldiers are better educated and more inquisitive than their forebears. Third, clearer explanations from political authorities of why operations are necessary in terms of advancing the national interest. Fourth, a greater openness among uniformed leaders to discussing issues and addressing concerns relating to the moral dimensions of modern warfare.

Since 1990 and the prelude to the 1991 Gulf War, there have been an undisclosed number of ADF personnel (my guess is nearer to tens than hundreds) who have indicated their unwillingness to deploy on operations they cannot reconcile with their ethical principles or to engage in activities they consider morally unacceptable. The approach to individual cases of selective conscientious objection taken by the Australian Defence Force

(ADF) in recent years is to deal with them quietly and confidentially. To date, this approach has been workable because there have been few such cases, while public controversy has been avoided because those involved prefer privacy and anonymity. But this approach is unsustainable in the longer term on two grounds.

First, the number of objectors is unlikely to decline in the current climate. Second, 'ad hoc-ery' is a flawed foundation on which to build a consistent personnel policy with conscientious rigour. The ADF does not have the legislative authority to formally recognise selective objection among its members but it usually (although not always) has the ability, through its posting mechanisms, to send those with an objection to a particular deployment or a specific operation to another unit or locality if the conscientious objection cannot be resolved. Given evolving weapons, tactics, scenarios and the corporate risk aversion associated with current and likely future operations, a procedural review cannot be avoided and should not be delayed. Australia's operating partners have all endured controversial courts martial involving volunteers and conscientious objection over the last decade. The United States Army was obliged to deal with the cases of Sergeant Travis Bishop and Specialist Victor Agosto, who claimed conscientious objector status in 2009 and refused deployment to Afghanistan because, in their view, the conflict did not meet the criteria for lawful war. Bishop was sentenced to twelve months in gaol and Agosto to 30 days. A British soldier, Joe Glenton, refused to deploy to Afghanistan in 2009 because he felt the use of military power against the Taliban was an illegitimate use of force. He was sentenced to nine months imprisonment. Nearest to home is the case of the Australian-born RAF medical officer, Flight Lieutenant Malcolm Kendall-Smith. After refusing to deploy to Iraq in mid-2005 because he believed the initial invasion and subsequent occupation were illegal and therefore immoral, he was charged, court-martialled and convicted of disobeying lawful orders. In April 2006 Kendall-Smith was imprisoned for eight months, directed to pay £20 000 in costs, and discharged from the British armed forces.[1]

A large part of the present problem for Australia arises from the unintended consequences of the *Defence Act*'s recognition of a right of selective conscientious objection (SCO), also known as objection to particular wars. The inclusion of SCO in the Act was a substantial departure from previous practice. In 1901 the newly formed Commonwealth Government assumed sole responsibility for national defence and was empowered by the Constitution to raise and maintain naval and military forces. The 1903 *Defence Act* determined that uniformed service would be voluntary, except in times of war, when men could be conscripted for home defence (within the geographic confines of the Commonwealth of Australia).[2] A bill for universal (meaning compulsory) military training for Australian men aged 18 to 60 was introduced by the Deakin Government in 1909. The electorate accepted the need for conscription in times of national crisis and continued to do so.[3] The original Act also made provision for exemption from service on the grounds of 'conscientious belief', which was defined as 'requiring a fundamental conviction of what is morally right and wrong, which is so compelling that the person is duty-bound to follow that belief'. The *Act* recognised the validity of conscientious belief for 'those who could prove that the doctrines of their religion forbade them to bear arms or perform military service' (section 60). Exemption was limited to combatant duties and was restricted to individuals who could demonstrate membership of an organisation that formally professed pacifism. Australia was the first nation to grant complete exemption from military service on these grounds. The religious test was abolished in 1910 to allow for recognition of objection on secular or philosophical grounds.

After the two world wars of 1914–18 and 1939–45, Australian forces consisting entirely of volunteers deployed to the Korean War (1950–53), the Malayan Emergency (1948–60) and the Indonesian 'Confrontation' (1964–66),[4] although compulsory military training was re-introduced in 1951 as part of a national service scheme[5] that continued until 1959.[6] In anticipation of possible higher level armed conflict with Indonesia, conscription was reintroduced using provisions contained in the *National Service Act* (1951) without parliamentary debate (not that it was technically required) on 10 November 1964.[7] The Act exempted conscientious objectors on the grounds of religious and non-religious beliefs from either all military service or from combative military service, the distinction reflecting the nature of the conscientious beliefs held by the person seeking an exemption. Total exemption was granted on the basis of 'deep seated and compelling' conscientious objection. Conscientious objection was, of course, always available to volunteers during peacetime through the process of administrative discharge.

It was not until late 1968 that the courts clarified the scope of conscientious belief. In *Thompson's Case* heard before the High Court, Bruce Thompson claimed that the phrase 'any form of military service' in section 29A(1) of the *National Service Act*, meant that exemption was possible if an individual objected to 'any form of military service', including a particular war. The court was split. Chief Justice Barwick disagreed and Thompson lost his case. The Department of Labour and National Service used Barwick's judgment to point out that:

> it is open to a national service registrant, whose objection
> to military service is of a selective nature in that he holds a

belief against participation in a particular conflict, to opt
for part-time service in the Citizen Forces at the time for
registration as an alternative to call-up for the full-time
National Service.[8]

Furthermore, there were fears that legal recognition of selective
objection could open doors to a general theory of selective obedience to law. The distinction between a person conscientiously
opposed to participation in a particular war and one conscientiously opposed to the payment of a particular tax, for instance,
was apparently rather slight. Such recognition had the potential
to erode public authority and destroy the fabric of government.
There was also the additional complicating factor of distinguishing between political beliefs and party loyalties. The latter could
involve all of the members of a political party seeking exemption
from military service on the grounds that their party opposed
a war. Those defending a right of selective objection note that
it applies in the sole area where the Executive Government can
compel personal service (which is different from paying taxes and
obeying the speed limit). Personal service can also be compelled
by the judiciary in the form of jury service and by the legislature
in the form of compulsory voting. Both of these obligations are,
of course, also accompanied by opt-out provisions.[9]

Disagreements about selective objection continued until the
end of Australian involvement in the Vietnam War and the proclamation of the *National Service Termination Act* (1973). Provisions
relating to national servicemen were removed from the *Defence
Act* in 1975.[10] The debate was moribund until Michael Tate, a
Labor senator from Tasmania, proposed legislation to recognise
a right to selective conscientious objection.[11] He later introduced
a Private Members Bill into the Senate proposing changes to the
National Service Act (1951). The matter languished until 1990

when Senator Tate, by now Justice Minister in the Hawke Labor Government, circulated the first draft of a *Defence Legislation Amendments Bill*. It included recognition of SCO for conscripts, although the last national service trainee had been discharged from the Army in 1973. The Service Chiefs were mortified by the prospect of SCO being offered even to conscripted personnel because they contended that some of the principles that applied to conscript service could (and would) be applied to volunteer service or create unhelpful confusion. These fears soon materialised when Leading Seaman Terence Jones failed to report to HMAS *Adelaide* before the ship deployed to the Gulf of Oman in August 1990 to enforce United Nations' sanctions against Iraq after its invasion of Kuwait.[12]

Leading Seaman Jones defended his action by saying (while he was absent without leave): 'I am not a coward and I would be prepared to fight for my country, but *I am taking a political stand* because this is not our war, we are just following the Americans. I am prepared to die to defend my country but not to protect the United States' oil lines' [emphasis added]. He implied that he was morally compelled to be politically active in this instance. Although the *Defence Legislation Amendments Bill* was still in draft form when Jones was declared absent without leave and liable for arrest, the Independent (former Nuclear Disarmament Party) Senator for Western Australian, Jo Vallentine, introduced a private bill into the Senate for *An Act Relating to Conscientious Objection to Certain Defence Service*. She praised Leading Seaman Jones for being 'aware, informed and intelligent'. Vallentine sought to protect his 'political stand' as a matter of conscience that was essentially indistinguishable from a moral stand. The further inference was that a person's political beliefs were part of their moral conscience and therefore worthy of protection.

At his subsequent court martial, Jones was found guilty of

being absent from his lawful place of duty without approved leave. He was sentenced to 21 days' detention, reduction in rank to able seaman and forfeiture of four days' pay. Jones then sought a 'discharge at own request'. Despite the severity of the punishment, which was intended to make an example of Jones and to highlight the operational seriousness of his untimely abstention, a confidential paper prepared within the Naval Support Command shortly after the court martial noted that:

> In practice a considerable degree of flexibility has been shown in attempting to accommodate personnel who have genuine difficulties in participating in particular operations. This flexibility was exercised in the Gulf deployment where commanding officers agreed to allow a number of people to post off the ships for a variety of reasons, some less compelling than conscientious objection. The ability for commanders to do this is obviously useful and should be retained provided it is not seen as a *de facto* right of conscientious objection on the part of the individuals concerned.[13]

The court martial of Jones prompted an inquiry from the Human Rights and Equal Opportunity Commissioner, Brian Burdekin, who was concerned that the absence of any right of selective conscientious objection offended against the spirit of his Commission's act of parliament and was contrary to the *International Covenant on Civil and Political Rights* (ICCPR) which was incorporated into Australian law by the *HREOC Act*. In reply, the ADF insisted that:

> an expectation that all *lawful* orders will be obeyed is fundamental to the maintenance of discipline [...] Concomitant with this expectation there must exist a

right [...] to take disciplinary action where breaches of this fundamental obligation occur. In other words the right to enforce the obligation to serve is reasonable and not discriminatory. Accordingly, so far as volunteers are concerned, there is no scope for allowing for conscientious objection with respect to specified operations, or indeed combat generally, unless the matter is raised as a ground for discharge at own request.[14]

Recognition of conscience became a 'hot issue' again with the planned invasions of Afghanistan in 2001 and Iraq in 2003. Both operations provoked a great deal of vigorous discussion within and beyond the ADF about the justification of Australian participation given the absence of any clear, unambiguous, immediate or direct threat to the Australian people and the national interest by either Afghanistan or Iraq. In trips around the country to units and bases as the then Anglican Bishop to the Defence Force, I heard laments and complaints about both operations and detected that many previously apolitical servicemen and women felt they and their skills had been used for domestic political advantage and the generation of international goodwill. This was very far removed from defending Australia and its national interests, some felt, and led them to question the moral justification for using force. Matters of conscience and the nature of obligation were at the forefront of conversation. Based on my observations then and since, I would contend that the vast majority of ADF members have not actually thought much about the difference between moral objection and political dissent; the majority do not know how to differentiate between them or how and when they might overlap, and even fewer have thought about what they would do if confronted by a moral objection within their service.

The distinction is not, on face value, unclear. Moral objections arise from personal convictions about right and wrong. Convictions are stronger than beliefs in that they embody firm conclusions that must be honoured as they are part of a person's identity and cannot be violated without damaging a person's integrity. A person is entitled to refuse to participate in any action that adversely affects their identity or integrity. The *Defence Act* puts it this way: a conscientious objection 'is so compelling in character for that person that he or she is duty bound to espouse it; and is likely to be of a long standing nature'. Conversely, political opposition is usually an expression of individual disagreement based on beliefs about possibilities and preferences. These beliefs are essentially opinions or judgments with respect to competing courses of action. Political dissent is often disagreement with a government decision or policy on practical grounds, such as economics or efficiency. At this point complexity is apparent. The words 'usually' and 'often' are necessary because it is possible to object to a decision or policy – and their implementation – on moral grounds. For instance, a decision or policy might be entirely consistent with a person's beliefs and convictions but be implemented in a manner that is discriminatory or punitive, or have unintended consequences and produce unexpected outcomes that are inconsistent with a person's moral principles and ethical standards. The tradition in a liberal democratic society is to protect conscience by respecting moral objection and seeking to accommodate its demands. Political dissent is handled differently. It is considered routine, almost inevitable, and best managed through the ballot box. If an individual does not approve of a government decision or policy they can vote for a change of government and perhaps a change of policy at the next election. But it is not difficult to see how morals and politics can be intertwined, and often are.

It is the existence of moral objections to political decisions, the kind that Leading Seaman Terence Jones claimed to profess, that has become the most pressing issue for the Commonwealth Government, the ADF and, indeed, the Australian people. What is to be done when a uniformed person claims that a deployment is illegal or an operation is immoral because it lacks a legislative mandate or fails a necessity test? In 2003, a number of serving ADF personnel concluded that the invasion of Iraq by a Coalition consisting of the United States, Britain and Australia was either illegal (because it was not undergirded by a specific United Nations mandate) or immoral (because the case for entering Iraq lacked urgency and cogency). From my observations, the majority of those holding these views were not deployed to Iraq and were not required to express their objection and to endure the consequences. They were able to breathe a sigh of relief that their personal assessment of the deployment did not have professional ramifications. A small number of personnel did object to being deployed and sought alternative service. They paid a professional price for their personal convictions.

Since joining the ADF nearly 40 years ago, I have noticed a substantial shift towards showing greater respect for the personal convictions of uniformed personnel. For the greatest part this shift is welcome. It reflects the liberalising of Australian society and a growing confidence in the ADF's corporate culture, where differences of opinion are not routinely categorised as displays of insubordination or signs of disloyalty. The nation wants ADF members to be thoughtful and questioning, hence the substantial investment in education and training, especially in relation to morals (which deal with principles) and ethics (which is concerned with practicalities). But conceptual challenges remain. I would contend that the two most pressing challenges are managing the distinction between objection and opposition, and ensuring that moral conversation (which is how many people grow in ethical maturity and moral stature) is not proscribed as incitement to mutiny.

Trying to pursue mission objectives with both effectiveness and efficiency while giving conscience due regard is never easy. I realise there is impatience with suspected or declared conscientious objection among volunteers, an impatience reflected in the retort: 'If they don't approve they are free to leave'. But I would respond in two ways. First, what if an individual's objection is valid because a planned action is morally objectionable? The practice of moral conversation and the presence of conscientious people in an ADF unit may be crucial to preventing immoral and potentially illegal behaviour from starting and spreading. Second, should an otherwise successful career be ended because a person thinks that their participation in one activity is incompatible with their moral conscience and seeks an alternative? Specific objection is not the seed of general disobedience. Should there be some scope for restricted recognition of selective conscientious objection? I am not suggesting that a person who objects to the use of all force should be retained in the ADF, nor am I wanting to excuse sedition or, worse, treason. But in the context of limited wars, armed interventions and peace enforcement, there will be competing accounts of the causes and consequences of using force and there will be different interpretations of why Australian uniformed men and women need to be placed in harm's way. Given that ADF personnel receive ethics education during their initial entry training and in subsequent professional courses, uniformed men and women are bound to exercise their critical faculties. It is not surprising that they will ask hard questions, they will question political rhetoric and they will conduct their own assessment of the pros and cons of using force in any given situation. Sometimes they will conclude that the use of force is not justified. Such conclusions do not undermine the whole fabric of democratic government nor threaten the political impartiality of the ADF.

The pressing issue is not so much respect for conscience but differentiating moral principles from political preferences. Many people claiming to profess a moral objection are actually declaring political dissent. They think that something is bad (by which they mean a poor option) rather than wrong (by which they mean defying a principle). To help soldiers better understand the issues and to differentiate between objection and dissent, I believe the Army needs to invest deeply in even more nuanced ethics education and training, and perhaps to engage the assistance of UNSW Canberra with its expertise in ethics and sociology. The following practical proposals are offered as a way forward.

First, it is plain that much of the language used in discussions about the character of armed conflict is loose, undisciplined or lacking in precision. There is scope for a small handbook to be produced that distils the consensus that exists among philosophers and social theorists about what certain words mean when used in the context of compulsion and conscience. Clearer definitions will help to bring clarity to conversations involving leaders and followers, soldiers and civilians.

Second, initial entry training and continuing education programs need to be augmented with an *aide memoire* that mirrors the content of the ethics courses undertaken during a service person's career and that covers the legislative dimensions of uniformed service together with the ADF's commitment to conscience. Such a document will ensure that every uniformed person is aware of institutional expectations and their personal entitlements.

Third, the just war tradition shapes most ethical reflection on armed conflict in the Australian context. Just war thinking is dynamic rather than static because the conduct of armed conflict and the shape of international relations are forever changing. Therefore, the Army could convene an annual roundtable that focused on emerging insights drawn from both operational experience and critical scholarship over the previous twelve months. The roundtable's proceedings would produce an annual review of the just war tradition – in principle and practice – and be distributed among educators and trainers, strategic planners and unit lawyers.

Fourth, there is a need for the Army to convene regular community consultations that consider attitudinal changes to individual liberties and entitlements, government objectives and ADF policies. Given the 'can do' attitude that prevails across the ADF, focusing on human rights without any cognisance of strategic priorities will work against achieving practical progress in the direction of enhanced respect for moral integrity. At the moment, a mission-minded ADF is constrained from seeing the importance of being morally minded as well.

Fifth, while there is merit in lawyers turning their minds to the shape of future legislation bearing upon the recognition of conscience (section 61 of the *Defence Act*), philosophers need to explain the general principles upon which recognition of conscience is grounded, the values any amendment might seek to promote and the objects any amendment will attempt to secure. The wording of the current *Defence Act* makes the state's attitude to conscience look like adhering to an administrative procedure rather than honouring a democratic principle. Indeed, a group of like-minded philosophers might draft an Explanatory Memorandum to any amendments that would be available to parliamentarians to ponder in the context of future changes to the Act.

These initiatives recognise the increasing complexity of modern military operations, the politically contested nature of many national deployments, the greater likelihood that individuals will seek exemption from service, the convergence of moral objection and political dissent, and the absence of a consistent means and an adequate procedure for dealing with instances of selective conscientious objection among volunteers. Adopting one or more of these initiatives would signal the importance the Army attaches to matters of conscience, reduce the incidence of moral objection being confused with political dissent and ensure that missions are not disrupted by needless debates that have the capacity to damage morale and diminish cohesion. As other contributors have noted, the need for expanded ethics training and education is compelling and the demand for action is immediate.

PART 4: THE ARMY AND COMMUNITY EXPECTATIONS

An Australian soldier with East Timorese civilians as part of the United Nations' peacekeeping mission. *Commonwealth of Australia*

8

HUMANITARIAN VALUES AND MILITARY OBJECTIVES

BETH EGGLESTON

If most of us choose to be principled, practical, daring, courageous and thoughtful, and keep struggling to stay close to affected communities and create solutions with them, then humanitarian action stands a good chance of being relevant, effective and respected [...] ethical character and practical virtues, like roses and rice, need to be cultivated carefully.

Hugo Slim, Senior Research Fellow, University of Oxford
Institute for Ethics, Law and Armed Conflict[1]

The ethical dilemmas facing humanitarian workers, their organisations and partners are ever-present and are increasingly complex. The need for principled military leaders and the ethical use of force are also much discussed. Humanitarian ethics struggles with how best to save the most lives; military ethics grapples with how to avoid unnecessary deaths. Personal ethics and motivation are central to humanitarian action, and the decisions around what the humanitarian–military interface looks like in conflict is critical to humanitarian operations around the world. This has been my experience.

I had a difficult day at the office in February 2007. As I co-chaired a humanitarian civil–military co-ordination meeting at the United Nations Assistance Mission in Afghanistan (UNAMA), I learned that United States forces had acquired the office of one of our partners. The non-governmental organisation (NGO) in question was Afghanaid, a British aid agency who had been one of the only groups providing aid and development programs in the Kamdesh district of Nuristan province, and had been doing so for more than nine years. American forces had entered the Afghanaid compound without prior warning, bringing with them blindfolded and handcuffed detainees, and occupied the premises for the reason of 'military necessity'. Being perceived as supporting the international military effort in Afghanistan has always been a challenge for the aid community and for Afghanaid in particular; this had just got a whole lot harder. Indeed, the outcome of this situation was that Afghanaid had to cease operating in the area, leaving behind the nine years of relationships and programs it had developed, and thousands of people without life-saving services and assistance. It is situations like these that highlight why humanitarian civil–military co-ordination and dialogue is an increasingly important and necessary element in situations of conflict.

The Oxford Institute for Ethics, Law and Armed Conflict outlines these issues and the ethical complexities facing humanitarian organisations. These issues include the difficulty in reconciling political and military agendas that are at odds with humanitarian principles, the tensions between assisting in a way that does not jeopardise safety, problems of equity between competing operations, negotiation with non-state armed actors, perception of being complicit with regimes and when and how to speak out.

For me the ethical challenges are all too real. Having stood in a military hospital in Afghanistan seeing rows of wounded International Security Assistance Force (ISAF) personnel, and being told the vehicle-borne improvised explosive device that had sped toward them at a checkpoint was packed full of children, I understood why they did not shoot to stop it. I left Afghanistan with camps of hundreds of thousands of internally displaced people (IDPs) unvisited despite the offers of military armed escorts and air assets. Working with the ISAF mission was too dangerous both for the humanitarian workers and the IDPs themselves. And then I learned from the United Nations (UN) Headquarters in New York that admitting that there was a humanitarian crisis in Afghanistan was 'politically unpalatable'. Our unit resigned en masse as a result.

For all the differences and tensions between humanitarian agencies and militaries, ethical dilemmas are an area in which there are similarities and shared challenges. Indeed, both humanitarian and military actors are united in the reality that our actions can often mean the difference between life and death. We both strive to improve the quality of our leaders, the standards to which we operate and the interface between us. Humanitarian actors, which include UN funds, programs and agencies, the Red Cross and Red Crescent Movement, and national and international NGOs, face challenging ethical dilemmas working in complex emergencies including: negotiating access to affected populations, understanding the impact of accepting armed escorts for convoys, ensuring aid supplies are not causing long-term social problems or dependency and adhering to the 'Do No Harm' principles. I hope that enhancing the understanding of the ethical dilemmas facing NGOs may facilitate more effective dialogue and interface with militaries when operating in this complex space.

The current humanitarian landscape

The interface between humanitarian actors and militaries is a critical one and it is becoming more so in the face of the current massive humanitarian caseload and the reality that the international humanitarian system has been overwhelmed. Indeed, with the significant reduction in the Australian aid budget and aspirations to increase defence spending, the Australian Defence Force (ADF) could be delivering more and more of the government's emergency assistance.

Western nations cannot escape the horrific reality of humanitarian need in the world today. There is an ethical imperative to assist the more than 95 million people in need of humanitarian assistance, 65 million of whom are being displaced. With 76 per cent of people who live in extreme poverty living in countries that are politically fragile or environmentally vulnerable is it clear that poverty and crisis reinforce each other. The nature of global displacement is outlined in the 2016 Global Humanitarian Assistance report:

> A number of conflicts continued and intensified in 2015, bringing the number of people displaced by violence and persecution globally to over 65 million and generating severe suffering and humanitarian need. While attention grows on the rising numbers of people reaching Europe, the majority of displaced people are in the Middle East, North of Sahara and South of Sahara regions, and 60 per cent of those forced to flee remain internally displaced.[2]

To address this unprecedented situation and moral challenge, the UN Secretary General, Ban Ki-Moon, called for a World Humanitarian Summit, the first in the UN's 70-year history. This summit, held at Istanbul in May 2016, recognised the increasing humanitarian caseload and the reality that the international humanitarian system is not fit for purpose. The summit also recognised the critical role played by militaries in responding to crises, and the need to strengthen the interface through co-ordination. NGOs are under pressure like never before to deliver more with less, in more hostile environments, where they are often a target. This summit reminded us that there are no humanitarian solutions to humanitarian problems and that political will is the key to reducing conflict and suffering. I saw a lot of goodwill at the summit but political will was lacking.

The shape of the humanitarian caseload is also changing. Crises are fewer in number, but are more long-term, affecting many more people for longer periods. These crises are complex, often across porous borders, and are exacerbated by factors like climate change and involvement of non-state armed actors. The numbers of humanitarian agencies working in these contexts are huge, with more than 4500 organisations and their 250 000 staff working to provide humanitarian assistance globally. In 2014, humanitarian funding was more than US$20 billion and of the US$10 billion that was spent by international NGOs, 31 per cent of that funding went to the five largest 'mega-international NGOs': MSF, International Rescue Committee, Oxfam, Save the Children and World Vision.[3] NGOs play a critical role in implementing more than 80 per cent of the UN's humanitarian response operations. But just as not all militaries are the same, NGOs can work to different standards, levels of training, codes of conduct and operational priorities.

Militaries need to understand some of these standards and

the ways in which humanitarian actors operate, including the differences in organisational culture. It is often said that for NGOs the process is as important as the product, meaning the way in which humanitarian programs are implemented is central to their work. Ensuring that the actions of an agency 'do no harm', instill dignity and ownership, build resilience and do not create dependence are all elements agencies consider when they respond to crises. This approach can be incredibly frustrating for militaries needing to show tangible and short-term wins during a relatively short deployment. For the humanitarian community that often makes decisions by consensus, time is needed to consult and to shape a bottom-up approach. These processes are at odds with the hierarchical military culture of control and command. This friction can cause serious problems in the heat of a rapid-onset emergency.

Humanitarian agencies work in the way that they do for very important reasons. They are obliged to uphold the humanitarian principles of humanity, impartiality, neutrality and independence. These are the principles that carve out humanitarian space. The concept of humanitarian space, although contested, refers to the access to people and the ability to adhere to the principles. Essentially the idea is that humanitarian actors will have the independence, flexibility and freedom of action necessary to gain access and provide assistance to the affected population in a humanitarian crisis. A practical example is military actors providing area security that in turn creates a co-operative operating environment allowing aid agencies to access populations and to deliver assistance in alignment with their mandate. If these principles are disregarded, this operational environment, or humanitarian space, is undermined and will cease to exist. There is an ethical imperative to preserve humanitarian space, even and especially in times of armed conflict.

There is a view that how the principles are interpreted and adhered to is also changing as the make-up of the international humanitarian community shifts. This is a challenge not just for Western militaries but also for traditional players such as UN agencies, Red Cross and Red Crescent Movement and NGOs. The increase in funding from Gulf states, such as Kuwait and Saudi Arabia, and also the BRICS (Brazil, Russia, India, China and South Africa) is significant. These contributions often do not go through formal co-ordination mechanisms. The role of the private sector is steadily growing as well, much to the dismay of the humanitarian purists. But the humanitarian community must shape what that will look like rather than seek to stifle this engagement. Technology is also having an impact and is often touted as the answer to many humanitarian challenges. It can be a double-edged sword. For instance, even as technology has allowed for electronic transfers to get much-needed cash to affected populations in the face of disasters, crowd-sourced crisis-mapping can put other communities at risk as belligerents trace the flow of information.

Recognising that humanitarian action is a broader concept than just the delivery of physical goods is equally important. While humanitarian action does involve assistance such as the traditional tents and food, it has a focus on protection and ensuring that affected people have their rights upheld under international law, human rights convenants and refugee conventions. These two pillars are supported by a third aspect, that of advocacy, both in the public and private sphere. From an operational point of view, as the recent contexts of Iraq, Syria, South Sudan and Afghanistan have demonstrated, humanitarian workers are not just caught in the crossfire, they are deliberately targeted. MSF has made the significant decision to not share the GPS co-ordinates of some of the hospitals it supports, an unprecedented move considering hospitals are protected structures under international humanitarian law. This underscores that humanitarian workers are having to review and revise how they operate in these complex emergencies, and that has implications for how they interact with various militaries as well.

I have often listened to military personnel cite the need to engage in relief operations as there is a perceived lack of civilian actors to do so. The argument that NGOs are simply not present in hostile or high-threat environments to provide assistance, that there is a vacuum of actors and that militaries need to fill the space is not always the reality. At the time of writing, at Aleppo in Syria there are community-based organisations such as the White Helmets who are providing much-needed humanitarian assistance. There may be rare occurrences where humanitarian agencies are not present but this is limited to the most extreme circumstances. The majority of international NGOs work through local partners. Just because Western observers don't see white four-wheel drives bumping along badly formed roads with foreign aid workers doesn't mean that such work isn't happening. By way of illustration, Oxfam conducts 80 per cent of all its work through local partners. These partnerships not only build local capacity, they ensure aid can be delivered in the most appropriate means to the most vulnerable, boost the local economy and increase access by getting aid to those areas where expatriate aid workers and white four-wheel drives are targeted as foreign interveners.

How can we provide an ethical framework?

To ensure that humanitarian action is perceived as ethical, impartial and effective, there is a significant difference in how humanitarian actors and militaries interact along the continuum, ranging from peacetime, peacekeeping and peace enforcement to combat. This results in the relationships between humanitarian and military actors ranging from co-operation, through to co-ordination through interlocutors, to coexistence with indirect contact through third-party conduits. Context is everything and perception is reality. The relationship is dynamic and must respond and adapt to emerging developments to ensure the interface is appropriate and is supporting humanitarian space. Much of the thinking behind decisions in this space hinge on short-term versus long-term impacts. If your aid organisation accepts an armed escort today and transports its humanitarian assistance goods from A to B, will the perception that you are aligned with military forces in the area preclude you from accessing large populations in need into the future? Will a larger number of people suffer tomorrow because some of those being assisted today have received military support? How do we face these ethical challenges where there is seemingly no 'right' answer? And how do we engage in dialogue when there are few alternatives available?

Having been in the situation where I was asked to utilise humanitarian assistance to 'hold' an area after a security operation, being able to promote and protect humanitarian principles is a key skill to continue to ethically engage in such a complex environment. Humanitarian civil–military co-ordination is meant to guard against the instrumentalisation or politicisation of assistance, and to protect those who are in need. There is the argument that the reasons or intentions behind actions (be those military, political, religious or commercial) should not 'contaminate the action' – that is, it should not matter why militaries do life-saving work, the outcome is still saving lives. If only it were so simple. Although actions may be lifesaving in the moment there are often short and long-term impacts of such action. The question is, what if all future action to assist people has been thrown into jeopardy? Indeed, has it actually put them in harm's way? There is also the matter of how the action is undertaken. Is the action co-ordinated? Is there a clear exit strategy? Have internationally agreed guidelines been followed? Thankfully, a way forward is starting to emerge.

The concept of humanitarian civil–military co-ordination (UN-CMCoord) aims to address these tensions in a constructive way. The United Nations Office for the Coordination for Humanitarian Affairs (UNOCHA) defines UN-CMCoord as:

> The essential dialogue and interaction between civilian and military actors in humanitarian emergencies that is necessary to protect and promote humanitarian principles, avoid competition, minimise inconsistency, and when appropriate pursue common goals. Basic strategies range from coexistence to cooperation. Coordination is a shared responsibility facilitated by liaison and common training.[4]

In many ways, this initiative provides an ethical framework, a decision making process and a space to bring disparate views together to discern a way forward. This function is led by UNOCHA. On the ground, CMCoord officers are the first point of call when interacting with the humanitarian community and NGOs in particular. These officers will provide neutral meeting spaces and a mode of communication intended to enhance and support dialogue.

Humanitarian civil–military co-ordination also adds value in the quest to gain humanitarian access and protection of civilians in situations of armed conflict. If done effectively, humanitarian civil–military co-ordination can have other positive impacts. At the World Humanitarian Summit, the importance of localisation was highlighted, supporting and strengthening local structures, decentralising decision making and committing finances to the local level rather than through the international actors. Humanitarian civil–military co-ordination can support the process of localisation if national structures are respected rather than negated, which can often happen in large crisis responses.

Can militaries be humanitarian?

Although an unpopular perspective in military circles, the humanitarian principles preclude militaries from being seen as humanitarian actors. This is not to say that militaries do not provide life-saving, timely, and effective assistance in times of crisis. Indeed, appropriate use of military capabilities can be critical to an effective response. Further, as the UN Chief of Humanitarian Affairs, Stephen O'Brien, recently explained: 'We are in a region that has demonstrated that military actors can make a critical contribution in responding to natural disasters'. Indeed, there was the case of even MSF calling for military involvement in the response to the 2014 Ebola crisis in West Africa, acknowledging that there are some circumstances that call for the speed, scale and capability of military assets. But militaries have a mandate and role that ultimately sets them apart from humanitarian aid organisations. The latest version of the UNOCHA civil–military field handbook makes this point plainly:

> Military forces that deliver aid – be it fulfilling
> obligations under international humanitarian law
> (IHL), offering assistance to affected populations as
> part of a wider stabilisation mandate, in extremis,
> or in support of humanitarian operations – are not
> considered humanitarian actors. They might very well

fulfil or support humanitarian tasks, without changing
their original *raison d'être*.[5]

If this concept was more widely accepted and understood there
would be much less friction between NGOs and military actors,
bringing greater clarity to the roles and responsibilities of most
actors and leading to less blurring of the lines. There still seems to
be reluctance from the military viewpoint to accept that humanitarian actors are not part of a 'unity of effort' and should not be
viewed as such. Fully understanding that humanitarian NGOs
are not intelligence partners, force multipliers or part of a stabi-
lisation agenda or counter-insurgency strategy (COIN) is critical
for an effective working relationship in conflict environments.
Humanitarian NGOs rely on the community acceptance model
of security. Perceptions that they are aligned with a military-
political mission are highly problematic, not just for the safety
of their staff but also for the affected populations they seek to
assist. For these humanitarian actors, it is unethical to disregard
humanitarian principles. Upholding these principles needs to
frame their engagement with militaries.

Uncivil militaries

Private Militaries and Security Companies (PMSCs) have a
unique role in conflict contexts. They are commercial entities. In
offering services to non-state actors, PMSCs challenge the norm
in which the state has monopoly over the use of military force.
Indeed, major military operations can no longer take place without these support elements. The use of a contractor is often cost
effective, flexible and politically expedient. But ethical questions
about the place and the conduct of PMSCs have come to the

fore, especially after the behaviour of large PMSCs during the post-1991 Balkan wars.

Working in the same space as PMSCs is an area where both military actors and humanitarian agencies can have similar challenges. The lack of distinction of these operators can cause problems on both sides, along with the lack of clear channels for communication. There have been recent concerns about PMSCs wanting to 'cut out the middle-man' and start delivering assistance themselves rather than being contracted to the agencies that do. As PMSCs do not work primarily to humanitarian principles, this is a grave concern for the agencies that do and the resulting confusion can be deadly. The humanitarian civil–military co-ordination mechanisms described above do not include PMSCs. There is often confusion about the status and functions of PMSCs: to whom do they answer? How ought NGOs communicate with them, especially after security incidents? While there seems to be an understanding that states that are signatories to 'The Montreux Document on Pertinent International Legal Obligations and Good Practices for States related to Operations of Private Military and Security Companies during Armed Conflict of 17 September 2008' have legal obligations, the force and effect of this agreement does not pertain to non-state actors who also contract PMSCs.[6]

Towards a more constructive and ethical dialogue

There have been low points that have made the humanitarian sector reflect on itself. They include the 1994 Rwandan genocide, the 2004 Indian Ocean Tsunami, the collapse of civil order in the Darfur region of Western Sudan after 2003, and the continuing civil war in Syria. There are many more forgotten emergencies in which the international community has failed to protect and to assist. They are too numerous to mention. In all of these contexts there is an interesting question: whose mission has primacy? Both humanitarian and military actors believe in their mandates above all else, protect their people at all costs and pay the price when things go wrong. With so much in common there is no wonder certain elements believe they are 'on the same team'. This is a common misunderstanding.

Humanitarian civil–military co-ordination becomes more important with growing perceptions that aid is simply an instrument for advancing the interests of some states and when political–military objectives seem to trump humanitarian principles. For its part, the humanitarian sector is professionalising; investing in its leadership and management; institutionalising minimum standards, benchmarks and guidance; and mainstreaming key best practice approaches. In an effort to further improve humanitarian civil–military co-ordination on the ground, common standards are currently being developed globally to guide and support interaction. Humanitarian notification systems seeking to de-escalate conflict situations are intended to enable the work of humanitarian organisations in an area of military operations by sharing locations of humanitarian personnel, facilities and other essential public infrastructure in contexts such as Yemen. Not all humanitarian actors are taking this approach, however. Due to the unprecedented number of attacks on hospitals in the last couple of years, MSF has decided it will no longer share the GPS co-ordinates of its hospitals due to concerns they will be subject to deliberate attack. This is a significant and worrying trend that indicates the erosion of international humanitarian law.

Foremost is remembering that ethics are about people's welfare, personal choices and moral principles. It does not matter how many standards, how much training or how many pages of doctrine are produced, it is how people act in the heat of the moment and what decisions they make, often under extreme pressure, that will make the difference. If politics does not reflect or even respect the humanitarian principles, no number of guidelines or procedures will prevent a catastrophe. Although militaries act on behalf of the governments that deploy them, uniformed personnel need to be conscious of the humanitarian principles and to act always and everywhere in the light of their own humanity.

9

OPERATING WITHIN AN NGO: A UNIFORMED PERSPECTIVE

LEE HAYWARD

Working with a Non Government Organisation (NGO) as a member of the Australian Army presents a particular set of challenges; in my case these challenges arose in the course of advocating for gender equality. As I reflect on the source of these concerns, I realise they resonate across both my personal and professional experiences. Broadly, the Western conviction that we have the solutions to the problems faced by those living in developing nations is at the root of my concerns. Consequently, we seldom look back, critically examine our actions and understand how and why our 'accomplishments' have not achieved the intended results: how can a behaviour be ethical when we fail to consider its effects?

I will begin with some biographical information to establish the context for my choices and perspectives. I will then provide a broad overview of the NGO programs with which I have some experience before offering some detail on similar ethical concerns that arose from one particular operational experience with the Army. Next, I will use the Australian National Action Plan on

Women, Peace and Security 2012–2018 (NAP) – a plan which sees Defence as the responsible agency for multiple actions and strategies in the pursuit of gender equality – to highlight why I believe the similarities between the two experiences were so strong. Finally, I want to explain why I conclude that contemporary Western-originated programs aimed at establishing gender equality in developing countries, whether during war or peace, are unethical despite the best of intentions.

My background

I have a passionate interest in gender issues. I have a Masters in Defence Studies, majoring in International Security, and a Masters in Economics Studies, majoring in Development, and my personal library is full of books on gender issues. From an intellectual perspective I understand the complexities of gender relations, how gender equality can contribute to economic growth, national and international security, counter-terrorism, the United Nations' Millennium Development Goals (for addressing extreme poverty in its many dimensions – income poverty, hunger, disease, lack of adequate shelter, and exclusion – while promoting gender equality, education, and environmental sustainability), transnational crime-fighting and any number of other issues. On paper, I can provide conclusive arguments as to what the solutions are and how to implement them.

I highlight my background not to boast, but to emphasise that I did not go into these situations with a lack of foresight or an absence of a basic understanding of the complexity of the issue. But my years of study and all my 'book learning' did not change the fact that I was naive at best, ignorant at worst and I thought I knew enough to know how to stimulate change. I was wrong. My first challenge came from accepting I did not know the answers and rapidly making the change from being a planner to becoming a searcher.[1] Once I accepted that and started to critically examine my actions, the ethical challenges began.

The NGO programs

I have taken two breaks in my military service to undertake volunteer work overseas. Both times I contributed financially to the programs, as is expected with the majority of programs, a factor which raises significant ethical concerns in certain situations. The first time I worked with a local NGO in Zambia, the second time was with an international NGO in Senegal. I selected the NGOs and particular programs based on their commitment to female education, which has long been accepted as fundamental to the goal of achieving gender equality in developing nations.

In Zambia, the program I selected was theoretically aimed at empowering school age girls, encouraging them to stay in school and finish their secondary education, teaching them that they had more options than getting pregnant, becoming a mother in their early teens and dying of HIV/AIDS in their thirties.[2] I am not being flippant. At the time of my placement the average life expectancy in the communities in which I was working was early thirties.[3] I remember walking through the streets one day and realising how common funerals were, almost daily, and how rare it was to see someone who was middle-aged or older.

In Senegal, I initially signed up to work in a school, working with pre-teen girls. However, French was the language of the education system, and my French wasn't at the required standard to teach classes. So instead I found myself having a crash course in Wolof, the national language, and providing health care to *Talibe*

– young boys, usually aged from five upwards, who were sent away from home to live with *marabouts* (Islamic religious leaders and teachers) in *daaras* (Islamic boarding schools) where they spent their days studying the Quran. *Talibe* are not technically street children, but in reality they are. My days were spent either at a centre where the children could come to shower and have something to eat, or accompanying a locally employed nurse to various *daaras* to give the children first aid. I found this to be significantly more rewarding than anything I had done before, predominantly because I knew I was making a difference, no matter how small. I could also see first-hand where my financial support was going: food, bandages, medicines and local employment.

Like many others who volunteer or serve, my actions were founded on the best of intentions. And yet, years later as I reflected on the ethical challenges I had faced, I wondered if sometimes when an individual or organisation tries to change the world it is done with a focus on achieving short-term 'wins', and results in a disservice to those it was intended to help. Additionally, in trying to address local problems with Western solutions, the underlying issues are neglected, and medium- to longer-term results seldom reflect the well-intentioned actions of the initiator.

My study and personal experience has led me to realise that Western solutions will *never* solve the problems of developing nations. It is not a viewpoint that is universally shared and, frankly, when I first found myself reaching these conclusions and questioning what I had for so long believed to be true, it was incredibly confronting. Fortunately, I have now reached a point where I am confident and comfortable with my conclusions.

This means I am very conscious of the pitfalls of applying generic Western solutions to complex and sensitive issues in non-Western cultures. In the West and in my own country, I am an advocate of forcing social change to achieve the goal of gender equality. In developing nations forcing social change is potentially dangerous to the women I am seeking to help. Certainly it is pointless. This is not to suggest there is no hope: where developing nations have found their own solutions, or had equality forced on them through internal factors outside of their control, we have seen progress in gender equality. It is possible.

The ethical challenges I faced in Africa

The first principle of aid work is 'do no harm': a good phrase to live by and one familiar to most Westerners from the Hippocratic Oath. To me, the greatest gift you can give another human being is the gift of hope. This is why I joined the military and why I did the volunteer work. I wanted and still want to make the world a better place through giving people real hope for a better future. Sometimes in trying to give the gift of hope, however, we give false hope. This is a terrible thing even when it comes from a place of well-intentioned ignorance.

The first words I learned when I arrived in the central community in Zambia were *nguzo musimbi*, which in the dominant local dialect meant 'girl power'. I learned those words specifically, and as it turns out they are words I will never forget because they were meaningless: girls had no power. I was only in Zambia a few days when I realised that what I was trying to achieve was unrealistic for two reasons. The first was that the local NGO I was working with wasn't interested in empowering women. The way the volunteering system worked in this instance was that a large multinational NGO was subcontracting to local NGOs in different countries. The well-known multinational would advertise the program, be contacted by the volunteers and after accepting the fee and facilitating the initial communication between the volunteer and the local NGO, they would step back. I am not even sure how much of the money made it to the local NGO. On the other side, the local NGO would send out proposals for how the work they were doing fit in with the aims of the various multinationals it was targeting for support. Gender equality and female empowerment is high-profile, so they get volunteers (and the money they bring) by advertising programs with this goal. It is a universal truth that women's rights have been commercialised, and there are pros and cons that come with this reality. Sadly, all too often those who want to help are ignorant of the cons.

I found the whole set-up disappointing and frustrating, partly because it highlighted how 'voluntourism' can result in NGOs exploiting volunteers and locals for money, and partly because the potential to give false hope through the actions of such NGOs was not insignificant.[4] I am not suggesting all NGOs are the same. But I had done my research and the NGOs I considered were reputable. This is an ethical dilemma that anyone considering volunteering should reflect on prior to signing up: would the people I am seeking to help be better off if I just sent money and stayed at home? In many cases, the answer is 'yes'.

The second issue was that the girls I was working with knew I was kidding myself. This was perhaps a good thing, because I was not telling them things they believed only to later discover they were untrue. I was not giving false hope. The girls didn't turn up every day to listen to me wax lyrical about how they could become doctors or lawyers. Fortunately, I realised within about 48 hours that this was never going to be their reality. So I stopped. I stopped trying to tell them, from my place of white Western privilege, that they could do whatever they wanted – because they couldn't. With very few exceptions, their fate was already determined. In the community I was engaged in, finishing secondary school was never going to be the reality for many of the children, male or female. Zambia is one of the poorest countries in the world and the Zambian government didn't have the resources to make high school a reality in the communities in which I was working. So, instead I found a different way to make a difference to these girls. We played games and sport, and I was able to provide the means for them to forget about real life, if only for a couple of hours in the day, and just have fun. They could just be children.

I believe that the underlying problem here, and in many developing nations with similar cultural beliefs, is that gender inequality and the attitudes towards women are too deep-seated for the efforts of short-term volunteers to have much of an effect. There are no quick fixes. The problems of gender inequality will take generations to address in a meaningful and sustainable way. The NGOs who rely on short-term volunteers will invariably fail as they simply cannot provide the consistent effort required to develop medium- to long-term solutions and achieve cultural change. These solutions must be generated from within the developing country.

Additionally, gender equality, or its absence, was not the primary reason many of these girls had no future beyond early motherhood and early death. I deliberately chose a community where HIV/AIDS was rampant. I was surprised to find that the biggest killer in the community was depression, leading to alcoholism and liver failure, violence or suicide. This depression was founded in the absence of hope in a better future, and measures to address gender issues were so low on the priority list they weren't even on the radar.[5] I think I ended up doing more good than harm in Zambia, but only because I changed my focus or, in military-speak, I changed my line of effort to adapt to the tactical situation.

In Senegal I felt I made more of a difference to the children

I encountered. I dressed wounds, I helped teach the *Talibe* about hygiene, I played games, and I gave hugs and kisses. Some of the boys were five or six years old, they slept on a dirt floor, their clothes were essentially rags, and they spent their days begging for food and money and rote learning the Quran. Additionally, it was my experience sometimes when they made mistakes or did not bring 'home' enough money, they were beaten or whipped. Some of the wounds were truly horrific: providing basic first aid made a significant difference to their welfare. The broader community supported the program because we were helping look after the *Talibe*, thereby alleviating some of the burden on the wider community.[6]

Again, I think I did more good than harm because I was more realistic in my approach. I tailored my good intentions accordingly. Obviously, there was the concern that the children would form attachments to the volunteers, but because we moved around so much and saw so many children, the concern was seldom realised. Additionally, the children understood that the volunteers came and went, and did not appear to get over-invested in any one individual. Finally, many of the NGO employees were local nationals, so I knew I was not excluding local employment by being there. In Senegal, my ethical dilemma came about because I could not assist the young girls who sometimes lived in the *daara*s, because the program was not aimed at their welfare. The girls, all of whom were pre-teen, would cook and clean and were expected to remain in the background when we visited. While I understood that attempting to intervene on their behalf would not help them, more than once I asked myself if I was contributing to their ill treatment by failing to address it. I still don't know the answer to this question.

My operational experience in Afghanistan

In Afghanistan I experienced many of the same ethical concerns that I felt working with the NGOs. The role of Female Engagement Teams (FET) illustrates my point.[7] Although my exposure to these teams was peripheral (I did not go out on patrol as part of an FET mission), I was involved in mission planning for their host unit.

The logic behind establishing FETs was solid: all-male patrols could not engage with 50 per cent of the population in countries like Bosnia, Iraq and Afghanistan due to cultural sensitivities. These teams were established with the specific remit of engaging local women, building enduring relationships with them and addressing their issues.[8] At the tactical level they also proved to be an effective tool for commanders to assist with situational awareness and broader community engagement. Regardless of the intent behind the individual patrol, the use of FETs and their inclusion in other programs, such as those developed by the Provincial Reconstruction Team, publicly broadcast the acknowledgment of the role women have in peace and war, a role that is encapsulated in various United Nations Security Council (UNSC) resolutions and the NAP. The flaw in the process lay in the next step: I never saw these engagements translate into national agendas, or even continuing or sustainable agendas at the local level.

Gabrielle Cook, an international relations student at the University of Massachusetts, lists many reasons why FETs did not have the desired effect in her thesis on FETs in Afghanistan.[9] For me the reasons are less important than recognising that tactical level engagement by the FETs made little to no lasting difference to the women of Afghanistan, which should be the measure of their success. I would be happy to be proven wrong and to see gains made in female education, healthcare and economic opportunities continue after the departure of Coalition forces. I would warmly welcome seeing the 2009 law for the Elimination of Violence against Women (EVAM), the most high-profile 'achievement' of the West in terms of addressing gender issues in Afghanistan, make a long-term difference in the lives of women. But the signs are not positive. If the 2015 Gender Inequality Index is used as the measure of effectiveness, these efforts have made no difference in the short term either. Afghanistan is still one of the worst places in the world to be a woman.[10] This fact has not changed since 2001 when the Taliban were in power.

During the war in Afghanistan, women's issues were accepted as important throughout strategic-level negotiations primarily because the people with whom we were negotiating knew the value of telling us what we wanted to hear. However, when 'women's issues' such as gender equality, child marriages, or gender-based violence did make it to the negotiating table at the national level, they were invariably some of the first to be removed. Those who were in positions with power to bring about change had no intention of addressing the status of women. There were some token efforts but the impetus to enforce change simply did not exist. The situation remains unchanged. As Martin Luther King observed 40 years ago of the struggle for civil rights in the American south, 'lamentably, it is an historical fact that privileged groups seldom give up their privileges voluntarily'.[11] While he was talking specifically about racial tension, this observation remains relevant within any debate relating to equality. The failure of 'women's issues' to feature in peace agreements did not come as a surprise. It is not a phenomenon unique to Afghanistan. The United Nations' Women, Peace and Security initiative reported in 2014 that only '16 per cent of peace agreements in the last two decades have contained a reference to women and gender'.[12]

How do this experience and these realities relate to my ethical concerns? Media reporting and public commentary from prominent Afghan women such as Mahbouba Seraj suggests that women who stepped forward and spoke to the FETs and other Western organisations did so at their peril but with a reasonable expectation that it would be worth it. After all, they reasoned, women's liberation was a significant part of the American justification for deploying to Afghanistan. Given their raison d'être, the continuing use of FETs coupled with other gender-specific programs showed that the West believed these issues mattered. But in the context of gender, was it the right thing to do? What has been achieved? What has changed? Are there any realistic medium- to long-term improvements for women in Afghanistan? The depressing answer to these questions can be found with a quick online search. And if this is something the West didn't actually consider a priority, why did we suggest it was? And as we argued for change with no real consideration of underlying issues, using Western templates for solutions, did we give these women false hope?

Furthermore, by attempting to place these women into positions that their culture was not ready to accept in a society that is already one of the most violent in its oppression of women, were we increasing the personal threat they faced? The former UN Force Commander in Afghanistan, Major General Patrick Cammaert, observed: 'it has probably become more dangerous to be a woman than a soldier in armed conflict'.[13] In sending out FETs to talk to women, how mindful were Coalition forces of increasing this danger, raising women above the detection threshold and making them targets? Were those we said we would help set up for failure, and possibly quite violent backlash? While I do not know the answer to this question, I suspect it is 'yes'.

The National Action Plan

The National Action Plan (NAP) is Australia's response to, among other resolutions, the United Nations Security Council Resolution 1325 (UNSCR 1325). The NAP:

> sets out what Australia will do, at home and overseas, to integrate a gender perspective into its peace and security efforts, protect women and girls' human rights, and promote their participation in conflict prevention, management and resolution.[14]

It recognises that 'women are often excluded from formal decision making processes around preventing conflict, building peace and relief and recovery efforts', and highlights the need for women's inclusion in these processes.[15] This recognition is supported by several studies which have found that 'there is increasing evidence that women in government positions reduces the likelihood of collective violence in the form of state-sponsored human rights abuses [...] civil war [...] and interstate conflict'.[16]

The NAP is, of course, well-intentioned. Some of the aims are realistic and can result in medium-term changes. My questions are simple: when the military or other government agency leaves, have they left behind a legacy that suggests their stated belief in the importance of gender issues is credible? Or did these issues fall by the wayside during negotiations? Additionally, do the countries and communities they leave behind have the capacity and the intention to follow through? What has been the result for the women? Have we done the right thing by them and helped them achieve real and lasting change? Or have we applied templated Western solutions to a problem we don't understand? The 2004 report on UNSCR 1325 laments: 'in no area of peace and security work are gender perspectives systematically incorporated in planning, implementation, monitoring and reporting. An outstanding challenge is increasing the numbers of women in high-level decision making positions in peacekeeping operations'.[17] While the report is slightly dated, anecdotal evidence suggests the reality has not changed since then.

Through the NAP and UNSC resolutions, even the use of FETs, Australia indicates an awareness of the importance of gender issues in peace, stability and security. Yet our actions detract from our commitment as we consistently treat gender equality as a niche women's issue, not a general security issue. A review of post-conflict countries by the UN in 2010, which included Timor-Leste, found that only very limited resources were allocated to promote gender equality.[18] Ultimately,

> putting the UNSC resolutions on women, peace and
> security into practice requires changing our conception of
> international security to incorporate the provision of not
> just military and political security but also community
> security for women, men, girls and boys [...] eliminating
> violence against women in conflict depends ultimately
> on efforts to transform the social and economic gender
> inequalities that constrain women's participation and
> underlie their vulnerability in conflict settings.[19]

The concerns I have highlighted and the facts upon which they rest are not new. They should not be news. For me, the ethical challenges go beyond the foundational principle of 'first, do no harm'. As I reflect on these ethical challenges I realise that I should be judging the morality of my actions by 'deeds, not words'. The words are easy. They are found in the stock Western solutions we present, solutions that assume an understanding of the problem and the appeal of a universal fix. Such responses are invariably founded on the presumption that it is our place to dictate the societal changes to be made and how they are to be implemented by people who would prefer to be given a choice. Our deeds require more detailed consideration and this consideration applies not just to our actions but also our legacies. How many of us can reflect on the past and say our deeds tell the same story as our words?

PART 5: THE ETHICS OF EMERGING WARFARE

Members of militia groups preparing to surrender their weapons in the Solomon Islands, 2003. *Commonwealth of Australia*

WRONG

10

THE INDIVIDUALISATION OF MODERN CONFLICT

JAI GALLIOTT

For most people living in the relatively peaceful Western world, I suspect that war is a relatively distant and impersonal thing, even though some will have been to war in defence of their country and others may have dedicated their lives to researching it. When we hear the Last Post played at commemorative services on Anzac or Remembrance Day, or otherwise pause to think about those who gave their lives in defence of our nation, we picture them in their serried ranks, whether they be in the long line of headstones at a perfectly manicured military cemetery or the poppies adorning the seemingly endless wall of names at the Australian War Memorial. For much of the past few centuries, those who stand to become 'war dead' have also been relatively anonymous to their enemies.

Some will be inclined to say that this is not so. It is often argued that those who were killed in the world wars of 1914–1918 and 1939–1945 and more recent conflicts like Borneo and South Vietnam had the faces of those who they fought and killed permanently etched in their memory. But beyond these faces, soldiers on the opposing sides of those conflicts usually knew very little about the individuals they were charged with killing or how they became liable to be killed. Young infantrymen shot at waves of oncoming soldiers, simply because they were instructed to do so. Airmen aimed at formations on the same grounds, as did naval gunners who were rarely close enough to see the havoc caused by their bombardments.

At home, I have pictures of troops from the Australian Imperial Forces. In some of these pictures, among the young boys barely old enough to have been sent into conflict and the finely dressed but tired-looking officers, were people I now know to be my family members and who likely did exactly what I just described. Like many people from military families, I have been able to piece together the names and fates of those pictured from old family stories, faded notes on the backs of photographs and, more recently, internet archives that trace every distinguishing physical feature, their next of kin, how they served the cause and where they did it. Some of us will know that our grandfathers or great-grandfathers suffered from very particular injuries; that they were trained in using X weapon; that they were Y feet and Z inches tall. But the soldiers of bygone conflicts probably knew none of these or other more pertinent facts. Those killed in war were unlikely to have been surveilled for any extended period of time to fully understand their level of participation in the war or the aid they provided to the military effort, or even to have been on the figurative radar on the enemy's intelligence services. For the most part, the lives of soldiers, sailors and airmen were taken merely because they were on the wrong side, in the wrong place at the wrong time.

To understand how one might be shot just for being a soldier on the wrong side, it may be helpful to examine the work of the political philosopher Thomas Hobbes, who believed that the primal world of men is violent: a wretched landscape of war directed against all. To shield humankind from this lawless state of nature, Hobbes argued for the establishment of a sovereign who would organize a commonwealth of citizens to ensure peace. In the construction of this commonwealth, war shifted from being a civil conflict resolved by violence between individuals to battle waged between national communities. This concept of the state of nature is a mix of fact and fiction, but Hobbes essentially laid the groundwork for the nation states that we have today and the framework of international relations and law. He was also offering support for traditional just war theory and military ethics, developed by Christian thinkers in the Middle Ages and continuously honed and refined to this day. The great questions of recourse to war, or *jus ad bellum* in the ancient terminology, are delegated to states and to the sovereigns who rule them, whereas individual citizens and soldiers are subject to a more limited set of so-called *jus in bello* rules, a code of conduct covering what you may or may not do in the course of war. As long as soldiers do not directly target civilians or act disproportionately, they do not act wrongly if they fight in an unjust war. This is what Michael Walzer famously referred to as the 'moral equality of combatants', an important matter to which I will return.

The rapid individualisation of conflict

In any case, all of this is beginning to change. Emerging technologies, including artificially intelligent robotics and cyber systems, can alter our lives and have already begun to do so. The transformation will eventually disrupt most societal domains, and whether for better or worse, military forces and security industries lead the way. Indeed, over the past decade, militaries, particularly the United States military, as well as many private companies, have been actively developing technologies in the fields of robotics, cyber and information science, especially technologies that empower individual military actors and enable the targeting of particular individuals rather than formations. This is with the explicit aim of reducing costs, lowering risk and saving lives. There have been responses from social scientists to these questions and the applied challenges posed by these new technologies.[1] Yet these responses are problematic in that they focus on single technologies (drones or cyber, for instance) and ignore important meta-trends, as they do not pay adequate attention to the key role of 'individualisation' in the design, implementation and use of military technologies. The few initial explorations of individualisation see the process as being driven by normative changes in international law rather than technology or some other combination of factors, limiting understanding of the importance of technological design and how it feeds into this process.[2] I want to change this approach and build the relevant understanding while outlining a number of challenges for individualisation.

It must first be acknowledged that individualisation is not a new concept or phenomenon when considered beyond the military domain. Over the course of the past few decades, individualisation has emerged as a characteristic of contemporary society, particularly Western societies with strong American influences. Explored by influential sociologists such as Anthony Giddens and Zygmunt Bauman,[3] the concept of individualisation is focused on the way that action is increasingly mediated through and by the individual person. There is, according to the theory, a new relationship forming between the individual and society through a continuing, multi-faceted and generally indirect feedback process. The changes linked to this evolving relationship are now influencing the military. In today's conflicts, we are increasingly likely to know our enemies on an individual basis, and are rapidly moving away from defining enemy forces in terms of groups and more toward definitions that are tied to individual acts by, and the roles of, particular enemy figures. That is to say that we are increasingly targeting select individuals at specific points in time and space, rather than enemy formations that happen to be in the wrong place at the wrong time.

Individualisation is commonly thought to be driven by the development of humanitarian-focused norms in international relations and international humanitarian law. More likely, however, is that individualisation is facilitated by dramatic military-technical developments in the fields of robotics, cyber and big data and that the relevant international norms are changing via an indirect feedback process. Sadly, the fact is that technology usually drives normative change. This is not necessarily to subscribe to a form of technological determinism, but rather to admit that humans are all too often left struggling to catch up once the technological 'genie is out of the bottle'.[4] We now have sophisticated surveillance aircraft and drones in such numbers that there is the potential for a voyeuristic relationship to form between drone pilots and their targets, who may be watched for days, weeks or months on end. These technologies do such a good job complementing human intelligence sources that some countries have 'kill lists', supported by large dossiers of information detailing individuals' activities, education, financial status, sexuality, browsing patterns and so on.

Of course, it is not so difficult to come across information that may support targeted killings in the modern age because more and more people store their data on the internet; governments keep data online; banks keep financial data; your phone provider stores your metadata, hospitals keep health data, and social media sites keep our photos, videos, and way too much personal information. Big data, social network analysis and the like are very much the domain of modern military forces. Add in rapidly improving face- and voice-recognition software and rapidly advancing data-analysis technologies, which go very nicely alongside wide-area persistent surveillance technologies like Autonomous Real-time Ground Ubiquitous Surveillance (ARGUS), and it is clear that war is getting personal. This will become even more true as the technologies of warfare continue to become more individualised, particularly with the prospect of highly autonomous robotic and cyber information harvesting systems, and the boundaries between targeted killing in regular warfare and targeted killing in broader national security operations are likely to become even more blurry than they are today.

Indeed, the American military lawyer and a contributor to this volume, Charles Dunlap, has argued that we are entering the age of the 'hyper-personalisation' of war, which will take things to a whole new level.[5] He sketches a future in which enemy forces will be able to launch swarms of drones equipped with facial recognition software to roam battlefields looking for very specific members of an enemy's force, and predicts that this may spill over into bioscience, with breakthroughs in our understanding of genetics opening up the possibility of personalised medicine (treatments tailored to a specific person's genetic code, for instance), which may eventually allow the development of DNA-linked bioweapons, such as a virus designed to disable or kill only a specific individual. The potential for an over-technologically optimised military operating environment would, of course, corroborate the primary role of technology in facilitating individualisation. Those who see the individualisation of warfare as a more deliberate and intentional move want war to become more like policing, with its focus on individual harms, individual victims, and individual culpability. If individualisation means war is becoming more tailored and deliberative, it will become possible, some like the American human rights scholar Gabriella Blum say, to add to warfare some of the due process protections common in law enforcement, but historically considered unfeasible on the battlefield.[6]

Problems and challenges

In many respects, the individualisation of warfare can be viewed as a good thing. Targeted killings may be troublingly intimate, but they are surely better than more indiscriminate forms of killing. Just war theory, after all, obligates parties to a conflict to avoid the intentional targeting of civilians and take all reasonable measures to avoid causing incidental civilian deaths. The individuating technologies of modern warfare represent a significant step forward in our ability to ensure that wars kill or harm as few people as possible, so long, of course, as the relevant decision makers do not fall into the trap of engaging in more warfare.[7] Compared to the firebombing of Dresden in February 1945, the dropping of atomic bombs on Hiroshima and Nagasaki in August 1945 or the not so precise bombing attacks on Kosovo in 1999, weapons capable of killing only specific individuals seem like a moral advance. I want to point to some of the problems and challenges associated with the individualisation thesis, however, and also the general implications of the individualisation of war.

To begin, there exists a problem in that individualisation has been utilised by revisionist just war scholars to advocate a revolution in the philosophy of war and military ethics, the implications of which have not been fully thought through. Revisionist theory is often associated with the moral equality of combatants, the idea encountered earlier, as well as a rejection of the so-called symmetry thesis: the idea that soldiers fighting in both just and unjust wars possess equal war rights and equal responsibilities. Revisionists argue that from the perspective of human rights this symmetry makes no sense. If soldiers are fighting in a just war, then how could they be fairly killed by enemy soldiers who are fighting for an unjust cause? Revisionists argue that we need more reason than we usually think to kill enemy combatants. The fundamental feature that we find in the revisionist theory, especially that of Oxford moral philosophers David Rodin and Jeff McMahan, is to deny that war rights and responsibilities are a matter of civilian or combatant status. This forces us to look in a more granular way at particular individuals within the conflict and ask: what is it that they are responsible for, what are they liable for, and what rights and protections do they consequently possess?[8]

In many respects, extending the 'law enforcement' analogy to the ethics of warfare is a good thing in that it limits the moral licence to inflict deadly violence on one another. But embracing the revisionist account and attempting to wage war according to it would require such granular individualism that it renders just war theory virtually useless. Even with the best of today's technology and that in the pipeline, no commander could possibly know the individual liability of all persons on the battlefield and tailor his or her use of force to suit. Individualisation might therefore lead to the setting of impossible standards that could work only in something close to a world government scenario, and do not reflect the reality on the ground. At worst, the revisionist theory supported by individualisation could encourage unipolarisation of international affairs and lead to an increase in unethical political or military conduct.

It also needs to be said that while war is becoming individualised in that targeting is increasingly based on an individuated assessment of specific combatants, and will obviously become even more so if the revisionists succeed in bringing about a revolution of the kind described above, this can only be determined through an almost evidentiary analysis and weighing operational relevance within a larger network apparatus that could, in the medium to long term, diffuse responsibility. Even with the dramatic transformation to the targeting criteria applied on battlefield over the past few decades, there has been a surge in the number of people required for this application. Warfare has become lawfare, with masses of lawyers and other high-level decision makers becoming involved in the targeting process in ways that the frontline soldier could not have imagined a century ago. It is apparent, from CIA-style strikes for example, that there are a significant number of decision makers involved in the authorisation of an attack, some would suggest including the office of the United States President. In these regards, conflict is actually becoming a more collective effort, but with power centralised at higher or more bureaucratic levels. In this kind of complex decision making environment, tracing the sequence of events that led to a particular event is likely to lead in a great number of directions, making it difficult or even impossible to identify contributing agents and take remedial and/or corrective action. This difficulty in identifying contributing agents is the so-called 'problem of many hands' identified by Harvard political scientist Dennis Thompson.[9]

On an operational level, it must also be acknowledged there are limits to individualisation. There are limits to all sensors, some of which will be overcome by technology, some of which will not. We must also be careful, as citizens of the developed world, not to take for granted the basic identity management functions of the modern state bureaucracy. This structure begins with foundational identity documents such as birth certificates, then expands through one's lifetime within a highly complex system of state credentialling that is required for full participation in civic and economic life in the developed world, but pretty much absent in much of the rest of the world. According to one recent estimate, as many as one in three children in the developing world do not have any kind of official identity registration generated at birth. The operational significance of this is not only a concern for counterterrorism and insurgency, but also in peacekeeping and humanitarian relief missions and, we might eventually come to see, regular operations. We must therefore be careful not to over-invest in a military ethics revolution or to become overconfident in the capabilities of technology. This is not to say that we will never achieve the granular individualism spoken of earlier, but rather that we must carefully map the elements of technological individualisation that will be most pernicious and plan to prevent or offset negative consequences, taking particular care to ensure that humans do not incorrectly 'fill in' the information or decision making gaps left by technology.

Another problem is that while individualised killing technologies are currently the prerogative of technologically advanced states, this will soon change. Al Qaeda, the Islamic State, and other malignant non-state actors are already attuned to the emerging possibilities of personalised warfare: in 2007, for instance, terrorist sympathisers hacked into the email and telephone records of Danish soldiers serving in Afghanistan and used the information to harass and intimidate service members' families. More recently, in March, an Islamic State website posted the names and home addresses of selected American military personnel and their families online, urging 'our brothers in America [to] [...] take the final step' of killing them. Drone and facial-recognition technologies are already commercially available. They have been developed in many places, including China and Russia, and have been provided to field operatives to test state defences. So even if we believe that the Australian government and others will use these technologies responsibly — not a foregone conclusion — we cannot rest assured that others will do so. This must be taken into account in the moral calculus when states resort to war, for if employing individualising technologies is likely to provoke retaliatory attacks, this could adversely affect the *jus ad bellum* proportionality criterion.[10]

More generally, I wonder where the individualisation of war is taking us. Will we end up targeting political leaders or extending combatant status to civilian programmers, weapons engineers and the like? The rise of this form of war, while promising to offer greater protection of civilians, in some ways seems to challenge the general prohibition against directly targeting political leadership and other people of similar importance and responsibility as a tactic of modern warfare. Historically, as professional militaries developed, political leaders no longer led armies directly into battle, thus creating a clear differentiation between those who conduct war at the policy level versus those who wage it on the battlefield. Those who designed weapons were always a long way from the battlefield. The practical implication has been that strikes against political figures and weapons designers have generally not evolved as a central or morally sanctioned component of military strategy. This observation is complicated, however, by the ambiguity of distinguishing between operational and political leadership in modern war and the blurry line between modern-day combatants, and engineers and programmers, who nowadays work near the theatre of combat in robot hospitals or digitise the battlefield. The technologically driven individualisation of war has complicated these distinctions, as status-based or functional criteria no longer offer a clear template for targeting.

Could it be that the individualisation of conflict amounts to the individualisation of the enemy more than anything else? We target more people, in more places, with automated technologies and adjudicative practices that in some respects seem to represent devolution. Think back to my earlier reference to Hobbes. The idea was that we handed power over to the sovereign because it was better able to protect the rights of individuals than the individuals themselves. Could it be that the technologies behind the individualisation of war are now changing the state of affairs such that we are beginning to (slowly) head back toward a Hobbesian state of nature? And what of the other problems and challenges?

11

THE ETHICS OF ENHANCED HUMAN PERFORMANCE

MATTHEW BEARD

Biomedical human enhancement of military forces presents a myriad of opportunities to those who want their personnel to perform better in the field. These include ethical advantages, where enhancement might reduce unethical conduct during war. As with most emerging technologies, however, it would be reckless to pursue these opportunities without first identifying the ethical risks such interventions may pose. Not only can these undermine the ethical advantages of enhancement, they may lead to reputational crises that could stymie further research and development. Enhancement poses some risks. But these risks are not insurmountable if suitable and adequate safeguards are observed.

These risks and the safeguards I describe do not constitute anything radically new in terms of theory, but I do hope to outline the ethical terrain without necessarily settling upon a particular moral position. I accept that the pragmatic and ethical benefits of enhancement are hard to ignore, but I hope that this discussion might help future development proceed in a spirit of ethical restraint, mindful of potential collateral damage and unintended side-effects.

What is enhancement?

The American genetic bioethicist Eric Juengst defines enhancement as 'a medical or biological intervention to the body designed to improve performance, appearance, or capability besides what is necessary to achieve, sustain or restore health'.[1] I note that this isn't a perfect definition, and epigeneticists, biologists and chemists would likely pick apart its understanding of what counts as a 'biological intervention', but I think it's intuitive enough to capture most of what I'm talking about: Captain America's super-serum is enhancement; Tony Stark drinking a triple espresso before a mission is not. Emotion-reducing pharmaceuticals are an enhancement; meditating prior to a mission is not.

The benefits of enhancement

Any piece of new technology offers a range of different advantages. New military technology, specifically, can create strategic opportunities, reduce costs, improve operational competence or more closely align activities with the core values of a defence force. I am going to focus on the *explicitly* ethical benefits of enhancement. Though any enhancement that allows a soldier to advance a just cause in an ethically defensible way is going to be of net ethical benefit, many are primarily strategic, pragmatic or functional in nature. The ethical advantage is incidental to the actual intended benefit (for instance, a soldier who can stay alert for extended periods may be in a position to make better ethical judgments due to a lack of fatigue, but the primary reason for keeping him or her awake is likely to be strategic). For reasons of scope, such enhancements are not my focus (although they also warrant consideration by ethicists). Instead I am going to look at two advantages I consider to be primarily ethical: decreased combat force size and enhanced moral decision making. I will also note some factors that will need to be addressed to maximise these advantages.

Decreased force size

All things being equal, if enhancement can improve the capabilities of individual soldiers then it should reduce the demand for combatants as a whole. That is, we would need to recruit fewer soldiers and therefore expose fewer people to the lethal risks posed by war. The decreased force size is not, in itself, an ethical benefit. The benefit lies in the assumed correlation between smaller forces and lower casualty rates. Seen through the lens of just war theory, which is the oldest and most influential ethical theory regarding the morality of war, this means more wars are likely to satisfy the 'proportionality' criterion. Proportionality stipulates that a war is only just if and when, among other things, the anticipated harms of war, including the death and injury to combatants and non-combatants alike, are justified by the overall benefits of waging conflict.[2] Even a just cause cannot be pursued ethically if the harmful outcomes of engaging in conflict would be worse than if no conflict were engaged in at all.

This observation means that the proportionality criterion will sometimes require us to stand by and allow injustice to transpire rather than taking action, because to intervene would only cause greater harm. One common situation in which this might occur would be when the number of personnel who would need to be committed to an operation, and potentially killed or maimed in the process for it to be successful are too great to justify. A historical example can be seen toward the end of the Second World War, when invading the Japanese home islands was seen as unjustifiable based on the anticipated casualties.[3] In these situations, deploying fewer, enhanced soldiers who are capable of performing the same operations as a larger, unenhanced force to achieve the same outcomes enables us to engage in morally justified operations in which participation would previously have been unethical. It is a matter of historical speculation, but the possibility that a smaller, more effective force might have enabled the military defeat of Japan without using atomic bombs against civilians is one I think we are obliged to entertain.

The same arguments also offer second-order ethical opportunities. Although the most substantial and dramatic consequences of war involve the loss of human life, the material damage to property and infrastructure is also significant and must affect judgments of proportionality. If human enhancement offers the possibility for smaller sized forces than are presently required to effectively wage war, a beneficial side-effect of this may be the reduced size of the theatre of war. This, in turn, may result in a reduction in the extent of damage or destruction to civilian infrastructure during conflict. The promise of reduced casualties and collateral damage is particularly significant because popular and political support for war in Australia and the West is important, and civilians and military decision makers alike are increasingly unwilling to accept even a small number of casualties. This reluctance may make it difficult to undertake morally justified (and tactically necessary) military engagements, such as 'Responsibility to Protect' missions, which some scholars might argue are increasingly important in the current global environment. 'Responsibility to Protect' is a political commitment endorsed by all United Nations members at the 2005 World Summit as part of a determined effort to prevent genocide, ethinic cleansing and crimes against humanity.

If enhanced military personnel are more physically adept, psychologically resilient, and more likely to survive, this may empower the military to engage in wars that are morally necessary, but which have been previously regarded as politically untenable because civilians would not accept the possibility of military casualties.[4] This means states may feel less reluctant to deploy to conflicts overseas. In sum, we might see more just war and less unjust peace. Such a transition would be morally dubious because of the inherent ethical complexity of war, but offers the potential for significant ethical benefits to the victims of injustice around the world.

Maximising the benefits of a smaller force

The proportionality criterion is only one among many considerations that need to be satisfied before a war can be justified. There is a concern that reduced casualties and increased effectiveness will make it easier to resort to military intervention in situations where there are other ethical reasons to abstain from conflict. Because one major objection to military engagement, both ethically and among the voting public, is the risk of death to a nation's soldiers and to innocent civilians, reducing this possibility may be seen as a force multiplier.

The transition from states of unjust peace to states of just war is (as noted above) ethically vexed. Although some scholars, like Michael Walzer, argue that it is always morally justifiable to fight back against an unjust peace,[5] most believe war can only be justified if (among other things): the harms it inflicts are proportionate to the state of affairs it aims to generate; and the state of affairs generated by having gone to war is ethically preferable to the state of affairs which would exist if a decision was made against going to war. In both instances, due consideration must be given to the loss of life and property occasioned by war. A second concern is whether making force deployment more politically straightforward is likely to see the military used increasingly to advance or defend national interests rather than justice. Indeed, some have raised precisely these criticisms against the just war tradition as a whole. In brief, it provides self-interested politicians with a convenient ethical veneer for their self-serving warmongering.

In some sense, we need to concede that if there is less political objection to deploying the military abroad, it does inevitably increase the risk of unjust war. Removing one check and balance, in this case civilian scepticism, does increase this possibility. To manage this risk, those involved in military decision making, including civilian leaders, will need to remember and reassert their commitment to the other principles of just warfare such as just cause, right intention, last resort and the like. Ideally, such principles would also be enshrined in the laws of a nation as much as possible in order to regulate the use of deadly force. Furthermore, we might turn to some of the insights from the just war revisionist school led by the Oxford moral philosopher Jeff McMahan,[6] who argue that combatants can generally, under certain conditions, be held morally accountable for their involvement in just wars, to 'tighten the screws' on the military's own responsibility for the wars in which it participates. In this way, the scepticism once provided by civilians might be embraced by military leaders to varying degrees. While not a perfect solution, this might allow nations and governments to enjoy the ethical benefits of easier deployment whilst managing the ethical risk as best we can.

Another ethical concern prompted by force reduction is the mass unemployment it might trigger. If a larger force is now redundant, it follows that a number of military personnel will be out of work. Ethically responsible force reduction would need to be implemented slowly and carefully to ensure that the ethical advantages do not impose burdens on the broader community or the Department of Veterans' Affairs. A large-scale force reduction over a short period of time risks leaving a far greater population of veterans facing re-integration issues than the Department of Veterans' Affairs could reasonably hope to manage efficiently. With processing difficulties in the early stages of discharge already a factor in the number of veterans either unemployed or homeless in Australia,[7] the failure to patiently and gradually reduce force sizes in line with the existing rate of retirement from the Army is likely to lead to a whole new category of ethical difficulties.

Enhanced decision making

Enhancement does not just involve changing combatants' physical abilities. It can also involve making positive changes to a soldier's neural functioning. For example, the United States Air Force provides pilots with Modafinil, a drug that improves alertness and enables a person to function for up to 60 hours without sleep.[8] Other drugs have been proposed to reduce aggression and incidents of psychological trauma. Similar kinds of intervention may improve decision making in a way that produces ethically desirable outcomes. The opportunities presented by these forms of enhancement are not aimed at improving the moral *character* of soldiers (that, I believe, is a task for moral education rather than enhancement),[9] but rather at their ability to comprehend complex situations and reach ethical judgments quickly, as well as to control emotional responses that may make ethical judgments more difficult.

Protecting non-combatants

Avoiding the deaths of innocent people as far as possible is perhaps the most sacred principle of military ethics. Enshrined in international law through the idea of civilian immunity; this ethical principle requires that combatants avoid intentionally targeting non-combatants and also take reasonable risks to prevent their being harmed as a side-effect. The advantage of cognitive enhancements in this regard is twofold. First, the ability to comprehend complex, high-pressure situations clearly is likely to lead to decisions that more accurately reflect the reality of the situation. Enhanced soldiers might be able to more quickly distinguish a civilian fleeing an urban combat situation from a combatant moving to a position of cover. In this case, the enhancement is actually to neural processing, but with second-order ethical advantages.

Second, enhancement might be able to reduce incidence of 'counter-moral emotions' that can cloud and corrupt ethical judgment. The Oxford University philosopher of applied ethics, Thomas Douglas, explores this possibility:

> Enhancement might consist in the attenuation of counter-moral emotions: emotions that interfere with moral reasoning, sympathy, and all other plausible candidates for 'morally good motives' [...] Biomedical moral enhancement might sometimes consist in the biomedical attenuation of these emotions.[10]

For example, American soldiers responded to the death of a member of their company from a roadside bomb in 2005 by killing 24 Iraqi civilians in the nearby town of Haditha. Military philosopher Nancy Sherman contends that 'the events of Haditha [should be seen] through the lens of traditional revenge and honour. The Haditha rampage took the form of a reprisal raid, inspired by the US brigade experiencing the killing of one of their own'.[11]

It is plausible to assume that the visceral reaction to seeing the death of a person who is not merely a colleague but also a brother- or sister-in-arms would result in overpowering feelings of hatred, diminished empathy or aggression that ideally would not be in the psychological make-up of military professionals. The clinical psychologist Jonathan Shay describes these situations as 'berserk states', 'in which abuse after abuse is committed'.[12] To Shay, 'the berserker is figuratively – sometimes literally – blind to everything but his destructive aim. He cannot see the distinction between civilian and combatant or even the distinction between comrade and enemy'. Berserk states are, Shay suggests, uncommon but not unheard of in complex military environments. They tend to result in a soldier losing all sense of vulnerability and propriety and entering into a state of 'reckless frenzy'. They are also, in a sense, natural responses 'when a soldier is trapped, surrounded, or overrun and facing certain death, the berserk state has apparent survival value' and, because of this, it is difficult to predict who will be susceptible to the berserk state, or when it might occur.

Maximising the benefit of
cognitive enhancements

Before exploring emotional suppressants, it will be necessary to fully understand their role in moral decision making. The assumption underpinning emotional suppressants as enhancements is that our emotions are, at least some of the time, not informative or significant for decision making. The emotions are, at least occasionally, pathological in nature and therefore a distraction to rational decision-making. This school of thought, which finds its strongest intellectual ally in the work of Immanuel Kant, is only one philosophical account of rationality.[13] Other accounts see the emotions as inseparable from the way human beings evaluate events and the world around them, such that to dull or repress emotion would not enhance decision making, but detract from it. Sherman argues that 'emotions [...] are complexes that include evaluations and affects, and that in some cases, though not all, lead to desires to act'.[14] If so, simply to repress the emotions may restrict unethical behaviour, but it may also restrict ethical behaviour motivated by the appropriate emotions.

An example possibly better known to Australians is useful to illustrate this concern. In 2011 while the Australian Special Forces were operating in Afghanistan, Corporal Ben Roberts-Smith silenced three Taliban machine guns at great personal risk. He later said: 'I saw my mates getting ripped up so I decided to move forward, I wasn't going to sit there and do nothing'. If his commitment to his mates had been suppressed, would he still have performed his heroics that day?[15] The point to be noted is this: it seems at least possible that interventions designed to suppress 'counter-moral' emotions might not be precise instruments. Although the desire for vengeance might be suppressed, so too might the feelings of loyalty and camaraderie that define a 'band of brothers and sisters'.

A second consideration is whether these kinds of cognitive enhancers will be voluntary or mandatory for military personnel. The case for voluntary enhancement is weaker in a military context than in other medical areas because military personnel do not enjoy the same rights to patient autonomy as civilians do. Uniformed personnel forego particular rights, including some medical rights, to improve the ability of armed forces to defend the nation. Soldiers commit to a relationship of 'unlimited liability' when they enlist, the former British Army officer and ethicist Patrick Mileham claims,[16] and in doing so waive particular rights including, as the ethicist Michael Gross states, 'their autonomy, privacy, right to informed consent, and right to refuse particular treatments'.[17] Western militaries are, however, seeing increasing pressure to conform to broader civilian values. Australia has seen recent demands for greater transparency and accountability, including pressure for a Royal Commission into sexual abuse within the military. This development suggests the standards that previously justified mandatory medical intervention might be subjected to broader bioethical norms, including patient autonomy. Even if this doesn't transpire, there are reasons to be hesitant around mandatory enhancement. For one, mandatory enhancement might serve as a disincentive for enrolling in the military, depending on broader social attitudes toward human enhancement, and therefore compromise the armed forces' ability to perform a necessary service to the nation.

For another, if suppressants are made mandatory and later found to have led to illegal or unethical behaviour, the military will face complex legal and ethical challenges in identifying responsibility. Maxwell J Mehlman, Director of the Law-Medicine Centre at Case Western Reserve University, argues that '[t]he system by which the military holds superiors accountable for unreasonable acts must apply to the unethical or illegal command decisions concerning enhancement'.[18] This implies that those involved either in ordering the mission or in making enhancements mandatory might be held solely accountable for any problematic consequences arising from them. The position is ethically defensible, but entails serious enough consequences to warrant close reflection by leadership before implementing any 'live' trials of emotional suppressants. On the other hand, voluntary enhancement also creates concerns. As Monash University bioethicist Michael Selgelid notes:

> A reason to worry about reliance on voluntary moral bioenhancement, in any case, is that those most likely to commit heinous acts with catastrophic consequences are probably not especially likely to volunteer for moral enhancement.[19]

The risks of enhancement

From considering how the benefits of enhancement could be maximised, I now turn to a couple of the ethical risks implied and suggest some principles we might use to minimise those risks.

Challenges to core values

The Australian Army holds the values of courage, initiative, respect and teamwork as the cornerstones of all its activities.[20] As well as being praiseworthy in their own right and the type of values likely to develop ethical combatants, being seen to act on these values situates our soldiers in a broader community of warriors. These institutional values form part of what Case

Western University ethicist Shannon E French calls 'the warrior code of honour'.[21] Embodying these values, and the virtues by which they are expressed, represents part of what it means to be an Australian soldier. Christian Enemark, Professor of International Relations at Southampton University, argues that drone pilots challenge our existing notions of military virtue because they face almost no risk of harm (and therefore opportunities to practise courage).[22] If the same can be said for enhanced personnel due to their improved physical and cognitive abilities, then there is a possibility that enhanced soldiers might suffer a loss of morale if they are disconnected from existing Army values.

It seems to me the most obvious way to work around this potential challenge (which, I should note, at least one former senior officer has told me is no challenge at all) is to reframe the conversation around courage as a value so that it is no longer intimately connected to accepting physical risk. Were the Army to come to see courage not as the acceptance of possible harm but more broadly as the willingness to do what is right despite the difficulties involved (no matter what the difficulties of doing so entail), it would be possible to reframe the discussion in a way that avoids potential challenges to morale.

Treatment of enhanced veterans

Unlike 'go pills' and other medications, some enhancements are likely to be permanent. This creates a substantial area of ethical complexity regarding ownership of enhancements and responsibility for enhanced personnel once they have resigned their positions and returned to civilian life. How enhanced veterans would be able to return to civilian life with new abilities that radically separate them from their neighbours is a question with implications ranging from the seemingly inane to matters of national security. Many authors have noted that veterans already face difficulties re-engaging with civilian society, and risk being 'exiled' in various ways.[23] If these personnel are also equipped with enhanced physical or cognitive abilities, the dissonance between war and peacetime (itself a source of psychological distress) is likely to deepen.[24]

For instance, if a soldier can run as quickly as an Olympic athlete, should they be permitted to compete in local sports leagues? If not, they are cut off from a major source of community, which is a considerable issue given our growing awareness of existing veterans' struggles with re-entry. Can they serve as police officers, who presumably will have different legal and ethical permissions around enhancement? Will neurological alterations affect their ability to flourish in relationships? These questions do not present easy answers but before implementing an enhancement program, I believe defence forces have a duty of care to develop management programs around these issues to ensure that those who have been submitted to unusual, lasting enhancements continue to flourish.

The stakes are even higher when considering who owns an enhanced body. Once a soldier is discharged, all of the rights they possessed as civilians are generally restored to them – including total autonomy over their bodies (which, for a range of reasons, is not available to them as enrolled personnel). As Australian military ethicist Nicholas Evans and American bioethicist Jonathan Moreno note, 'enhancement might well turn out to be forever. Whether a warfighter is able to consent to this type of relationship, and whether they should be able to do so, should be a serious question in future works on the subject'.[25] For enhanced soldiers, should this mean they are permitted to offer themselves as research subjects for universities, private companies or even foreign governments? How the military manages the interplay between individual rights and classified research in these cases is largely unprecedented.

Some of the questions around human enhancement are deeply philosophical and existential. Such questions warrant close consideration. There is a temptation to pursue these deeper and more heavily contested questions at the expense of addressing more imminent, pragmatic and applied questions. I do not believe the thoughts offered here represent the totality of applied questions around enhancement, but it seems clear to me that the current 'ethical stocktake' the defence forces are undertaking, including identifying some moral principles and governing values, also needs to identify what enhancement offers and what the costs might be.

In *Alice in Wonderland*, Alice approaches the Cheshire Cat. 'Will you tell me please, which way I ought to go from here?', she asks. 'That depends a good deal on where you want to get to', the cat replies. Principles and values will keep us moving on an ethical path that ensures our exploration of enhancement is free of transgressions. It is only by being aware of where we might want enhancement to take us, however, that we'll have any use for these principles at all.

12

THE ETHICS OF EMERGING TACTICS

JOHN HARDY

The military tactics currently being developed by Western nations reflect a range of changing circumstances, adversaries, equipment and weapons on the contemporary battlefield. Many of these tactics have little impact on the ethical questions that traditionally arise during the prosecution of war. Some ways of warfighting, however, add new dimensions to longstanding ethical challenges. The new tools and technologies available to modern militaries are wide-ranging in scope and nature. These tools range from the relatively unsophisticated, such as an action camera combined with a hobby-grade treaded remote control vehicle, or a human-placed remote ordnance detonator, to the highly developed: a remote weapons platform mounted to the turret of an armoured vehicle, an unmanned underwater vehicle used to detect mines at sea, or semi-autonomous and potentially armed robots which can be used to assist or replace humans in conflict. The possibilities presented by emerging technology are endless, as are the questions that arise from their exploitation.

Many of these technologies reflect long-term trends in military systems' increasing adoption of technology[1] and, more recently, the widespread development of robotics for military uses.[2] But the line between incremental and potentially transformative or disruptive innovation is blurred. Increasingly, the factors distinguishing weapons, systems and platforms are often ambiguous. For example, Case Western University statistician Patrick Hew argues that Improvised Explosive Devices (IEDs) are a form of robot-enabled warfare rather than simply the ambush weapon they are often considered to be.[3] Precisely what differentiates a remote weapon or automatic trigger from a robot is still open to interpretation and debate, so the influence of emerging technologies on tactics remains unclear.

New tactics employed by the Army are not only emerging but are also *emergent*, in the sense that they result from interaction and self-organisation at scale and rarely appear to be linear progressions of behavioural adaptation. Therefore, emerging tactics not only reflect advances in technology, training and doctrine, they also reflect the Army's reaction to the way similar tactics and technologies are used against Australian soldiers. Put simply, emerging tactics are a process of negotiation and the Army's actual and potential adversaries will have a direct influence on the process of emergence. Many of these examples are incremental advances of existing capabilities but some incorporate design features offering altogether new capabilities that will enable entirely new tactics, as well as new considerations for existing tactics. Two types of particularly influential technologies are information and communication-enabled platforms which generate, display or disseminate battlefield data and which allow remote control of systems. These technologies provide tangible ways of enhancing soldiers' situational awareness. They also carry the potential to complicate the already fraught process of ethical decision making at the tactical level.

Emerging tactics reflect the changing relationship between distance, threat and presence on the contemporary battlefield.

One example is the use of remotely operated platforms; another is the incorporation of small robots alongside ground forces to provide niche capabilities. These changes, combined with the proliferation of precision munitions, have altered expectations about military tactics held by commanders, political leaders and the public in Western societies. The implication of these changing expectations is that emerging tactics will likely continue to address the Army's obligations to correctly identify targets and to engage them with the least amount of force necessary by utilising the most advanced information and communication technologies available at the tactical level. Emerging tactics will reflect both the availability of advanced platforms, weapons or information and also the expectations of the Army, individual commanders, the state and the general public on the ethical use of force. This will further expand the range of skills that soldiers will need to make effective and ethical tactical decisions.

The ethics of precision

Over the past twenty years, widespread expectations that Western military forces will use precision weapons to the greatest extent possible have tempered debates regarding the ethics of new and emerging tactics. At the tactical level, targeting decisions have come to include both traditional tenets of ethical warfare, such as the *jus in bello* principles embedded in International Humanitarian Law,[4] and consideration of new and additional information collected, generated and disseminated by new weapons and equipment. One consequence of the proliferation of these weapons is that emerging tactics rely increasingly on decision makers' access to information. The tactics of 'high-tech violence' provide benefits and challenges to soldiers and commanders alike.[5]

Critics of high-tech weapons and tactics lament the simple correlation that is often inferred between precision and ethicality. For example, Maja Zehfuss, Professor of International Politics at Manchester University, contends that precision in targeting is an ambiguous concept and easily confused for accurate targeting in effect rather than in intention.[6] It is important, then, to examine two distinct aspects of precision: accuracy in identifying a target and accuracy in striking it.

Precision first involves locating and positively identifying a target. This is no small feat on the contemporary battlefield. Despite many advances in intelligence, surveillance and reconnaissance technologies, cutting-edge equipment is only as useful as the intelligence it provides. Two key considerations for high-tech military systems are: first, that the quality of technologies used to gather targeting intelligence does not necessarily improve decision making and, second, that the availability of information can diminish as well as enhance tactical decision making. In essence, precision involves successfully destroying or disabling a target and limiting harm to non-targeted people and infrastructure to the greatest extent possible.[7] The objective of enhanced precision in new weapons and emerging tactics is to maintain or improve the military effectiveness of offensive action, while decreasing the risk posed to non-combatants and civilian infrastructure.[8] This risks significantly raising the information requirements for commanders and weapon operators, who cannot engage targets with purely speculative value and who are obliged to use proportionate and discriminate weapons in their tactical engagements.[9]

Targeting precision is widely linked to greater adherence to the core ethical principles governing armed conflict. The consequence of this link is that precision has a significant political value. Greater precision has reduced the risk of collateral damage without sacrificing the capability to engage legitimate targets. In some circumstances this can reduce, although not eliminate, the ethical burden of military commanders who are weighing up the military necessity of tactical actions against the potential for unintended harm to civilians and non-military infrastructure.[10] Despite the essentially incommensurable values of civilian death and injury with calculations of military advantage,[11] the language of precision used by Western governments has been used to validate military campaigns as ethical. This has fuelled rising expectations that the conduct of war will further limit the risk to non-combatants.[12] Western militaries also face an ethical dilemma involving risk to their own forces, particularly as remotely operated, semi-autonomous and robotic systems proliferate on the modern battlefield. The principle of unnecessary risk proposed by Bradley Strawser, Assistant Professor in the Defense Analysis Department of the United States Naval Postgraduate School, captures the essential contradiction between the inherent risks of using military force and the ethical obligation to limit risk to only what is strictly necessary.[13]

The implications of deploying high-tech systems, particularly those involving remotely operated or precision munitions, for the ethics of emerging tactics involve four key considerations. The first concerns the concept of distance. On the contemporary battlefield, distance has well and truly outgrown the linear calculation of proximity to target. Remote operation of vehicle-mounted weapon stations, uninhabited vehicles and emplaced detonators all serve to complicate the traditional concepts of distance that have, in any event, been in doubt since before the turn of the century. The second consideration is that immediacy of a threat is not directly related to distance. Although the debate regarding the ethics of stand-off weapons still rages, the disconnect between the immediacy of the threat posed by direct and indirect fires has never been so stark. The third consideration is the use of sensor data in targeting systems, particularly where sensor data does not correspond with information absorbed by human senses. These systems are altering the information requirements for ethical decision making on the contemporary battlefield. Finally, the fourth consideration is that emerging technologies and tactics will influence levels of and requirements for situational awareness. Soldiers' ability to perform the three components of situational awareness – to identify, process and comprehend information – will be affected by the tools and technologies used to generate, analyse and distribute tactical information.[14]

Two concepts of battlefield distance

The notion of distance between a soldier and a target features prominently in most debates about the ethics of military tactics. The convergence of advanced surveillance technologies, remotely operated platforms and individual targeting tactics have attracted attention to the politics of conflict and the military values of honour and courage.[15] These issues have risen to prominence in poorly informed mainstream public debates and obscured the ethics of distance in emerging tactics.[16] For example, Christian Enemark, Professor of International Relations at Southampton University, has called 21st-century warfare 'post-heroic' as he believes the risks to operators and the targets of stand-off weapons are incongruent.[17] This claim represents, however, a limited and strictly linear understanding of distance between weapons and their effects. The renowned American just war theorist James Johnson grappled with these very same issues when discussing cruise and ballistic missile technology and nuclear weapons in the 1980s.[18]

Despite simplistic arguments that the distance between combatants and theatres of operations offered by remotely operated weapons is unprecedented,[19] the relationship between distance and risk on the battlefield is not direct or linear. A basic tenet of combined arms warfare is that opposing forces can use indirect fires to attack each other and, as such, the operators of stand-off munitions are rarely under direct threat from their targets. Regardless, the ethics of war do not require every individual combatant to be under direct and specific threat from their targets prior to using military force. In combat, the purpose of using force is primarily to attain military objectives. Immediate self-defence certainly occurs in combat but it is generally a by-product of tactical engagement for a military purpose. It is difficult to imagine a situation in which it would be ethical and responsible to deploy personnel for the express purpose of defending themselves from attack rather than for the purpose of securing a military objective or for wider force protection.

The concept of distance as it is used to discuss the ethics of tactical engagements is a product of two variables: proximity and battlefield presence. These deceptively simple terms encompass a range of counterintuitive possibilities. For example, immediate presence, direct observation and individual risk seem to be mutually entailed. Soldiers can operate remote weapons stations from inside armoured vehicles and rely entirely on sensor-generated information to engage targets only metres away that pose a direct threat to their own safety. Conversely, soldiers can remotely operate mine-clearing vehicles while relying almost entirely on their own direct observation of the situation, but still be a safe distance away from any potential explosions from buried mines of unexploded ordnance. Proximity, observation and presence are not mutually entailed and require further specificity. There are at least seven measures of proximity from the perspective of a weapon operator making a decision to effectively and ethically engage a lawful target. The first four focus on the operator, platform and weapon relative to a target. The fifth through to the seventh measures focus on weapons effects and potential retaliatory strikes.

The first measure of distance is the proximity of a weapon operator to their target. This is the way that distance is most commonly discussed in ethical debates and reflects the space between a human decision maker and the potential target of a weapon. The second is the proximity of the weapon to the target. This reflects the 'bows and arrows' argument regarding stand-off weapons which are outside the range of direct counterattacks. The third is the proximity of a weapon operator to their weapon. This captures the distinction between the weapon and the operator, a feature of remote systems that is often emphasised as novel. This distance is equally applicable, however, to many other weapons, such as cruise missiles on naval surface combatants that can be launched from a command station a significant distance from the weapons themselves to engage distant targets. The fourth measure is the proximity of a weapon operator to the platform that carries or delivers their weapon. This can range from a few steps to thousands of kilometres due to tele-operation technologies that are not affected by connection distance.

The fifth measure of distance is the proximity of a weapon operator to the effects of the weapon. This measure has proven to be a confounding issue in the current debate on remotely operated weapons. Critics argue that distance from the violent effects of military weapons reduces the psychological impact of violence on combatants.[20] If true, it is likely that this would actually be commensurate with the Army's ethical obligation to reduce unnecessary risk of psychological trauma by reducing stress on its soldiers.[21] However, research conducted by the United States

Air Force into the combat stress endured by pilots and operators of remote systems indicates that occupational burnout is not reduced by distance from weapons effects.[22]

The sixth measure is the proximity of a weapon operator to direct retaliation by the target. This is a point of contention regarding the ethics of stand-off weapons in general. The widespread acceptance of snipers, body armour, bombs, missiles, attack helicopters, tanks and numerous other weapons and platforms suggests that there is little appetite for compelling combatants to fight exclusively within direct retaliatory range of each other. The seventh measure of distance is the proximity of a weapon operator to indirect retaliation by the target or associated forces. This is where remote systems are often posed as unique or unethical. In reality, they are closely related to any long-range stand-off weapons currently in use. Arguments that remote systems are exceptional tend to revolve around the claim that drone pilots are immune from counterattack while flying combat operations on the other side of the world.[23] But, like sailors who fire cruise missiles outside the retaliatory range of adversaries, American continental missile launch sites such as Nevada are not out of reach. Rather, they are beyond the range of indirect fires from a particular opposing force.

Battlefield presence is a measure of an individual decision maker's immersion in and experience of a tactical situation. This is a product of their observation and interaction with the situation, their indirect experience of the situation through sensors and battlefield data, and the combination of subjective and objective interpretation of the information available to them. Unlike distance, which has changed little with the advent of new technologies, the concept of presence has been dramatically altered by new forms of data generation, communication and distribution. For example, the kinds of data used to make tactical decisions can be tangentially influenced by distance in ways that proximity is not. The closer a weapon or system operator is to a potential target, the more likely they are relying on direct observation with its attendant subjectivity. At mid-range that same operator must rely on a combination of observation, communicated information and sensor data. At longer ranges the experience leans more heavily on indirect observation and data, becoming more objective but less experiential in nature. Fully remote systems, where an operator is not physically present in an Area of Operations (AO), engender total reliance on sensor data and only limited subjectivity in interpretation of data. This spectrum of presence is not exhaustive, but provides a discrete variable for the knowledge component of distance separately from physical proximity. Separating proximity and presence is a crucial step in exploring the information requirements for situational awareness for emerging tactics.

Evolution of emerging tactics

The most significant differences between emerging and traditional tactical information flows relate to the volume and variety of data. New forms of data create a qualitative difference between existing and emerging tactics. Meanwhile, the sheer volume of battlefield data generated and disseminated by military systems creates a quantitative difference that necessitates new information processing skills at the tactical level. More tactics now rely on data-enhanced situational awareness, but the changing nature of the information that soldiers use on the battlefield creates new challenges for ethical decision making. Sensor data can contribute to soldiers' situational awareness in a variety of ways, but tend to share three important characteristics: sensors rarely duplicate human senses, sensors can exacerbate tunnel vision, and sensors include non-sensory information which requires advanced skills and training to interpret.[24]

In some ways, these challenges replicate the coevolution of technology and society. People have come to rely on a wide variety of non-sensory information in everyday life, including weather data, two-dimensional pictures and video recordings that only narrowly approximate human eyesight. But in other ways, military tactics involve unique challenges. For example, combat skills can utilise innate senses such as balance and pressure detection to identify the location of gunfire or explosions while other senses are overwhelmed. Some of these skills are developed from pre-existing individual aptitudes while others are learned. Radio protocols are a good example of skills taught to enable rapid tactical exchanges of relevant information. The Army's challenge for emerging tactics will be to meet its requirements to inform tactical decision makers to enable ethical targeting while also training soldiers to process data and communications quickly enough to make effective decisions. This will require new skills in using sensor data alongside sensory perception at a range of distances, distributing data across teams and overcoming the human tendency to focus on what can be seen rather on what might not be easily detected.

Emerging tactics will put additional pressure on the Army to train its soldiers with the skills to rapidly interpret and process multi-source sensory, sensor-based and communicated data. This has the potential to both increase and diminish situational awareness at the tactical level, meaning that soldiers' capacity to make ethical decisions could be influenced by emerging technologies and tactics. Situational awareness could potentially be diminished by constraints on direct observation due to limited sensor data, such as field-of-view limitation from remotely operated cameras, disconnection from weapons effects both friendly and hostile, or from the tunnel vision which sensor data can engender in weapon operators. Situational awareness could potentially be enhanced by the rich availability of data, including much better observation of routes, objects and targets, by the integration of live observation and battlespace management data, and through risk reduction strategies which risk consumable equipment rather than human lives.

Overall, emerging tactics utilising high-tech systems have the potential to lead to significantly different decision making processes that have implications for ethical tactics. A range of new technologies has altered situational awareness. These technologies have enhanced the soldier's ability to identify, process, comprehend and apply information. These experiences offer insight into the ethics of emerging tactics. The soldier's ability to identify potential targets has been substantially enhanced by better identification and pattern-of-life analysis.[25] The consequence of enhanced situational awareness has led to new tactical procedures for high-value individuals, including higher approval levels to ensure that lawful and ethical targeting decisions are made.[26] The soldier's capacity to process information has been altered by the combination of direct and remote observation and control mechanisms and the wide inclusion of non-sensory data alongside observed experience. The soldier's ability to comprehend information has been altered by the necessity to integrate data from multiple input streams and from multiple angles, including different forms of communication and different data types, particularly where that data combines familiar and unfamiliar or specialist information.

Managing the consequences of emerging tactics for ethical military practice will likely necessitate new skills and training for the next generation of soldiers. Such training will need to develop advanced individual skills in data processing and combat stress management to overcome information overload. Emerging tactics will almost certainly involve further integration between manned and unmanned systems and will require greater aptitude for and training in rapid processing of sensor data at the tactical level. Soldiers will also need decision making processes that consider a much wider array of information streams and accommodate higher thresholds of knowledge for targeting decisions. This means that effective and ethical tactics tomorrow will require a new set of skills in addition to those that are needed today. It is unlikely that technology will alleviate many of the complicating factors that contribute to friction in contemporary conflict, but it will enable the Army to manage the co-evolution of tactics and expectations while maintaining its high level of professionalism and individual skill.

The increasing development of high-tech military systems continues to drive the emergence of land warfare tactics in an attempt to improve weapon precision and combat effectiveness. Precision, proximity of weapons to targets, battlefield presence of combatants and situational awareness all have the potential to significantly influence ethical considerations for emerging tactics. To manage these influences, the Army will need to consider how it trains combat and support personnel, particularly remote systems and robot operators, in the principles of ethical and legal targeting. The Army will also need to consider approaches to delegating authority to remote and semi-autonomous systems at the tactical level. Human operators will require further training to process and comprehend the scale, volume and variety of situational data presented to them to avoid information overload and to maintain combat performance.

Emerging tactics will introduce both push and pull factors that could contribute to enhancing or diminishing situational awareness and ethical decision making. Historically, increases in targeting capabilities have been quickly followed by increases in expectations regarding informed decision making and precision. Should that trend continue, emerging tactics will not only enable, but also oblige, soldiers to make better informed decisions. Tomorrow's soldiers will need to balance the benefits offered by new technologies against any limitations that may reduce awareness or certainty on the battlefield to ensure that emerging tactics remain ethical and just in the conflicts to come.

PART 6: ETHICS AND THE FUTURE BATTLE SPACE

Trooper Scott Newman, 2nd/14th Light Horse Regiment (Queensland Mounted Infantry), runs through a cyber battle near Samawah in Iraq. It was Cavalrymen's first mission specific training at Shoalwater Bay in preparation for deployment to Iraq with Overwatch Battle Group (West)-4.
Photo by Warrant Officer Class Two Graham McBean

13

WEAPONISING SOCIAL MEDIA

SHANNON BRANDT FORD

Terrorist groups have begun to use social media to incite violence. The defence and security agencies need to prevent or minimise the harm of these attacks but this practical problem relates to a complex set of theoretical problems that are reflected in a broader academic debate. Some argue that contemporary conflict involves new and unique features that render conventional ways of thinking about the ethics of armed conflict inadequate at least or redundant at most. As the internet has become an international asset that is vital to global commerce and communications, new questions have emerged that have produced new challenges. While there has been discussion of 'weaponising' social media, what does it mean and what tactics are involved? I contend that what we are in fact seeing is a process of militarisation and outline three broad 'non-conventional challenges' for the use of military capabilities, as well as sounding a cautionary note about processes of militarisation that expand the boundaries of war.

Social media and violence

Terrorist groups are using social media to further their goals, including as a tool to instigate violent acts to create fear within a target population. For example, Charlie Winter, senior research fellow at the International Centre for the Study of Radicalisation, and Haroro Ingram, a lecturer at the National Security College in Canberra, describe the two men who opened fire outside a Muhammad cartoon contest at Garland in Texas during May 2015 as being 'in contact with low-level jihadis on Twitter' but having 'little going for them in terms of organisational ISIS connections'.[1] They were not trained by the so-called Islamic State in Iraq and Syria (ISIS) nor directed to carry out an attack by its command. Rather, suggest Winter and Ingram, they were merely inspired by its propaganda.[2] Winter and Ingram also examine the impact of the incident on 12 June 2016 when Omar Mateen walked into Pulse nightclub in Orlando, Florida and shot 49 of its patrons and staff. According to Winter and Ingram:

> When rumors of his ideological inclination first went public, observers stopped talking about Mateen as if he was an 'ordinary' mass shooter and effectively put the full force of ISIS behind him. He stopped being a mere man with a gun and was transformed, via the media and politicians, into a fully-fledged ISIS operative, a human manifestation of the group's international menace.[3]

There are clearly some important differences between these two incidents. But the overall goal remains the same for groups such as ISIS. Social media is an important means of proliferating messages to instigate random violence that induces fear in the target population about future attacks.

In a monograph produced for the Royal Danish Defence College in 2015, the strategic communications analyst Thomas Nissen suggests that this type of incident clearly demonstrates that social media has been 'weaponised'. He argues that it provides actors with 'stand-off' capability to deliver effects or 'remote warfare'.[4] Social network media, he suggests, are weapon systems in their own right, providing actors with new intelligence, targeting, influence, operations, and command and control capabilities. They are not, he believes, just a new, technologically provided way of communicating and exerting influence.[5] Nissen describes weaponisation as the adaptation of something existent or developed for other purposes so it can be used as 'a weapon (platform/system) in order to achieve "military" effect(s)'. He suggests that such a 'thing' could be a chemical or bacillus that is modified to be used as a weaponised chemical agent (for example, gas) to produce weapons-grade uranium for nuclear weapons, or just dirty bombs; to use or adapt existing computer code to create military effects in the cyber domain (for example, Stuxnet); or as in this case to use and/or modify social network media algorithms, code and platforms for 'warfighting' purposes.[6]

Can social media really be described as a weapon? According to Thomas Rid, Reader in War Studies at King's College London, and Peter McBurney, Professor in the Agents and Intelligent Systems Group of the Department of Informatics at King's College London, a weapon is an instrument of harm.[7] More specifically, they describe a weapon as 'a tool that is used, or designed to be used, with the aim of threatening or causing physical, functional, or mental harm to structures, systems, or living things'.[8] Cyber-weapons, for example, are software designed to attack and damage other software (or data within computer systems). Randall Dipert, Professor of Philosophy at the State University of New York, suggests that some cyberweapons damage software by infiltrating (or injecting) unwanted data into an information processing system that alters the database. They might also do damage by interfering with intended ways of processing that data (such as is the case with malware).[9] Social media is not a weapon in this sense. It is not the instrument or tool that is doing the harming. Rather it is enabling a message that intends to incite others to do harm. For this reason, it is more accurately described as propaganda. In effect, the use of social media to incite violence *is* dissemination of information designed to influence people's opinions and behaviour.

This is no less morally problematic. After all, Nissen notes a number of legitimate ethical concerns with using social media in this way. For instance, what are the ethical implications of conducting 'military' activities against threats on social media? Using social media for warlike activities is counter to their 'social' or 'civilian' purposes. Trying to deny audiences the ability to speak freely on social network media sites and platforms can be ethically problematic, especially for Western liberal democracies where the notion of keeping the moral high ground and defending freedom of speech are deeply rooted values. It might also make them 'dual-purpose' objects and thereby lawful military targets.[10] Nissen also observes that when we refer to social media as weaponised, we 'securitise' the issue, which might unnecessarily undermine human rights. Such labels frame the activity as being conducted in a state of emergency and render all responses to be a security, intelligence or defence issue.[11] The problem described by Nissen is, however, one of *militarising* the use of social media rather than *weaponising* it. Militarisation is where something designed for civilian use is adapted for a military function or purpose. This is appropriate in some circumstances, particularly in warfighting. But it can develop into a problem when it leads to an overarching ideology of militarism. The American military scholar and ex-Army officer, Andrew Bacevich, helpfully defines this problematic type of militarism in terms of the following three elements: 'the prevalence of military sentiments or ideals among a people; the political condition characterised by the predominance of the military class in government or administration; the tendency to regard military efficiency as the paramount interest of the state'.[12]

Non-conventional challenges

One reason to militarise social media is that modern conflict presents non-conventional challenges. These involve new and unique features that render conventional ways of thinking about the ethics of armed conflict inadequate or redundant. Several scholars are currently looking at this problem. For example, Joseph Margolis argues that these conflicts involve non-state actors, high civilian-combatant casualties, the participation of mercenaries, and the use of unconventional tactics such as terrorism and human shields.[13] Jessica Wolfendale suggests that modern conflicts no longer conform to the conventional model of interstate conflict motivated by concrete political aims.[14] Authors such as Mary Kaldor and Herfried Münkler use the term 'new war' to describe current forms of armed conflict.[15] Paul Gilbert suggests that these modern wars are characterised by low-intensity intrastate conflicts motivated by 'identity politics'.[16] Michael Gross attempts to articulate the modes of warfare that deal with modern dilemmas but in a way that still meets the just war conditions of necessity and humanitarianism.[17] Simon Bronitt and his colleagues suggest that the 'War on Terror' provides a new context in which legal systems have struggled to determine the legitimate boundaries on using force to prevent acts of terrorism, including the development of lethal force.[18]

So what are these non-conventional challenges? One set of challenges is the non-conventional threats we now face. For example, Christopher Kutz argues that recent developments in modern violent conflict have meant the increasing use of 'asymmetrical' tactics, such as guerrilla raids, hiding among either one's own or one's enemies' populations, infiltration of enemy lines, sabotage, and joint operations with collaborating civilians.[19] According to Rod Thornton, such asymmetric tactics allow a weaker actor to target the vulnerabilities of a much stronger opponent using unexpected methods, including actions outside the conventional norms of warfare.[20] Furthermore, contemporary terrorism is now a major focus for defence policy revisionists who, David McCraw suggests, believe that the current era is dominated by unconventional rather than conventional warfare.[21] Michael Gross also describes the problematic move towards criminalising armed conflict. He contends that the tendency to view non-conventional conflict as a criminal activity creates a problem because adversaries are more likely to conclude that their enemies are despicable villains rather than honourable foes. This outcome, he believes, signifies a sea change in the conventional way of thinking about war, since an important norm of conventional war asserts the moral innocence of combatants on any side.[22]

A second set of challenges is the *emerging technologies* that are transforming the norms of armed conflict. The development and use of social media is one example. Another is military robot technology and its use in targeted killing. Outside the conventional battlefield, Mary Ellen O'Connell suggests that the use of military drones has created more opportunities to employ targeted killing against terrorist groups.[23] Another example of the influence of transformative technology is developments in cyberwarfare.

Patrick Lin and Shannon Ford suggest that the modern world's dependence on digital or information-based assets, and the vulnerabilities of critical national cyber-infrastructure, mean that a non-kinetic attack (for example, cyberweapons that damage computer systems) could do serious harm.[24] This is why the United States, for example, takes the cyber threat seriously, declaring that, as part of its cyber policy, it reserves the right to retaliate to a non-kinetic attack using kinetic means. Or as one United States Department of Defense official remarked: 'If you shut down our power grid, maybe we will put a missile down one of your smokestacks'.[25] There are a host of other emerging technologies that will pose significant challenges in the future, such as artificial intelligence, human enhancement, autonomous weapons, and the possibilities go on.

A third set of challenges is the non-conventional uses of the military to serve a wide range of institutional roles and purposes. Military capabilities are not only used in wars. Military operations encompass a wide range of tasks including peacekeeping, supporting civil authorities, counter-terrorism, disaster relief, enforcement of sanctions, and so on. Many of these activities do not require the military to use force. In some cases, because they are working in an environment of dangerous conflict, the military are prepared to use force. In particular, in the past two decades the military has increasingly been used for purposes other than fighting conventional wars. This is due, in part, to the emerging norm in the 1990s favouring military intervention to protect civilians whose lives are seriously threatened.[26] The international response to the popular uprising against Muammar Gaddafi in Libya during 2011 and the country's descent into civil war in 2014, for example, demonstrates how the politics of humanitarian intervention have shifted to the point where it is harder to do nothing in the face of atrocities.[27]

Another reason for the increasing use of the military outside of war is the recognition, by some, that the military can perform a variety of political functions in peacetime. The heightened attention to the threat from international terrorism has already been noted. But military capabilities might also be used to affect a target's decision making without resorting to (or intending to use) actual violence. Barry Blechman and Stephen Kaplan, for example, argue that most uses of the armed forces have a political dimension because they 'influence the perceptions and behaviours of political leaders in foreign countries to some degree'.[28] They hold that a political use of the armed forces occurs when physical actions are taken by one or more components of the uniformed military services as part of a deliberate attempt by the state's authorities to influence, or to be prepared to influence, the specific behaviour of individuals in another nation without engaging in a continuing contest of violence.[29]

Extending the boundaries of war

It is necessary in some cases to use military capabilities to respond to non-conventional threats.[30] But we potentially create a moral problem when we allow the boundaries of war to extend too far; when, as Rosa Brooks describes it, everything becomes war and the military becomes everything.[31] We should resist the notion that violent conflict is a normal element of human social interaction, which too easily permits the uniquely destructive activities that should only happen in war. This is because such action contradicts the conventional view of civil society that considers '*bellum omnium contra omnes*' (or 'war of all against all') as a feature of the state of nature that should be avoided. As the political philosopher Thomas Hobbes remarked more than three centuries ago:

> Hereby it is manifest, that during the time men live without
> a common Power to keep them all in awe, they are in that
> condition which is called War; and such a war, as is of *every*
> *man, against every man.* For War, consisteth not in Battle
> onely, or the act of fighting; but in a tract of time, wherein
> the Will to contend by Battle is sufficiently known.[32]

In this state of nature, Alex Bellamy claims that individuals can never be sure of their security and are forced into a war of all against all.[33] Tom Sorell describes how in the classical social contract theories of Hobbes, John Locke and others, the state of nature is the human condition before there was a state order and the condition that human beings would be returned to if an existing state were to dissolve.[34] Sorell describes the state of nature as a state of generalised insecurity in which the concept of morality has no footing.[35] In this state, Sorell asserts that each person has the right of nature, taking whatever seems a help to his own self-preservation and prosperity.[36] Bellamy explains that to avoid this situation, individuals agree to the establishment of states to meet their most fundamental needs. That is, the people agree to a social contract in which they place a monopoly of power and the right to rule in the hands of a sovereign. In return, the sovereign promises to protect the political community from the twin dangers of internal anarchy and external aggression.[37]

Yet recent scholarship has sought to apply the principles of war to an increasingly wide variety of practices, contexts and institutions. The terrorist use of social media is one of these areas. But there are a number of others. John Stone, for example, demonstrates the way in which cyber-attacks can be construed as acts of war.[38] Randall Dipert also applies the conventional principles of the just war tradition to cyberwar. He concludes that existing international law and principles of just war theory do not apply to cyberwar in a straightforward way.[39] Michael Quinlan uses just war thinking to morally evaluate intelligence practice. He argues that just as we cannot morally engage in any war we like and fight it any way we like, so we cannot engage in any intelligence activity and conduct it in any way we like.[40] There is even an influential literature that seeks to apply the principles of war to business practice.[41] Mark McNeilly, for instance, uses Sun Tzu's ancient text *The Art of War* to formulate six strategic principles that apply to the world of business.[42] In similar fashion, Andrew Holmes adapts Carl von Clausewitz's *On War* to business practice as 'part and parcel of man's social existence'.[43]

There is nothing wrong with seeking to develop such inter-disciplinary insights. There is a risk, however, that we can miss the point of the exceptional nature of the destructiveness that we apply to military combatants in warfare. A patently absurd example of this inattentiveness is William C Bradford's argument that academic 'scholars, and the law schools that employ them, are — at least in theory — targetable so long as attacks are proportional, distinguish non-combatants from combatants, employ non-prohibited weapons, and contribute to the defeat of Islamism'.[44]

Plainly, war needs boundaries because in war we permit substantially more harm than we do in normal life. Most nations treat war as something that allows moral exceptions to the prohibitions against destruction and killing. The just war tradition is an important source for understanding and limiting this form of moral exceptionalism. Michael Walzer refers to this limitation as the adaptation of ordinary morality to the 'moral reality of war'.[45] Shannon French argues that the strong moral prohibition on murder produces a dilemma for those who are asked to fight wars and are directed by their political masters to kill an enemy. Soldiers must learn to 'take only certain lives in certain ways, at certain times, and for certain reasons [...] otherwise they become indistinguishable from murderers and will find themselves condemned by the very societies they were created to serve'.[46] David Luban contends that the military paradigm offers much freer rein than normal life. He suggests that in war, but not in law, it is permissible to use lethal force on enemy troops regardless of their degree of personal involvement with the adversary.[47] Luban observes that one can attack an enemy without concern over whether he has done anything wrong. He further notes that, in war, 'collateral damage' (that is, foreseen but unintended killing of non-combatants) is morally permissible and the requirements of evidence are much weaker.[48] In his history of war and the law of nations, Stephen Neff identifies a set of normative features that make war different to the rest of social life. He asserts that war is a violent conflict between collectives rather than between individuals, thereby distinguishing it from interpersonal violence.[49] He proceeds to argue that wartime is distinguishable from peacetime.[50]

The just war tradition attempts to explain the 'rightness' or 'wrongness' of the decision to fight a war and the way in which a war should be conducted. The purpose of the first set of just war principles (*jus ad bellum*) is to prevent the *harms of war* by limiting its initiation. The second set (*jus in bello*) aims to minimise the *harms in war* by restraining its conduct. This stipulates that military combatants should *only* do the harm that is justifiable because it is necessary to secure victory. But this still permits much more destruction and killing than normal life. The harmful means employed by military combatants in war are unlike, say, those of a police officer in a well-ordered society. As Geoffrey Corn and his colleagues explain:

For the soldier, the logic is self-evident: the employment of combat power against an enemy – whether an individual

soldier firing her rifle, a tank gunner firing a highly-explosive
anti-tank round, or an Apache pilot letting loose a salvo of
rockets – is intended to completely disable the enemy in the
most efficient manner in order to eliminate all risk that the
opponent remains capable of continued participation in
the fight.[51]

According to the British ethicist David Whetham, the just war
tradition provides an ethical framework for distinguishing justifiable military action from mass murder. It provides a common
language within which the rights and wrongs of armed conflict
can be intelligibly discussed and debated rationally.[52] That is,
destructive acts that are disproportionate and/or indiscriminate
are off limits. So the just war tradition demands that military
combatants exercise restraint in their pursuit of military goals. By
way of contrast, theorists such as James Turner Johnson emphasise the judicial function of war. This approach suggests that the
just war focuses on a 'conception of sovereignty as responsibility
for the common good of society that is to be exercised to vindi-
cate justice after some injustice has occurred and gone unrectified
or unpunished'.[53] I am not disputing that the just war thinking is
concerned with justice. But these notions are not incommensu-
rate. The just war tradition is a complex, long-standing historical
discussion about both harm mitigation *and* the pursuit of justice.

The use of social media to incite violence creates a number of
practical ethical problems. But it also highlights a broader (and
more complex) set of non-conventional ethical challenges for
the military. In particular, we are facing more non-conventional
threats and we should expect novel uses of emerging technologies. The upshot is that Western nations need to put much more
effort into thinking about how they use military capabilities in
conflicts short of war. This includes responding to the use of social

media by terrorist groups. But there is good reason to be cautious about extending the boundaries of war. Such an approach can end up ignoring the fundamental tenet of modern international society that identifies the state of nature as a problem to overcome. Instead, the better approach is to emphasise the underlying principle of restraining violence that is promoted by the just war tradition.

14

WHAT CYBERWEAPONS TELL US ABOUT OUR JUST WAR

ADAM HENSCHKE

The introduction and use of new technologies in the military space, specifically, the use of cybertechnologies as weapons, has created a range of ethical issues. Rather than present an argument about the ethics of cyberweapons or the use of cybertechnologies as part of modern warfare,[1] exploring the ethics of cyberweapons can tell us something about the existing beliefs we have about the ethics of warfare. In particular, new technologies like cyberweapons challenge our existing beliefs and can act to reveal particular intuitions about moral situations.

One particular problem provides a starting point: if offered the choice to use a cyberweapon or not as part of a traditional military operation, should a commander favour targeting civilians or causing physical damage? This problem highlights a tension in just war theory's *jus in bello* criteria: that on the one hand, a decision maker should adhere to the principle of discrimination, while on the other, they should respect the principle of proportionality. Following a method of case-based reasoning, the core moral values underpinning the tension are highlighted as they relate to cyberweapons. The first case looks at the demands of discrimination when military forces deliberately put people's lives at risk rather than target civilians for non-lethal harm. Proportionality is then drawn out when one adds cyberweapons to the options. Cyberweapons pose a special challenge for these issues, because of the civilian reliance on cyber-infrastructure, which poses a dual-use challenge. This is a common problem to the just war tradition that, at its core, is a pluralistic doctrine. Decision makers must choose between different moral values. Some may disagree with this characterisation, but thinking about cyberweapons can actually act to *uncover* our existing beliefs about which moral value takes precedence in a situation of incommensurable values. That is, the ethical questions new technologies bring up can both challenge *and* reveal our existing beliefs about things like the just war theory.

The challenge and the just war tradition

Consider this challenge: a military commander has a cyberweapon and has the option of using it as part of a military campaign that is also using traditional methods including soldiers, bombs and bullets. The challenge arises as they are faced with a situation that requires them to decide between two options:

- Option 1: use the cyberweapon to deliberately target civilian infrastructure that will substantially affect a large number of enemy civilians for a significant period of time, but will most likely cause no loss of life;
- Option 2: use traditional military methods (soldiers, bombs and bullets) that will definitely kill enemy soldiers, and more than likely cause casualties on their own side.

They do not have any other options. There is no Option 3. Furthermore, the military outcome is the same and is equally likely to occur, whichever option is chosen. That is, in all but the means chosen (and their direct impacts) everything else between the two options is equivalent.

To explain why this is a problem, we need to turn to the just war tradition. As it is usually understood, the tradition contains two core areas: the *jus ad bellum*, concerned with the justice of decisions around going to war, and the *jus in bello*, concerned with the justice of decisions around what you can do in war.[2] Tensions in *jus in bello* come to the fore when thinking about cyberweapons. The underlying concept of the just war tradition as a morally pluralistic doctrine, meaning it actively draws from different moral values or normative traditions to create a theory that appeals to means as well as ends, is worth examining first. For instance, the Australian philosopher Tony Coady explains that:

> my exploration of just war theory will treat it as a non-utilitarian, indeed, broadly non-consequentialist moral theory. By this I mean that it does not determine moral issues *only by recourse to the maximising or optimising of outcomes* [...] there are moral imperatives, such as the prohibition on attacking non-combatants, that are not principally justifiable *solely* in terms of their beneficial outcomes. But *this is not to say that consequences are of no importance in the just war tradition* [...] The approach will merely reject the idea that the whole of morality is to be treated in this fashion and will suspect that the sort of large-scale maximising calculations characteristic of utilitarianism pose illusory prospects for understanding the moral enterprise.[3]

For instance, in *jus in bello* discussions, there are two core principles which limit and guide what a soldier can do while fighting a war: the principle of discrimination and the principle of proportionality, which track to rules and outcomes, respectively.

On discrimination

The principle of discrimination holds that a soldier cannot deliberately target civilians/non-combatants. The Ontario-based philosopher Brian Orend observes:

> The requirement of discrimination and non-combatant immunity is the most important *jus in bello* rule [...] The substance of the rule is this: Soldiers charged with the deployment of armed force may not do so indiscriminately; rather, they must exert every reasonable effort to discriminate between legitimate and illegitimate targets. How are soldiers to know which is which? A legitimate target in wartime is anyone or anything engaged in harming.[4]

On a traditional reading, this is a rule that cannot be broken. It is what philosophy calls a deontological principle. As Orend's account has it, 'all non-harming persons or institutions, are thus ethically immune from direct and intentional attack by soldiers and their weapons systems'.[5] Every effort must be taken to avoid hitting civilians and their institutions with weapon systems. Simply stated, discrimination means that the military commander cannot use cyberweapons on civilians or their institutions.

When thinking of cyberweapons, however, discrimination seems to be over-demanding and impractical. For instance, it seems problematic to say that we should sacrifice the lives of the enemy and put our own soldiers' lives at risk to avoid causing disruption to cyberservices. If a military could achieve their ends by shutting down the enemy country's social media sites like Facebook, or by full-scale military invasion, the principle of discrimination holds the seemingly counterintuitive position that one should choose a full-scale military invasion with all its death and destruction. Simply stated, despite the principle of discrimination, common sense suggests that one should choose the cyber-option over the traditional option.

Recall however the description of Options 1 and 2 above. In Option 1, using cyberweapons, it is specified that the cyber-attack will have *substantial* impacts for a *significant* period of time. While shutting down Facebook for a day feels trivial, as computers and the internet become ever more integrated into our worlds, we are becoming increasingly vulnerable to cyber-disruptions, though perhaps indirectly. For instance, should a cyber-attack shut down international air freight for a significant period of time, access to food and countries' export economies could suffer quite substantially. Furthermore, new generations may be particularly vulnerable to cyberdisruptions. Consider that many people in the developed world have spent their entire lives connected to and connected *by* the internet. Given that many, and in some cases all, of their important social relations are enabled and assured by cybertechnologies, these 'digital natives' could suffer significant emotional trauma from a loss of access to social media in the same way that a person would suffer from being cast out of their community or excommunicated.[6] The point here is to say that cyberdisruptions can have substantial and significant impacts indirectly and in some cases directly.

Still, we might consider that human lives are more important than substantial and significant interruptions. In armed conflict there are, however, legal bans on the military use of non-lethal weapons.[7] Consider an acoustic weapon that substantially deafens a large number of civilians for a significant period of time. Despite being non-lethal, this kind of weapon is prohibited by both the laws and the ethics of war. That is, if you have the option of using the non-lethal acoustic weapon or bullets, you are required by law and ethics not to use the acoustic weapon. While this may seem counterintuitive, as the Australian ethicist Stephen Coleman has argued, there are a number of good moral reasons to consider that militaries should be banned from using non-lethal weapons on ethical grounds.[8] Given that the impacts of some cyberweapons can be substantial and significant, the same restriction would hold for cyberweapons. The point here is that though it may seem counterintuitive, we have reasons and precedents for adhering to the principle of discrimination, and not selecting Option 1; cyberweapons that deliberately target civilians are prohibited by the principle of discrimination, even when they have non-lethal outcomes.

On proportionality

This leads us to the second element of the *jus in bello*, the principle of proportionality. The basic idea of *jus in bello* proportionality is that you must choose the option that causes the least damage to your target to achieve the given military ends. The decision metric is a consequentialist one; you are morally required to choose that option which will likely cause the minimum amount of harm. The Canadian philosopher Thomas Hurka describes it this way:

> [a]s many writers have noted, the structure of just war
> theory closely parallels that of the morality of self-defense

> [...] An act of self-defense is wrong if the harm it causes the
> attacker is out of proportion to the harm he threatens, *or if
> the threat could just as well have been averted by less violent
> means.*[9]

In essence, if you have less violent means at your disposal then
you ought to use them over more destructive ones. In this way,
proportionality is a consequentialist principle, where one's decision making is prescribed by the consequences of one's acts.
Simply stated, if you have two options, and one would likely
cause less harm than the other, then proportionality requires you
to select the one which causes the least amount of harm.

When thinking of proportionality, however, it seems problematic to say that you must take the least damaging option when
targeting the enemy:

> War is a world apart, where life itself is at stake, where
> human nature is reduced to its elemental forms, where
> self-interest and necessity prevail. Here men and women do
> what they must to save themselves and their communities,
> and morality and law have no place. *Inter arma silent leges*:
> in time of war the law is silent.[10]

The basic idea is that you must do what will win the war. Consider allies fighting against Germany during the Second World
War: the threat posed to the world by the Nazi war machine was
so great that the allies could and should have taken all means
necessary to defeat the enemy. Given the threat posed, the simple
fact is that we must win. Hence the adage 'all is fair in love and
war'. As long as the enemy is defeated, why should we care if the
choice is disproportionate?

To explain proportionality, think of it this way: if you have two options that will produce the same result, and one kills 1000 enemy soldiers while the other kills just five enemy soldiers, proportionality holds that you must choose the second. Michael Walzer opens his seminal text *Just and Unjust Wars* defending just war theory against a realist position by arguing that in war moral principles do apply.[11] This is perhaps *the* core premise of the just war tradition. Even in conditions of war, ethics do apply. So, if either option would produce the equivalent military outcome, the principle of proportionality applies – you must choose the one that causes least harm, in this case, the second.

The *jus in bello* principle of proportionality is, however, complex. Hurka highlights this complexity when he says:

> [an] act in war is wrong if the relevant harm it will cause is out of proportion to its relevant good. This raises three questions: (1) What are the relevant goods that count in favor of a war's or act's proportionality? (2) What are the relevant evils that count against it? (3) How do these goods and evils weigh against each other?[12]

In addition to measuring the harm caused against the military aim being pursued, included in the proportionality calculation are elements such as the loss of your own soldiers' lives. Consider now that you have two options that will produce the same result: one will cost you 1000 dead soldiers and the other will cost you five. Proportionality here requires you to choose the second.

The common sense intuition underpinning this is that there is an ethical responsibility to take seriously the lives of those under your command, which is clearly supported by a practical responsibility to not waste the lives of your own soldiers needlessly. Tony Coates, a political scientist at the University of Reading, captures this approach when he cites a statement made

by General Norman Schwarzkopf, the Coalition commander in
the 1991 Gulf War:

> My nightmare is anything that would cause mass casualties
> among the troops. I don't want my troops to die. I don't
> want my troops to be maimed. Therefore, every waking and
> sleeping moment my nightmare is the fact that I will give an
> order that will cause countless numbers of human beings to
> lose their life.[13]

The idea is expanded by the Oxford University ethicist Bradley
Strawser in what he calls the principle of unnecessary risk (PUR):

> it is wrong to command someone to take on unnecessary
> potentially lethal risks in an effort to carry out a just
> action for some good; any potentially lethal risk incurred
> must be justified by some strong countervailing reason.
> In the absence of such a reason, ordering someone to
> incur potentially lethal risk is morally impermissible.
> Importantly, PUR is a demand not to order someone to
> take unnecessary risk on par with alternative means to
> accomplish some goal.[14]

Taking us back to issues of cyberweapons, proportionality now
presents the commander with two strong reasons to favour
using the cyberweapon. First, this option would cause less harm
to the enemy than the traditional military methods, thus proportionality gives the commander reason to use cyberweapons.
Second, given that cyberweapons would remove the need to put
their own soldiers at risk of lethal harm, again, proportionality
gives reason for the commander to select this. The point here is
that the commander has reasons for adhering to the principle of

proportionality, and selecting cyberweapons that deliberately target civilians are recommended by the principle of proportionality.

Cyber-infrastructure and dual-use objects

The tension is between the two *jus in bello* principles of discrimination and proportionality. On the one hand is the principle of discrimination, which tells the commander that they ought to avoid substantial and sustained impacts to civilians, while on the other, the principle of proportionality tells them that they ought to choose the option that causes the least number of soldiers to be killed. One principle gives reasons to choose Option 1, the other gives reasons to choose Option 2.

This tension poses a particular problem when considering the use of cyberweapons, as cyber-infrastructure is set up, maintained and used by private companies and civilians. Whether it is the physical superstructures that transmit communications, the programming that allows people to communicate and interact, or the particular services that rely on the hardware and programming, the majority of cyber-infrastructure is civilian. Which, following the principle of discrimination, would seem to preclude most cyber-infrastructure from being a military target. Civilian infrastructure like roads, bridges, dams and power plants is, however, a legitimate target in war if being used by the enemy military. In this sense cyber-infrastructure is no exception. As the international law scholar Michäel Schmitt has written, '[f]or example, Facebook has been used for the organisation of armed resistance operations and Twitter for the transmission of information of military value'.[15] In 2013, a group of international legal experts looked at the way the laws of armed conflict relate to cyberwarfare, and released the *Tallinn Manual on the International Law Applicable to Cyber Warfare*. The *Tallinn Manual*'s analysis of the permissions and limits of targeting cyber-infrastructure is a useful touchstone to help explore the tension between discrimination and proportionality.

Where things like infrastructure are used by both military and civilians, decision makers face the situation of dual-use objects, and the laws of war seem quite clear here: 'As a matter of law, status as a civilian object and military objective cannot coexist; an object is either one or the other. This principle confirms that all dual-use objects and facilities are military objectives, without qualification'.[16] On the first reading, then, this would seem to resolve the tension between discrimination and proportionality:

> When a civilian object or facility is used for military ends, it
> becomes a military objective through the 'use' criterion [...]
> For instance, if a party to the conflict uses a certain civilian
> computer network for military purposes, that network
> loses its civilian character and becomes a military objective.
> This is so even if the network also continues to be used for
> civilian purposes.[17]

If a piece of cyber-infrastructure is used by the military, then it becomes a legitimate military objective. The principle of discrimination no longer applies, and any military decision making can be guided by proportionality. But when considering a factory that produces hardware for cyber-infrastructure that is used by the enemy military, 'the issue of whether such a factory qualifies as a military objective by use depends on the scale, scope, and importance of the military acquisitions'. The Tallinn experts 'were unable to arrive at any definitive conclusions as to precise thresholds'.[18] So, there is a problem of identifying the threshold at which dual-use infrastructure becomes sufficiently militarised to qualify as a legitimate target. Furthermore, there is the issue of the temporary nature of dual-use objects:

> Civilian objects that have become military objectives by use can revert to civilian status if military use is discontinued. Once that occurs, they regain their protection from attack. However, if the discontinuance is only temporary, and the civilian object will be used for military purposes in the future, the object remains a military objective through the 'purpose' criterion. It must be cautioned that the mere fact that a civilian object was once used for military purposes does not alone suffice to establish that it will be so used in the future.[19]

The relevant cyber-infrastructure thus recovers its immunity when the enemy military stop using it for the military purpose, and previous military use is not enough to justify targeting. To determine the legitimacy of a target, the Tallinn experts stated that 'the legal question to be asked is whether a reasonable attacker would determine that the reasonably available information is reliable enough to conclude that the civilian object is going to be converted to military use'.[20]

The dual use of cyber-infrastructure draws out two key points. First, a great deal of cyber-infrastructure will be dual-use objects. Second, there is considerable interpretation and discretion about what counts as a dual-use object. That is, it is not always immediately apparent what will qualify as a legitimate military target, and it is possible for different people to disagree about whether some cyber-infrastructure is a legitimate military target or not. The dual-use nature of cyber-infrastructure draws out the tension between the principles of discrimination and proportionality.

The problem of incommensurable values

This all serves to bring us back to my initial challenge: in military decision making, a commander may have to make a choice between the principle of discrimination and the principle of proportionality, initially set up as choosing between two options. In choosing the first option, the commander deliberately targets civilians to avoid loss of life. In the second, however, the commander deliberately avoids civilians, but causes loss of life.

At its core, the commander is facing a problem of choosing between incommensurable values. Put simply, it is like asking which of the following is best: Fyodor Dostoyevsky's *Crime and Punishment*, Michaelangelo's *Mona Lisa*, a puppy or the film *Captain America: Civil War*. There is no obvious answer. Moreover, there is no definitive answer because reasonable people can disagree about which of these is 'the best'. But for any disagreement or discussion to be *reasonable*, people must be able to give a *reason* why they think one is better than the others. *Crime and Punishment* tells us core truths about the human experience, the *Mona Lisa* is aesthetically and historically remarkable, a puppy is a living thing, *Captain America: Civil War* provides a simple pleasure whose making employed hundreds of people, and so on.

I suggest that like choosing which of those things is the best, when making a decision between Option 1 and Option 2, the core tension is that discrimination and proportionality are *both* important moral values. Moreover, these values are of different kinds, so are incommensurable; discrimination derives its moral force from an adherence to the basic respect for humans, those innocent civilians not involved in any threat of harm. Proportionality derives its moral force from a recognition that we ought to minimise negative consequences, such as the deaths of soldiers, both enemy and the commander's own.

Technologies: challenging and revealing

Some, however, may be unconvinced by the general contention that the just war tradition is a morally pluralistic doctrine.[21] I could seem to have described a false dilemma; a sophisticated moral theory could resolve the given tension in such a way that discrimination and proportionality are, in fact, not in tension at all. Seth Lazar's recent entry on 'War' in the *Stanford Encyclopedia of Philosophy* is one such example:

> When they are properly understood, only proportionality
> and necessity [...] are necessary conditions for a war, or an
> act in a war, to be permissible [...] Both the necessity and
> proportionality constraints involve comparing the bads
> caused by an action with the goods that it achieves. They
> differ only in the kinds of options they compare.[22]

In response, this shows the value of looking at new technologies as they relate to things like warfare and how exposure to the options offered by new technologies can challenge our existing moral beliefs. To explain this challenge, recall that I said the just war tradition is a pluralistic doctrine, and claimed it is founded on a set of different moral values. Insofar as there *is* a problem of incommensurability, I proposed that these values will, and do, come into tension. In this sense, the challenges of cyberweapons are nothing new. Such tensions, insofar as they exist, are familiar to military decision making. Technologies present us with the problem of deciding from within a new set of options, thus making us rethink how we normally make these decisions. This then makes us think about the values underpinning those normal decision making processes. That is, the options new technologies offer that can *challenge* what we take for granted.

Returning to scepticism about just war tradition being morally pluralistic, there may be some who see no tension between the two principles, or offer a sophisticated line of reasoning that explains how one moral theory resolves the tension. What I suggest here is that, rather than just posing a challenge to one's existing moral beliefs, the new options offered by technology *reveal* those existing beliefs about which values take precedence over other values, and which moral theory is best suited to resolve our issues.

PART 7: ETHICS EDUCATION AND TRAINING

An Australian senior NCO and a Rwandan Patriotic Army Liaison Officer prepare to destroy a live M79 rifle grenade while conducting explosive ordnance disposal action. *Commonwealth of Australia*

THE AUSTRALIAN DEFENCE FORCE AND MILITARY ETHICS

HUGH SMITH

I was recruited to UNSW's Faculty of Military Studies at the Royal Military College Duntroon in 1971 to teach international politics to undergraduate officer cadets. Taking a broad interpretation of the subject, I covered issues such as the causes of war, the dynamics of nationalism and the evolution of international law. Most required excursions into disciplines such as psychology (does war 'begin in the minds of men'?), sociology (why is nationalism so powerful?) and ethics (should states obey international law?). I later offered a course on nuclear strategy (the Cold War still raged at that time) which posed psychological, sociological, ethical and legal questions even more acutely: could it ever be right to use weapons of mass destruction? Was it justified even to threaten their use? Could military commanders justifiably refuse to 'press the nuclear button'?

These courses were offered in the Department of Government (later Politics) but there were no corresponding departments of psychology, sociology, ethics or philosophy. This deficiency in the education of future officers was noted during planning for the Australian Defence Force Academy (ADFA) in early 1980s, when UNSW proposed to establish a Department of Behavioural Science after ADFA was opened. Support also came from ADF quarters including Nick Jans, a former Army officer who later specialised in military sociology, who argued strongly for the teaching of behavioural science.[1] In the event, the proposal faded away as other more pressing priorities emerged at the Academy.

The advent of the Academy in 1986 did, however, make possible other developments. A new postgraduate course, the Master of Defence Studies, began enrolling military and civilian students in 1987. Offerings came mainly from Politics and History, with classes scheduled for late afternoon or evenings to encourage part-time study. My contribution was a semester-long course on 'Legal and Moral Problems of International Violence' (a title chosen more for its acronym LaMP than its brevity). After a slow start, it attracted numbers of bright and articulate military officers who were keen to debate the ethical and legal issues surrounding war. What is a just war? Can weapons be 'inhumane'? Who qualifies as a 'non-combatant'? Can personal morality ever come before duty? Teaching these students was a delight, as they had previously enjoyed few opportunities to debate the ethical foundations of their profession frankly and openly.

In the early 1990s, having developed a strong interest in military sociology over the years, I offered another postgraduate course entitled 'Armed Forces and Society'. Focusing on the ADF it looked at questions such as: what motivates people to enlist for military service? Why do they stay or leave? What is military culture? How are minority groups treated? Again, I found many uniformed students welcomed the opportunity for uninhibited discussion on such issues. One student working in Army Personnel proposed that all officers posted to a personnel position should be required to take the course.

In the past decade or so, courses and research at what is now UNSW Canberra have paid much more attention to some of the disciplines mentioned. The School of Humanities and Social Sciences has two or three staff specialising in ethical issues with courses at undergraduate and postgraduate level. The School of Business has taken up topics such as leadership, recruitment, retention and organisational theory. The Australian Defence Studies Centre and its successor, the Australian Centre for the Study of Armed Conflict and Society, have also raised awareness of ethical and sociological issues through conferences, workshops and publications. One factor making this possible has been strong growth in postgraduate student numbers.

But greater interest in sociology, ethics and culture in the ADF has also resulted from less welcome factors. Cases of sexual abuse, gender discrimination and bullying at the Academy, other training institutions and the ADF generally have demanded attention. Governments and parliamentary committees have taken an active and often critical interest. Nor have the media held back from reporting problems, sometimes becoming closely involved, as in the 2012 'Skype affair' at the Academy. External and internal inquiries into organisational problems have abounded, averaging about one a year. The ADF found that it could no longer dismiss instances of misbehaviour as 'one-offs' or the responsibility of a few 'bad apples'.[2] As one internal study put it: 'there are parts [of our current culture] that serve us poorly, which limit our performance, hurt our people and damage our reputation'.[3] The possibility of a 'bad barrel' had to be considered.

If the ADF is to grapple successfully with such problems it must have some grasp of what makes individuals and groups tick and of what holds them together, in particular the disciplines of psychology and sociology and the factors of culture and ethics. The role that ethics play in the profession of arms and their relationship to law and culture needs to be considered, as do the challenges to ethics presented by armed conflict. Peacekeeping and other operations such as counterterrorism, law enforcement and border protection, in particular the clash of ethical and cultural values between different societies and different armed forces, are significant. The ethical and cultural values of the ADF as they currently stand, and attempts to shape them, also require examination. My experience has equipped me to raise some questions and propose some guidelines for developing ethics education in the ADF.

Ethics in the profession of arms

An extended definition of ethics is not required here but several key characteristics ought to be noted. First, ethics is about what is right and wrong to do (or not to do) as judged by general principles – such as human rights, 'the greatest happiness' or 'love thy neighbour' – that are widely, if not universally, shared. Second, ethics involves choices which revolve around competing principles or competing interpretations of principles. Often some harm results and guilt is experienced whatever choice is made. This is often referred to as the phenomenon of 'dirty hands'. Third, ethical *behaviour* requires both choice and action. In some cases the ethical choice is clear but competing loyalties – for example, to peers, the unit or the service – push the actor toward unethical behaviour. This is a test of integrity rather than an ethical dilemma.[4] Fourth, ethical decisions are made by a free agent, aware of what he or she is doing and bearing responsibility for those actions. A soldier ordered to shoot an unarmed prisoner, for example, should not be regarded as lacking choice, though his very limited options may mitigate punishment. Fifth, ethics is not about 'correct' choices but about individuals assessing the consequences of different courses of action as best and as honestly as they can. Higher standards of judgment (and behaviour) are expected from some, not least members of the armed forces.

Law is closely related to ethics. In the military context the International Humanitarian Law of Armed Conflict (IHLAC) embodies the most important ethical principles for the conduct of war. But all laws are general and need careful and conscientious interpretation in each situation. Identifying legitimate targets in the midst of hostilities, for example, is notoriously difficult and offers plenty of scope for honest disagreement. While law usually reflects moral principles, the culture of a society may clash with ethical values. Embedded patterns of behaviour which members of a community unthinkingly or consciously accept as binding can seemingly justify practices such as racial discrimination, repression of women and brainwashing in education. Respecting another person's culture is thus not always as imperative as respecting another's human rights or moral worth. The same applies to religious beliefs, which are sometimes called upon to support less than humane practices.

Military culture may likewise clash with ethical standards. Desirable or even essential values can be taken to negative extremes. Dedication to achieving the mission may encourage soldiers to see any means as justified. Teamwork may lead to isolation of those who do not fit the team image or act like team players.[5] In the ADF 'mateship' is valued for increasing cohesion and effectiveness but can also mean covering for others' wrongful acts, hiding inefficiencies and beating the 'system'. Ethical awareness is an essential means of keeping the negative side of military culture in check.

Observance of ethical principles is not just a value in itself but essential to the ADF and Australian society for practical reasons. First, such principles if effectively inculcated determine how soldiers use force. When governments send military forces into action ethical and cultural values become vital means of control. Ethical failures may produce illegalities, adverse publicity, retaliation by an opponent and other damaging consequences. In particular, ethical integrity is vital in many contemporary operations that 'depend in part on winning the trust and co-operation of local populations'.[6]

Second, ethics are important for a military organisation in maintaining professional cohesion and pride. Failures on this front, such as sexual abuse, the bullying of recruits or gender discrimination, undermine the loyalty and dedication of members of the force and erode the esteem in which citizens hold the profession. Ethical sensitivity is also vital in allocating responsibility in the event of accidents, when balancing demands on individuals against military requirements, when ensuring equitable treatment of social groups and ethnic minorities, and so on. Australians rightly expect ADF members to be 'held to higher standards and greater scrutiny than the majority of Australian society'.[7]

Third, ethics are important in the relationship between a government and its armed forces. If there is a lack of trust in the ADF, a government will be reluctant to grant it authority to act effectively.[8] For their part, those in uniform owe loyalty and obedience to their commanders, their service and the nation represented by the government of the day. But loyalties can be strained if soldiers believe that government policies are illegal, wrongful or do not serve the national interest. A soldier who, for example, believes a conflict he is engaged in to be unjust, may follow his conscience and resign.[9] Governments may have an obligation to provide a convincing rationale for any commitment.[10] Perhaps the soldier's new creed should be: 'Ours *is* to reason why'.

Ethics at war

While some argue that ethics have no place in regular warfare or can be counterproductive because opponents will exploit ethical restraint, the fact is that most soldiers behave ethically most of the time. Prisoners of war are not killed out of hand; civilians are not deliberately targeted. Even those perpetrating such acts commonly seek to justify themselves on ethical grounds such as self-defence or necessity. Among soldiers at war a sense of humanity, a respect for laws, and professional pride may all underpin ethical behaviour. Ethical considerations in war may be weak and one factor among many but they are rarely absent altogether.

This is all the more remarkable in that combat itself makes ethical behaviour far more challenging than in most situations. Difficult decisions must be made in difficult circumstances, and pressure can result in 'ethical creep' down a 'slippery slope'.[11] Perhaps it is the stress of combat itself rather than a lack of education and training in ethics *per se* that makes otherwise good people do bad things.[12] Nonetheless, such education and training seems unlikely to make matters worse and might do some good.

Life and death decisions

A soldier is given the means and the legal authority to exercise the power of life and death over others. Even if under direct orders, he or she must make decisions about who lives and who dies among enemies, non-combatants and their personnel, and dozens or hundreds of lives may be at stake. By their nature armed forces seek to secure and exploit maximum disparities in power between themselves and others. And where great disparities exist ethical behaviour is especially needed but is also especially difficult.

Despite the pervasiveness of the media much action in war still takes place where no witnesses, no close supervision and no records exist. A soldier may be able to kill with impunity, knowing that no-one can discover the circumstances, or perhaps even that killing has taken place. In these circumstances ethical behaviour depends more than ever on the moral qualities of the individual. Oddly, some wrongdoers film or photograph their actions (the prisoner abuse scandal at the American-managed Abu Ghraib detention facility in Iraq for example) and bring punishment on themselves. But they are hardly acting out of consciously ethical motives.

Military ethics and law, finally, require personnel to distinguish between the lives of people in a way unique among professions. For the soldier, enemy combatants are legitimate targets but are often difficult to distinguish from non-combatants; once taken prisoner or wounded, combatants cease to be targets (*hors de combat*) but transition from one status to the other is often unclear. Non-combatants are protected by IHLAC and can be put at risk only if military action is judged to be necessary, proportionate to the objective and discriminating as far as reasonably possible. (Whether there is a moral distinction between one's own civilians, enemy civilians and third-party civilians is a source of debate.) Minimising casualties among one's own forces is usually a military and political – if not moral – priority, so dilemmas arise in deciding how much they should be exposed to risk in order to spare non-combatant lives.

Means and ends

Battle has its own imperatives: survival and winning. By instinct, training and culture soldiers tend to do whatever is necessary to save their own lives and the lives of comrades. There may be strong pressure to bend or break moral and legal rules to achieve this. Classic dilemmas include the patrol behind enemy lines sighted by a local civilian: can he be killed before he raises the alarm and jeopardises lives or the mission itself? How harshly can a prisoner be interrogated if he holds information that might save lives? At the very heart of military activity is a tension between results-oriented and rule-oriented behaviour.

This is also true at the national level. A war proclaimed to be in the national interest rouses patriotic support regardless of merit and encourages a readiness to do whatever it takes to secure victory. Yet over the centuries, scholars, lawyers, clerics and others have developed principles intended to guide those contemplating war: the just war tradition or *jus ad bellum*. Importantly this tradition does not permit a free choice of means even in the most justified of causes. Every war should be conducted according to the prevailing law of armed conflict (*jus in bello*) even if an opponent breaks the law and gains an advantage. The reasons for this distinction are both principled and pragmatic. Principle argues that to respond in kind to illegal and unethical behaviour will lead to a common descent into barbarism. Practice suggests that law-breaking behaviour in war often gives military advantage in the short term at best while leading to criticism from the international community, a nation's own citizens and its own armed forces. It may lose 'hearts and minds' while provoking an enemy into a greater determination to prevail.

Fog and friction

Military decisions in war are often taken in the most unpromising circumstances. First, reliable information is usually inadequate, out of date or lacking altogether. Commanders rarely have enough intelligence about the enemy, non-combatants or even their own forces. In this 'feeble light', as Clausewitz puts it, 'one has to trust to talent or to luck'.[13] Moral and legal judgments tend to have good illumination only after the event.

Second, the consequences flowing from different courses of

action in war are notoriously unpredictable. Friction intrudes into every plan. Civilians turn up where they are not expected. Bombs fall in the wrong place. The enemy fights more fiercely than anticipated. Choices must be made with only sketchy knowledge of how each possible course of action might turn out.

Third, the time available for decision making can be extremely short. At the tactical level the choice between shooting an approaching person and holding fire may have to be made in a split second. At higher levels even hours or days may not be long enough to gather as much information as a commander needs to estimate accurately the course of battle.

Finally, psychological and physical pressures distort decision making. Danger is inherent in war and soldiers naturally see their own survival and that of their unit as the highest priority. Commanders may unconsciously overestimate the strength of the enemy or their own weakness such that non-combatant losses appear more justifiable. And physical exhaustion, stress and sleep deprivation undermine any person's capacity for careful and reasoned ethical decisions.

Detachment and disconnection

Many soldiers lose their moral sensibility, devaluing human life as they become familiar with killing or due to remoteness from their victims. Death and destruction on a large scale or on a routine basis tend to produce emotional numbing in even the most compassionate human being. Common psychological defences include demonising the enemy so they appear less than human, regarding non-combatants as covertly supporting the enemy, and repressing compassionate feelings – often paying a price later in the form of post-traumatic stress disorder or moral pain.[14]

Ethical detachment also arises in that individuals are members of a larger organisation which sets objectives, applies powerful pressure on members to achieve those goals, and employs violence as a normal means. By their nature military organisations develop a 'can-do' and 'must-do' ethos that helps to get results but reduces the sense of individual responsibility. Members of a hierarchy thus find it easy to dissociate themselves psychologically from the actions they take in the name of the organisation. Their deeds are 'owned' by someone or something else.

Technology also contributes to psychological detachment by increasing the physical distance between soldiers and their human targets. The spear and longbow meant an enemy need not be killed in face-to-face fighting. Cannon, artillery, bombers and eventually nuclear missiles made long-range attacks on cities 'progressively' more feasible and destructive. Now electronic communications allow controllers, not 'soldiers' or 'pilots', to attack targets thousands of kilometres away. Soon intelligent weapons platforms will be able to seek out specified targets and fire munitions automatically. Ethical choices will no longer be made on the battlefield or in the war room but entered into computer programs.

Peacekeeping and other roles

Most professions encompass a range of activities but none wider than the military. Its expertise and capabilities can be directed toward a wide variety of ends in a wide variety of situations. If the ethical problems of lethal conflict are complex enough, other activities of military organisations such as peacekeeping, border protection, law enforcement and counterterrorism raise many additional ethical dilemmas.[15] There is clearly scope for greater study of and training in the ethics of peace operations.[16]

Peacekeeping

Peacekeeping takes place in a wide range of circumstances, from relatively stable situations to chaotic and dangerous internal conflicts. It is designed to promote peace or at least stability between states or, more commonly, between factions in an internal conflict. Some level of force may be needed but, unlike war proper, peacekeeping does not aim simply at the defeat of an armed enemy. Where military victory is a relatively straightforward goal, peace and stability are amorphous and complex objectives that require a degree of co-operation among contending parties.

In peacekeeping there are usually more players in the game than simply two identified armed forces, and each group is liable to have different ethical and cultural values. Should peacekeepers remain neutral or impartial towards warring factions regardless of their behaviour? Is it proper to do deals with local warlords who abuse human rights? Should a peacekeeping force give life-saving medical assistance, food and water to the civilian community if this directly or indirectly assists one of the warring factions? The reluctance of the UN to take active steps against impending and actual atrocities in Rwanda during 1994 and of NATO in the east Bosnian town of Srebrenica during 1995 exemplifies such dilemmas in the extreme.

Peacekeeping, moreover, may take place in situations where some of the parties are ignorant of the law of armed conflict or deliberately flout it. Yet peacekeepers are required to observe the principles of necessity, discrimination and proportionality and may have highly restrictive rules of engagement and orders for opening fire. One reason is that self-restraint, while carrying risks, is more likely to promote the peace process or at least avoid undermining it.

Peacekeeping forces are usually multinational in composition.

Thus it may be necessary to work with other military forces that have different values, such as lack of professionalism, willingness to accept bribes, brutal treatment of captives, and discrimination against women (whether locals or members of the peacekeeping force). Peacekeepers must also work with non-government organisations of various nationalities. Can these groups be trusted with military intelligence? Should scarce military resources be used to assist with medical supplies or transport of food? In all these areas international law provides little guidance.

Constabulary operations

Law enforcement, border protection and counterterrorism also present distinct ethical challenges. In some of these missions the military's role is closer to policing than traditional soldiering. Yet the philosophies of each activity are very different. Law enforcement does not distinguish between friend and enemy but between criminals and innocent citizens. Its preferred means is to use no or minimum force. The ethical dilemmas of constabulary operations are themselves complex. Inevitably soldiers will be less familiar with such problems and have less training in them than law enforcement professionals.

Another key difference is that whereas military organisations normally direct their efforts against an external enemy or operate in a foreign country, law enforcement and counterterrorism are often directed against one's own nationals. Soldiers may be required to use force against fellow citizens engaged in dangerous or criminal behaviour and are liable to question whether such actions are ethically right, however legal and necessary they appear. Since 11 September 2001, for example, the Royal Australian Air Force has at times been placed on alert to shoot down civilian aircraft, including hijacked passenger planes that might be flown into a high-value target. Governments are reluctant to promote debate on such issues. Yet it seems desirable that more public, professional and scholarly debate should examine these dilemmas in advance, rather than at the last minute or not at all.

Border protection, the phrase used to describe preventing unauthorised arrivals on a nation's territory, is another source of ethical challenges. The Royal Australian Navy, for example, has been tasked to intercept boats carrying refugees or would-be migrants to Australia, and from time to time has turned them around at sea. This duty can entail difficult judgments about whether a boat is seaworthy and able to be sailed to safety. The 'custom of the sea' is that the preservation of life is the first priority regardless of politics or practicalities. Thus one Australian ship's captain defied a direction to abandon asylum seekers at sea, believing it 'neither sensible nor ethically prudent'.[17]

Ethical challenges for the ADF

If ethical decisions are ultimately taken by individuals, it is essential for the ADF to ensure that those involved understand their ethical responsibilities and are encouraged to carry them out. It is a matter of both learning and character, of informed choice and appropriate action. The ADF therefore pays great attention to moulding the character and values of its members through formal and informal education, training and leadership. Those in uniform, however, are never totally isolated from the society from which they are drawn and with which they constantly interact. Two contemporary developments in Australian society have made the promotion of professional military ethics more difficult.

First, individualism has grown apace. The so-called 'me

generation' has good points, such as the desire to realise one's potential to the full. But this may undervalue the ideas of selflessness, loyalty and sacrifice that are traditionally central to the military ethos. Higher levels of education and skills tend to empower individuals, who may become more reluctant to subordinate their lives and actions to the control of others.[18]

Second, distrust of traditional institutions has increased, not least because many have blatantly failed to maintain the high standards they profess. Much-publicised abuses have occurred in the church, business, politics and government agencies as well as in the ADF. The burden is on all such institutions to demonstrate that they understand the ethical challenge and are taking effective steps to meet their proclaimed standards.

While almost everyone agrees that ethical development is desirable for those in uniform, almost everyone has different ideas about its purpose and about how it should be done. Traditionally the development of ethical behaviour in the ADF has relied on three approaches: the example set by individual leaders, the proclamation of values and codes of behaviour, and the creation of administrative systems. All have merits and demerits.

The first relies on leaders demonstrating by their actions integrity, responsibility, trustworthiness and respect for others. There is no doubt that good leaders are essential and can have a powerful positive effect. But bad leaders also set a powerful example, demotivating subordinates and encouraging cynicism. Ultimately, bad leaders may drive out good. No military force can guarantee it will produce good leadership all the time.[19]

Second is the ethical code, a list of 'virtues' such as honesty, integrity and loyalty that are expected of leaders and followers. While these qualities are admirable, such codes can be seen as: bland official statements which can be quietly ignored; unrealistic demands for a standard of behaviour little short of perfection;

unconvincing calls to backsliders who simply ignore them; and a source of resentment for those who do not need them. Sometimes the response is to remain within the letter of the code rather than embrace its spirit. But military organisations want more than mere observance of rules (which may be out of fear of punishment, peer pressure or concern for personal reputation rather than genuine conviction).[20] A more fundamental problem, as one cross-national survey indicates, is that such codes are mostly functionally oriented, exhorting virtues such as courage, loyalty and teamwork, which focus on the goal to be achieved rather than presenting intrinsic ethical demands.[21]

The third approach is to establish processes that punish wrongdoing promptly and effectively, reward good behaviour, and encourage reporting of improper behaviour while protecting whistleblowers.[22] Failure to deal with wrongdoers increases discontent among victims and observers, and may drive members to the media for support in exposing faults. More fundamentally, administrative approaches are generally *post facto* and often fail to change damaging 'habitual behaviour'.[23]

A thorough examination of ethics education and training in the ADF requires consideration of several complex sets of questions.

Aim

Is the aim of ethical development primarily functional (making the ADF more efficient and effective) or aspirational (making soldiers more virtuous)?[24] Are virtuous soldiers compatible with an effective military? If education in ethics 'needs to appeal to the emotions as well as the intellect', what is the balance between character development and providing intellectual understanding?[25] Many armed forces now seem to be aiming beyond creating virtuous soldiers by developing 'good soldiers who are also good *people*.[26] General Maxwell Taylor, a senior American military commander and later diplomat who was active in the 1950s and 1960s, believed that a bad man in private life could be a good soldier, even an officer, while the senior British officer General Sir John Hackett argued in the 1980s that this is simply not possible.[27] Who is to be believed?

Scope

Should ethics development focus primarily on what is relevant to the military mission or embrace as well peacekeeping, counter-terrorism, border protection and so on? Should it include ethical issues across Australian society? Is there also a need for the ADF to understand concepts of culture, religion and the working of societies very different from those of Australia?[28]

Approaches and methods

Should a distinction be made between ethics education and ethics training, the latter being more prescriptive than the former? Who should present ethics education? Should the responsibility be given to officers, chaplains, lawyers, or academics (ethicists or behavioural scientists)? Perhaps a variety of teachers with different approaches is actually beneficial in stimulating thought. Which methods are more effective: presentations, role-playing, case studies (real or imagined, ancient or modern)? Should personnel be directed to learn or encouraged to self-educate?

Organisational practicalities

If officers carry the greatest ethical burden, all military personnel at all levels are responsible in law for their behaviour.[29] Yet decisions must be made about who should be taught (officer cadets, officers, non-commissioned officers and other ranks); at what stage of their Service careers should the teaching be delivered;

at which institutions – cadet academies, staff colleges or within individual units; at what depth; and for what length of time?

Ownership

Who owns ethics in the ADF? If everyone owns ethics, as is sometimes asserted, this can mean that no-one really takes responsibility for it. Consequently ethics education may be consigned to what free space can be found in the program, who is at hand to teach it, and when personnel happen to be available to learn. Are the ADF institutions currently responsible for ethics education properly resourced and empowered? What is expected of the Centre for Defence Leadership and Ethics operating at the Australian Defence College – too little or too much? Should there be, for example, a 'Chief of Army Ethics', as in the British Army?[30]

Does it work?

The final question is the most difficult: how do we know if ethical development – whatever form it takes – is doing any good? Ethics, some argue, are 'caught' rather than taught.[31] Overdoing ethics education may lead to 'ethics fatigue'.[32] Youth, Aristotle argued, is not the best age for the serious study of ethics, since young people lack empathy and experience.[33] Perhaps ethics training is by its nature 'highly perishable'.[34] Yet attempts must be made in the hope or expectation that some ethical principles will be understood and followed sooner or later in a person's military career.[35]

Principles for an ethical ADF

What is required is a sense among military personnel that ethical behaviour can and should permeate all military activities, and that ethical behaviour results more from debate than *diktat*. This debate should take three forms. It must be personal, by which I mean within the thinking and conscience of each individual. It must be between members of the military organisation. And it must be between the military profession and the wider society. The aim of ethics education should be to promote such debate, recognising that ethical behaviour is a struggle for everyone, even (or especially) senior leaders. It is not a matter of observing 'unbreakable rules' but of wrestling with complex and in some cases insoluble problems. Values and ethics are things primarily to work out for oneself, with some help from others. As the English novelist John Mortimer put it in his autobiography *Clinging to the Wreckage*: 'My father [...] never told me the difference between right and wrong [...] that's why I remain so deeply in his debt'. What is needed are people in uniform who understand the nature of ethical thinking, who acquire and develop appropriate analytical skills, and who recognise the ethical dimension of a problem instinctively and immediately.

Debate within the ADF will be much aided by efforts to move its culture in the direction of greater self-learning, self-correction and self-regulation by groups and individuals.[36] Military forces have been 'learning organisations' for generations and there is no reason why they cannot learn ethics.[37] Debate also serves the purpose of informing those in uniform about the values they share with each other – or sometimes shows up differences in values that need to be resolved.

Ideas about military ethics also need to be shared with the wider community. It is an unfortunate fact that the subject is little studied in Australian universities and is often dealt with by the media only in sensational terms. Military sociology is likewise neglected in Australia.[38] While UNSW Canberra has taken important positive steps, it remains the case that 'Australia has no independent, university-based intellectual centre for the development of rigorous academic research on the human dimension of the military institution'.[39] Nor is there a network of military ethicists, such as the newly formed 'Compass Group' based at UNSW Canberra, involving a number of civilian universities and colleges committed to military ethics research and teaching.[40]

There is no best single method of education and training in ethics in the ADF. Debate, character development and leadership must all play a part. Nor are there clear and immediate measurements of the effectiveness of ethical development. Spectacular lapses in behaviour may be evidence of failure of some kind but in themselves do not prove that progress has not been made across the board or will not be made in the future. Ethical improvement is a long-term process that requires continuous effort while offering few opportunities for self-congratulation.

16

MILITARY ETHICS EDUCATION IN THE ARMY: AN ACHILLES HEEL?

JAMIE CULLENS

In addressing the vocation of uniformed service, the noted Canadian author, historian and public intellectual Michael Ignatieff explained that behaving ethically 'is not an optional extra [...] it is the absolute core of what defines you as the warrior profession. It is ethical restraint which makes the distinction between a warrior and a barbarian [...] your life is one continuous set of ethical challenges'.[1] This exhortation effectively and persuasively encapsulates the fundamental ethical challenge for uniformed men and women as members of the profession of arms.

The Australian Army's operational experiences in places like Somalia, East Timor, Iraq and Afghanistan have highlighted the responsibilities and professionalism required of its personnel to ensure tactical success on the ground. These traits have been demonstrated and tested in many ways, including the controlled and measured way in which personnel responded to crises and combat; the disciplined use of force; and the empathetic, positive and friendly engagement with local communities. Such leadership and professionalism, and the tactical success they engender, are the foundation for strategic, as well as battlefield, success. Most of these ideas have been captured in the Army's outstanding doctrinal publications that are updated on a regular basis.[2] Despite a great deal of change in technology and tactics, the *nature* of war is unlikely to change, as recent conflicts have demonstrated. A highly experienced Australian military leader, Steve Day, observed that:

> War is a dehumanising experience for all concerned. All
> our civilising influences – family, the comforts of home,
> regular meals, routine rest, personal safety – are removed.
> Soldiers live and sleep rough. They see and are involved in
> unspeakable events. And the constant fear of danger can
> slowly drain one's inner strength. A soldier's humanity and
> compassion for fellow human beings can begin to erode.
> In this atmosphere, the wall of integrity and discipline
> that separates an honourable soldier from an armed thug
> is severely tested. One of the great challenges in war is that
> you must at once use both extreme violence and extreme
> humanity.[3]

The generally high ethical standards in Army barracks and operations to date are due primarily to appropriate selection processes as well as the exemplary training and education provided to its personnel. The Army has also had the opportunity to validate its training and test its skills through participating in conflicts of choice rather than conflicts of necessity, with East Timor being the notable exception. Such an approach has resulted in the deployment of highly trained niche force elements in 'controlled' operations and the resultant casualties have been mercifully few. In this context it has relied on its people to 'do the right thing' in the inevitable chaos and uncertainty of war. Australia has also been fortunate in achieving positive outcomes while avoiding large-scale casualties in the operational environment for more than a decade. Steve Tilbrook, the Australian infantry platoon commander present at the 1994 Kibeho massacre in Rwanda, noted that the 'only reason there was a good outcome I believe was because we got lucky'.

While Australia's operational performance has been commendable, and has been accompanied by some good fortune, it is evident that from 'duty of care', 'risk mitigation' and 'reputation management' perspectives, the Army needs to put more effort into training and educating its people in the field of ethics and ethical decision making to mitigate the risk of failure in future conflict. What follows is a personal reflection based on more than a decade's experience working in the field of military ethics education in the Army and the wider Australian Defence Force (ADF). I have drawn on anecdotes and interviews from Army personnel, good and bad, positive and perilous, in developing my own views on a way ahead for ethics training and education within the ADF.

Training or education?

Are military ethics properly deemed a training or educational process? ADF doctrine attempts to explain the differences between the two and provides a good definition. Training is defined 'as a planned process to inculcate and modify attitude, knowledge or skill behaviour' to achieve effective performance 'against a pre-determined standard', while education aims at 'developing the knowledge, skill, moral values and understanding required in all aspects of life'.[4] Weapon handling, tactical procedures, the application of rules of engagement and orders for opening fire are training activities whereas interpretation and application of the law of war and ethical decision making are educational interventions. In sum, the Army's approach to military ethics needs to be a combination of the two.

This duality is recognised in current practice. The issues that require further attention include the need for structured programs on all professional development and promotion courses, consistent support from the chain of command and a culture that encourages discussion of challenging and sensitive issues in a non-threatening learning environment. Australia is the only Coalition partner to include the word 'ethical' in its definition of military leadership. This insistence is something of which the nation can be proud but its preservation is not a given without sustained effort.

In thinking about ethics the place to start is with intentions. Is the purpose of ethics education and training:

> to change character [...] or to build professional identity
> and change behaviour? Is it purely functional – designed
> to create soldiers who will possess the virtues to function
> effectively as soldiers – or is it aspirational – designed to
> create people who are in some sense morally 'good'?[5]

Ethics are essentially a combination of functional choices and aspirational ideals, focused on the question 'what ought one to do?' Discussions throughout the professional military education spectrum focus on inculcating Army values (courage, initiative, respect, teamwork) as a functional dimension, and they are aspirational in the sense that soldiers need to be prepared for making life and death decisions under the most trying circumstances imaginable. Perhaps an end point for this process is that all senior leaders should be capable of making decisions at the most advanced stage, the level of universal principles, in the American psychologist Lawrence Kohlberg's theory of moral development. Hugh Smith, a long-term and highly experienced educator of Service officers and a contributor to the volume, believes that ethical behaviour is essential in all military activities and that it can be developed through discussion, which can take three forms:

> It must be personal i.e. within the thoughts and conscience of each individual. It must be between the members of the military profession in its broadest definition. And it must be between the military profession and wider society.[6]

He also makes the insightful observation that the 'unexamined organisation is not worth working for'. This theme is applied throughout current courses in the ADF. The Army currently adopts more of a functional approach, as reflected in the content of the various character guidance and military ethics workshops. The aims of military ethics education should be both functional and aspirational, and further work is required to analyse precisely what the Army is trying to achieve. This work would require a much stronger focus on ethical theory and this could be delivered through contracted academics. This will be a demanding task and is best done by a multidisciplinary team, led by an experienced officer with the appropriate background and passion for the work.

Another key consideration for military ethics education is one of consistency of approach and delivery across the Army. Programs are currently delivered in an *ad hoc* manner and, in the case of star rank officers and senior non-commissioned officers, are significantly underdone. As the ADF continues its journey of adopting a holistic approach to education in military ethics there is an opportunity for the Army to look to kindred organisations and develop considerable synergy with this work while maintaining the specific cultural approaches to the issues.

Given that ethics can be taught and the Army recognises their importance, what are the pitfalls made in the delivery process? James Toner, professor of international relations and military ethics at the United States Air War College, argues that in some cases the assumption is made that military recruits of all persuasions are an ethical void and need to be built from the bottom up. Evidence would suggest that this is not the case with the majority of young people attracted to service in the Army. More effort should be exerted in the early stages of educational programs to develop an understanding of what the trainees know and to assess their experience of managing ethical dilemmas. Some would argue that a reasonable baseline is values education in Australian schools and that most programs are effective. Consequently, 'moral waivers' have not been considered in the local recruiting process, although the United States has relied upon them heavily in recent years as the pool of willing volunteers has diminished. In the most general sense, the Australian Army continues to recruit good people. Conversely, Toner notes it is a mistake to assume that soldiers have superior ethical judgement. There is no reason to suppose this is so. He points out that while the chaplains have a role in the character development process, the ethical climate of the unit set by the commander is far more important in developing ethical attitudes. In effect, 'ethics will be caught more often than they are taught'. If an ethical organisation is needed, ethical leaders need to be appointed. We cannot expect commanders to be capable of delivering lectures on ethics and to be 'conscience stricken by every act and every order'. The idea that every commander should be an ethical role model is fair enough but this does not mean that every commander possesses expertise in teaching military ethics.[7] Toner's views apply to the

Army and are important considerations as decisions are made on implementation plans for teaching military ethics.

Investment in recruitment, training, education and career development of the Army's most junior personnel and leaders continue to pay substantial dividends. Such dividends can include a national reputation for decisive and legal use of lethal force; a firm, fair and friendly attitude towards local populations; and a general absence of careless personal behaviour. This situation, however, could change pending the outcomes of continuing reviews, including examination of the culture within the ADF's Special Operations command. This increased focus on professionalism and additional investment in education needs to include provision for structured military ethics education on a 'cradle to grave' basis, as well as the use of 'ethics' language in the Army's senior leadership dialogue.

This whole-of-career education needs to be built around decision making frameworks designed to assist in the detailed analysis of ethical dilemmas. The framework in most use across the ADF is the St James Ethics Centre model. It is based on the Centre's work with the Australian Defence College and the Singapore Armed Forces over the past decade. The keynote presentation is titled 'Ethical Intelligence and Fitness for Command'.[8] The presentation combines aspects of moral philosophy with military command and leadership components to produce a framework for making ethical decisions. The framework is composed of a series of questions and decision points and has been well accepted by students over the years. The utility of this framework can be validated in various ways.

The existence of a series of unresolved issues in the organisation represents a greater challenge than a public scandal. A survey conducted by the Centre for Defence Leadership and Ethics (CDLE) at the Australian Defence College in 2008 with a reasonable sample of Army personnel (over 300) suggests we may have a sizeable number of 'little ethical problems' that should be systematically addressed. The survey also defined an ethical failure for the profession of arms as 'a situation in which unethical behaviour occurs on a significant/protracted scale (command level, scope or period)'.[9] My own engagement with officers studying at the Defence College suggests that the Army is an ethical organisation and for the most part tries to be ethical. But the Army's senior leaders recognise that there are problems. Several of Australia's Coalition partners have endured serious breaches of moral standards by their forces: the Canadians during the Somali famine relief operation in March 1993, the United States Army with the Abu Ghraib interrogation and detention facility after 2004, and the British Army with the murder of Baha Mousa in Iraq during September 2003. These incidents prompt the question: why should Australia bother doing anything more in this field of education when everything seems fine? Our selection processes are good; our training is good (probably outstanding in many areas); and our leaders are good. What else do we need to do?

Historical and contemporary challenges

The seminal work on Australian infantry culture in Vietnam, *Combat Battalion* by Robert Hall, examined the ethical behaviour of an Infantry battalion on operations in Vietnam during 1969–70. The war in Vietnam 'placed young Australian soldiers in positions of impossible moral ambiguity and expected them to cope alone. Still, the number and extent of moral or ethical failures was probably no larger than in earlier wars'.[10] Did this change with our more recent conflicts? Interviews that I conducted with Army personnel as part of a research project several years ago neatly encapsulated the nature and complexity of dilemmas faced by personnel on a regular basis on operations in Afghanistan. An officer recounted two compelling stories. In the first he explained that after clearing a village he was told to move on because the village would be targeted. He knew that there would be civilian casualties so he disobeyed the order and stayed *in situ* for two more days. He lied to his chain of command but displayed extraordinary moral courage in his actions. In the second he recalls:

> We got caught up in an intense and long running firefight.
> Things all of a sudden tapered off then stopped. After a
> few minutes of quiet, a solitary unarmed figure came down
> from the enemy position towards us. We motioned him to
> stop. He was very dirty and sweating but after searching
> him, found that he was only carrying a water bottle. He had
> clearly been involved in the fighting but was now unarmed
> and we could not prove anything. At that stage I had two
> Corporals and two soldiers with me. We discussed what
> we were going to do with him. The Corporals said let's
> just shoot him and bury him down the back and be done
> with it. The soldiers said nothing. I said let him go and the
> Corporals objected. I said let him go, and we did. I often
> wonder what would have happened if I had not been there.[11]

Both of these stories highlight the very strong moral position adopted by the youthful commander under very stressful conditions. His actions epitomised the values and actions that the Army expects in its leaders. Preparing young and inexperienced leaders for situations such as these needs to be a key focus of the professional education programs that individuals attend throughout their careers and it should be undertaken during periods of low operational activity.

The Army should also provide appropriate opportunities for personnel to reflect on the most confronting aspect of the profession, the act of killing. Again, I see this as a duty of care that cannot be neglected. The best environment to tackle this challenge is found in structured, facilitated discussions on leadership and ethics conducted in a non-threatening environment:

> From a first hand killing experience, I can break down emotions into three distinct phases. The first of these is the absolute and total dedication to the task of tracking down enemy soldiers who we knew were either commanding enemy cells or had already committed serious crimes against the coalition or the local populace. Emotions at this point were focussed totally on the mission and the importance of killing the enemy. At the time of killing the enemy, there was an initial feeling of euphoria at having completed the mission, closely followed by period of sympathy towards the target's family who were likely to never see him again. The final phase was transition onto the next target, which generally occurred immediately after returning to the base at the conclusion of the mission.[12]

Of comparable interest is the incidence of ethical issues encountered in the barrack or home-base environment. Perhaps the most compelling example of the way things can get out of hand is the experience, mentioned briefly above, of the Canadian Airborne Regiment that was part of the United Nations (UN) mission to Somalia in 1993. The catastrophic incident during the deployment was the torture and murder of a sixteen-year-old Somali youth by a small group of Canadian soldiers. The telling element of the case was that the poor behaviour of the perpetrators had been identified in the barracks environment before they were deployed overseas. The individuals' personal files had been stamped 'not to deploy on operations'. There are recent interesting Australian perspectives on these issues. In more than a decade of operations in Iraq and Afghanistan, many leaders highlighted their concerns about deploying with numbers of personnel deemed 'not fit for operations'.[13] During the delivery of the Canadian Somalia case study to young officers on a promotion course several years ago, the group concluded that we would be 'kidding ourselves' if we thought similar incidents could not occur in Australian deployments if there were leadership failures and a weak or unethical command climate.

Other ethical concerns raised in formal courses over the Army's many years of operations included inappropriate behaviour of commanders; witnessing foreign security service mistreatment of detainees; the challenges of local contract administration in operational environments where corruption is a cultural practice; inappropriate initiation activities in some units; sexual assault covered up by the chain of command; concerns about targeting processes when operating in an international coalition; abuse of detainees (on land and at sea); the possibility of hostile acts against minors; dealing with cultural issues concealing or excusing illegality; and the abuse of power by leaders. These issues reveal the range of challenges faced by the organisation's leaders at all levels and the need for continuing vigilance.

Teaching materials already exist to support education and training programs that deal with these issues. 'Project Achilles' involved a number of Navy, Army and Air Force officers between 2010 and 2012. The aim was to develop a series of half-day military ethics courses covering all promotion levels from new recruits to two-star rank.[14] Regrettably, the Army has accessed the material only occasionally over the ensuing years. The educational package includes case studies, video material and instructor notes. The material was designed specifically as a vehicle to generate discussion among students, covering a range of topics from reflections on the massacre of South Vietnamese civilians at My Lai in 1968 to the failure of UN forces to prevent genocide at Srebrenica during the 1995 Bosnian War.

The one-year Command and Staff College course for majors is a critical development intervention for officers aspiring to command and higher ranks. Due to the seniority of the students and the depth of their leadership and operational experience there are many opportunities to reinforce key elements of military ethics. As well as the personal testimonies of leaders who have had to deal with ethical dilemmas, there is ample opportunity for small group discussion of personal challenges in non-judgmental sessions with peers that are facilitated by more experienced officers. One presenter reflected on his experience with the course in its early years, remarking that some of the ethical dilemmas described by the students 'involved actions that were at the very least serious violations of the expectations of the military'.[15]

The more senior course (for those at colonel rank) is the culmination of a successful career. This course highlights the need for deeper and more creative thinking in a dynamic strategic and political environment. There are opportunities to discuss concepts such as the Bathsheba Syndrome,[16] the Melian dialogue from Thucydides, and ethical failings at the strategic level of Defence. As many officers do not get the chance to attend this course, the Services need to provide and promote other opportunities for those who will nonetheless exercise significant leadership responsibilities. In part, this is simple risk management and the discharge of a duty of care. Interventions should include the outstanding Melbourne-based 'Cranlana' program for enlightened and responsible leadership, organisational case studies and candid discussions with senior leaders about their ethical challenges. Such an approach would result in a marked improvement in the confidence with which senior leaders engage in ethical decision making.

A critical element of contemporary military ethics education programs is the use of personal testimony. In this educational approach leaders who have been involved in challenging situations and have had to make difficult ethical decisions in 'grey' environments where the decision has negative impacts tell their stories. Many of them find the experience confronting but the process cathartic. A former commanding officer discussing the poor command climate in his unit and the consequences of his court martial; survivors of helicopter crashes reliving their trauma; survivors of Auschwitz concentration camp; and commanders reflecting on unethical or inappropriate orders create unforgettable learning experiences.

The final observation relates to the need for an ethical climate survey. The Canadian Army displayed considerable institutional moral courage in conducting one in Kandahar several years ago, although the results have never been made public. I am aware that the questions included whether a uniformed person would report comrades mistreating non-combatants, whether they had observed a colleague causing unnecessary damage to private property, and/or had witnessed stealing from non-combatants.

Future development

The Army's commitment to ethics training and education fluctuates with the interest and commitment of the individuals who are responsible for its conduct. Consequently, the application of ethics education in the Professional Military Education (PME) continuum remains disjointed despite the experience of years of operations. Military ethics education and training in the Army would be enhanced by the following proposals. First, continue the annual Jonathan Church ethical soldier award. The award recognises excellence in soldiering while highlighting the ethical dimension of the profession of arms. Second, the Army currently posts Reservists to the Centre for Defence Leadership and Ethics (CDLE) at the Australian Defence College. Over the years a solid instructor capability has developed but each year the commitment varies owing to the vagaries of resource allocation. The demand for instructors from Army units and training institutions is high. A lot more could be done with limited investment. The Army should appoint a Lieutenant Colonel or Colonel into a 'Chief of Ethics' position. The British Army has recently established such a role. Third, the Army needs to adopt a systematic, structured approach across the professional military education continuum. This was endorsed and directed at one stage by a former Chief of Army using the Project Achilles course material but it has never been implemented properly. Some institutions stated that they were implementing programs (but without the Achilles material) whilst others claimed that there was no time in the program due to other mandatory training requirements. Fourth, partner with a university and engage their ethicists. Civilian ethicists could be brought into the Army 'tent'. The Army can also access the UNSW online military ethics courses. Fifth, support military ethics research in the Army and initiate an ethical climate survey similar to that applied by the Canadians in Afghanistan. This will require moral courage, given it has been suggested over the years but never pursued. There are also opportunities to update material such as the use of the ABC's *Australian Story* material on the Commando issues. Sixth, increase the emphasis on education in the Law of Armed Conflict and debate the challenges on all promotion courses. Seventh, moral courage sessions should be mandatory on Army promotion courses. The sessions delivered by CDLE over the years are very powerful and in high demand. The feedback is consistently very positive. Eighth, senior officers do not receive as much ethics education as their responsibilities require. As individuals rise in rank, the ethical challenges become more complex, particularly in relation to interactions with the political environment. The pre-command course has little emphasis on military ethics. Moral reasoning requires continual reflection and practice. The 'Cranlana' program gets excellent feedback but few officers get the opportunity to attend. Finally, commanding officers are responsible for the ethical climate of their units. Many are not comfortable using the language of ethics and values. Commanders need to be given the opportunity to debate the ethical challenges of the day and relate the experiences to their soldiers.

The Army's approach to the delivery of military ethics education has improved substantially since 2002. But after more than a decade of war it remains disjointed, *ad hoc* and unprofessional. The program relies heavily on osmosis and the efforts of enthusiastic amateurs as opposed to the delivery of a systematic curriculum by subject matter experts. It also suffers from the perceptions and personal bias of individuals in the chain of command. In essence it is routinely considered an optional 'add-on' as opposed to being core business in the Army's professional military education system. The standard response from education institutions facing so many mandatory demands on teaching time is usually, 'Where are we supposed to fit this in?' But the report of the Defence Abuse Response Taskforce (DART) tabled in Federal Parliament in November 2014 made clear there is no room for complacency when it comes to education in this field.[17] The

DART process cost the taxpayer $66.63 million and dealt with 1723 complainants. Some 846 people received the maximum compensation of $50000. A total of 133 complainants were referred to police. Two very powerful statements in the Report are worthy of close and continuing attention:

> if Defence leaders had not failed to act on their actual or constructive knowledge that abuse was occurring, much of the abuse reported to the Taskforce would not have taken place.

and:

> The Defence culture described in many of the complaints was that you do not jack (or dob) on your mates, even if those so called mates sexually or physically abused you. This flawed and dysfunctional culture discouraged some complainants from reporting abuse and, in other cases, complainants who did not report their abuse were further abused and mistreated.[18]

Cultural renewal is underway in the Army and a professional approach to military ethics education remains a pressing task. Until this positive change occurs and change is fully implemented, the paucity of this education remains an 'Achilles heel'.

17

THE PRACTICALITIES OF ETHICAL ACCOUNTABILITY

CHRIS FIELD

The Australian Army wants officers and soldiers who can blend, harmonise and put into action practical ethical behaviours with their land combat mission. Behavioural consistency requires an ethical framework, professional competence, practically applicable values, and continuous training, education and learning. I want to explore these ideas before concluding that ethical behaviour, in words and deeds, is a critical element of the Army's fighting power. For the Australian Army, fighting power 'is the way in which Army generates its capacity through the integration of the physical, moral and intellectual components at both the individual and organisational level'.[1]

Ethics

Ethics can be defined as: 'moral principles that govern a person's behaviour'.[2] The Australian Army's capstone doctrine, *Land Warfare Doctrine – 1, The Fundamentals of Land Power, 2014* makes three references to ethics:

> The profession of arms is unique because of the importance of its task, the moral and *ethical dedication* required to achieve it, and the lethal nature of its capabilities.[3]

> The Australian Army is committed to the profession of arms. Its members are experts trained in the *ethical application of land combat power.*[4]

> A professional soldier is an expert in the profession of arms. These men and women adhere to the highest *ethical standards* and are dedicated to the service of the nation.[5]

Schools of ethics in Western philosophy can be divided, very roughly, into three areas. The first draws on the work of Aristotle and holds that the virtues (such as justice, charity and generosity) are dispositions to act in ways that benefit both the person possessing them and that person's society. The second, defined particularly by the German philosopher Immanuel Kant (1724–1804), makes the concept of duty central to morality: humans are bound, from a knowledge of their duty as rational beings, to obey the categorical imperative to respect other rational beings. The third is utilitarianism, which asserts that the guiding principle of conduct should be the greatest happiness or benefit for the greatest number.[6]

The principal challenge for leaders and soldiers in the face of combat is the practical blending and harmonisation of Aristotle's virtues, Kant's moral duty and Utilitarianism's greatest good for the greatest number combined, for the Australian Army at least, with the requirements of *Land Warfare Doctrine – 1, The Fundamentals of Land Power, 2014.* This blending and harmonising aims to ensure the simultaneous lethal nature of our capabilities, the ethical application of land fighting power, and the application of ethical standards. How can ethics and lethality be harmonised in a manner that is practical for commanders and soldiers committed to the complexity of combat? As Carl von Clausewitz noted centuries ago, 'every war is rich in unique episodes. Each is an uncharted sea, full of reefs [...] meaning that the military profession constantly faces multitudes of complex challenges [...] ethical behaviour included'.[7]

Consequently, the ethical standards of uniformed personnel must hold firm every second of every day. Soldiers are always soldiers, in or out of uniform. They must, therefore, hold themselves to the highest ethical standards, making choices about conduct based on firm ethical foundations. With such a foundation in place, soldiers need to understand and prepare for 'factors that generate chance, friction and uncertainty for our people including enemy action, adverse weather, complex terrain, poor coordination, insufficient or inaccurate information and human error'.[8] This also means ensuring that Australian personnel maintain the ability to defeat a near-peer (i.e. comparable) enemy. To stretch collective thinking and increase the demands on training and education, the Australian Defence Force (ADF) must not think of 'near-peer' as nearly the ADF's peer but as nearly an adversary's peer. This means ADF members must be enabled to make ethical choices in complex situations to solve problems of strategy, operations, tactics, command and control, logistics, technology and, of course, ethics.[9]

The military profession

The requirements of the military profession are unique. The Australian Army is a professional 'entity that threatens and when necessary applies violence to achieve national objectives'.[10] Simultaneously, the Australian nation 'must trust the standing army to respect the law of the land and be capable of restraint and prudence in the use of appropriate and sanctioned violence'.[11] Eliot Cohen, the Army's inaugural EG Keogh Chair in Land Warfare Studies, contends that although the military is a profession, 'it does not, in fact, resemble [professions such as] medicine, [engineering] or the law' in four respects.[12]

First, unlike medicine, engineering or the law, the military profession responds to just one employer. The military profession binds itself to the government and has one fundamental structure. The ADF does not answer to individual State governments and cannot be sub-contracted by private entities for non-public activities.

Second, the military profession has an ambiguous purpose. All professional activities present difficulties of moral choice and ultimate purpose for their practitioners. The ultimate purpose of the medical profession is to cure patients of their diseases or, at the very least, alleviate any pain or suffering. An engineer's purpose is to construct objects to specified standards that reflect functionality and safety. Lawyers are servants of the courts whether they are acting as judges, prosecutors or advocates. By way of contrast, a military professional's ultimate purpose is 'altogether hazier'. It is 'the achievement of political ends designated by [government] […] but because political objectives are just that – political – they are often ambiguous, contradictory and uncertain'.[13]

Third, the military profession makes a virtue of adaptation. Medical, engineering and legal professionals generally require common technical expertise across time, nationality and place. Conversely, military professionals must constantly adapt their 'conception of professionalism to the war before them'.[14] For the Australian Army, operational requirements have changed markedly over the past century. Trench warfare is no longer a skill that need be taught. Each conflict comes with its own diverse expeditionary environments, and adaptive enemies are always seeking a new advantage against well-honed military capabilities. These demands require different conceptions of professionalism, equipment, force structure and leadership.

Fourth, the military profession is uniquely mandated to apply violence. According to Cohen, this mandate poses a series of dilemmas for uniformed personnel. He notes that 'lawyers continually appear in court or draw up legal instruments [...] doctors routinely operate or prescribe medication [...] [and] engineers build bridges or computers [...] [but] soldiers very rarely manage violence, or at least not large scale violence'.[15] Even military professionals who do apply violence in war 'do so for a very small portion of their careers, and rarely occupy the same position in more than one conflict'.[16]

When these four distinctions are considered together they presuppose the existence of an ethical framework that is clearly understood, well drilled and deeply inculcated. Plainly, this foundation must be emphasised and embodied in both words and deeds. The origins of our ethics are principles but the outcomes are practical.

Australian Army values

The ADF and the Australian Public Service have easy-to-remember and ethically grounded corporate values that can be employed to provide uniformed and civilian personnel with an inventory of what constitutes ethical behaviour. The specific values articulated by the Army are courage, initiative, respect and teamwork. The Army's aim in applying these values is to assure certain outcomes. Even under the most arduous conditions, when a person is cold, hungry, scared and uncertain, the Army's members can rely on their moral compass to discern and deliver ethically consistent conduct. Other contributors to this collection such as Matthew Beard, Ian Langford and Tom McDermott emphasise that the values underpinning ethics require a context. The Australian Army's values have a context of their own:[17]

Courage: Every Australian soldier is expected to demonstrate physical and moral courage. To be courageous in the Army is to believe in the Army's mission, its goals and one's mates, and involves doing what is right and fair in all circumstances and under the most demanding conditions.

Initiative: Every Australian soldier is expected to show initiative whenever required and to be committed to continuous learning and self-development. Initiative is fundamental to professional mastery and essential to the effective practice of mission command.

Respect: Respect is the glue that binds the other values together. It is the quality that will both temper and sharpen the hard edge that must be a part of military service in order to survive and prevail in war. Furthermore, the Australian nation must trust the standing army to respect the law of the land and be capable of restraint and prudence in using appropriate and sanctioned violence. Respect also extends to those whom the Army is entrusted to protect and support when deployed in Australia and overseas.

Teamwork: The Australian Army is a team of teams in which all soldiers are expected to be able to rely on their mates. Without a team a soldier is just another person. Robust, cohesive teams are the personnel building blocks of the Army's capability.

The ADF's three recruit schools, the Australian Defence Force Academy, and the single Service officer training colleges provide 'only a foundation upon which to build' the training and education of uniformed people.[18] Once the foundation is provided, all serving members in the trained forces of the ADF are obliged to undertake continuing self- and prescribed training and education across the demands of their profession, including ethics. If professional education and development for either leaders or soldiers were to stagnate or cease, their ability to function in an operational environment would be adversely affected. Indeed, it is likely they would become ineffective or, worse, detrimental to the national interests. Ethics are critical to mission success and the corporate health and wellbeing of the ADF.

Ethics applied to the military profession

The 3rd Brigade's *Human Performance Framework* is an example of complementary ethics education and training designed to reinforce the general need for ethical conduct. The framework stands on three pillars: support to families provided by the Geckos Family Centre; support to personnel who are wounded, injured and unwell provided by the Soldier Recovery Centre in North Queensland; and enhancing the performance of all soldiers provided by the Vasey Resilience Centre.[19] The 3rd Brigade works to empower leaders and soldiers by focusing on strengthening and enabling measures including building physical, mental, cognitive, emotional and ethical resilience in people. The aim is help personnel strive and thrive in combat and in life, and to create opportunities for post-traumatic growth.[20]

As Tom Frame observes in his chapter, the ADF will liberalise 'as Australian society liberalises'. The ADF cannot become isolated from the Australian community or indifferent to large-scale social change if it is to serve the Australian people and be responsive to their interests. The 3rd Brigade has sought a close and constructive partnership with the people of Townsville. This is the community in which Brigade members work and live with their families and from which ADF personnel derive another important sense of personal belonging. This partnership is being strengthened by the *Defence Community Accord* and the continuing development of the *Townsville Defence Community Panel and Forum*. These connections with the civilian community provide another dimension for enhancing the wellbeing of uniformed personnel and developing an ethical outlook that reflects the values and expectations of the nation.

The Australian Army strives to nurture leaders and soldiers who can blend and harmonise Aristotle's virtues, Kant's moral duty and Utilitarianism's greatest good for the greatest number within a professional outlook producing lethal capabilities, the ethical application of land fighting power and an adherence to ethical standards. Because war remains a profoundly human endeavour, the application of ethics by leaders and soldiers remains a deeply human enterprise. The need for clear and compelling ethics education and training will never diminish. Each year the Army inducts thousands of new recruits as future officers and soldiers who need to inculcate the Army's values and imbibe its ethical standards. As armed conflict changes and technology and tactics constantly evolve, more experienced personnel also face new challenges and fresh dilemmas. Consequently, discussions about ethics need to be vibrant and engage the very junior and the most senior, because each has a part to play in sustaining the Army's culture and the maintenance of ethical standards. Its ethical training remains a work in progress and complacency could be its greatest enemy.

POSTSCRIPT

ALBERT PALAZZO

This book contains varied viewpoints that underscore the complexity inherent to ethics and ethical decision making. The authors were asked to tackle the topic from many directions and they have done just that. In peace, in war, in uniform and sometimes out of uniform, ethics have played a central and often challenging role in Australia's military operations.

That ethics is a complex subject should not come as a surprise to the reader. Humans are complex at both the individual and collective levels. What we decide and how we act is a result of the intersection of our emotions with reason and our life experiences, as well as the residual instincts that evolution has bequeathed to us. War has been known from the start of the historical record and as far back into the archaeological as can be determined. Throughout, it has been and remains among humanity's most difficult and complex pursuits.

To regulate their actions humans typically set rules that define the boundaries of legitimate activity and decision making. To regulate war, there exists a copious array of treaties, agreements and theories that shape decision making and place limits on what can and cannot be done, by whom and to whom. Despite such rules, however, context remains the key variable in ethical decision making, thereby ensuring that ethical behaviour in war remains a challenging goal and a shifting objective whose attainment must never be taken for granted but must be continually pursued.

Also in these chapters there is another observation regarding ethical decision making. It is perhaps less obvious, but no less important. Ethics are a central component of war because waging ethical war is a key enabler to mission success. Ethical standards cannot be separated from war, if war is to remain useful and not devolve into something else, for example, genocide.

The Australian Army Mission Statement makes no mention of ethics. Arguably it should, although the Army and the wider Australian Defence Force (ADF) is alive to the need for a sound ethical foundation to everything that its members do. The mission is: 'Army is to prepare land forces for war in order to defend Australia and its national interests'.[1] That there is no mention of the application of violence or the destruction of property in the mission statement is simply a result of organisational jurisdiction. The Army prepares the land force for war whereas Joint Operations Command is responsible for its waging. But the absence of clear language on this point does not matter; violence and destruction are implicit to the mission statement and in a similar vein there is no need for a direct reference to ethics. Both are understood.

Military practitioners and scholars are well aware of war's tendency to violence and destruction. But they also understand that violence, and the death and destruction it causes, are not the end point of war. Nor is killing and causing suffering the objective. Rather, as those who comprehend Clausewitz's writings would understand, the aim of war is the attainment of a defined political goal.[2] At some point peace will be restored and with it the normal intercourse between peoples will be recommenced, whether the societies in question be at the state, tribe or clan levels of social organisation. Warriors must look beyond the waging of battle if they are to achieve the peace they seek.

Keeping the focus on peace is why ethics in war are so critical. Peace comes about when one side concedes to the other's onslaught. That is success in battle, but a lasting peace requires more. If a peace is to endure, the combatants and the people for whom they fight must not be brutalised. They must not kill or be killed simply for the sake of it. The force employed must be proportionate and just, and non-combatants must be protected. The seeds of the next conflict must not be sown. The restoration of normality should not be impeded by unethical behaviour by one or both sides of a conflict.

It is an overused example but one that speaks clearly to this point. The torture of Iraqi prisoners by a few very junior United States Army personnel at the Abu Ghraib detention facility had serious repercussions for the attainment of American policy goals, as well as for its global reputation.[3] Although under Saddam Hussein many more worse acts were committed by Iraqi security personnel, this was irrelevant to the condemnation the United States justly deserved.

The Australian Army understands this, as does the Australian society whom its soldiers represent. Ethics are central to the Army's values of Courage, Initiative, Respect and Teamwork.[4] These values are echoed in the Army's contract with the Australian people, to which all soldiers adhere.[5] In a series of public addresses, the Chief of Army, Lieutenant General Angus Campbell, has consistently stressed the need for the Army to understand the human side of war.[6] When he established the Australian Army Research Centre in 2016, for example, he stated that the ethical enhancement of the force was one of its principal aims.

Ethics instruction begins at the Defence Force Academy, the Royal Military College of Australia, the Recruit Training Battalion and other entry-level schools and it is refreshed throughout a soldier's career. Admittedly, it could probably be taught better or for longer, but it is not neglected and improvements are being made. The recently released 'Ryan Review' into the Army's education, training and doctrine needs, for example, identifies ethics as one of the pillars of building future land capability.[7] The 'Ryan Review' will drive reform across the Army's education continuum, and ethics will be a core learning requirement.

The Army values this investment in its people not just because it is right and is expected by the Australian people, but also because it is an investment in military effectiveness. The Army's most important capability is its soldiers. They matter more than the vehicles and weapons, and to build an effective force the Army must also build an ethical force. This is about more than preventing an Australian version of Abu Ghraib. Every good commander knows that their job is to prepare the men and women under their command for combat. Australian soldiers must be ready to face the horrors of war, and how they behave in the face of horror will guide how they fare in the struggle ahead and in the peace that follows.

Like all complex activities humans undertake, an ethical course of action is not achieved without effort. Behaviour must be watched, and there is need for periodic renewal and re-examination, and a constant striving to do better. The Army is committed to following and sustaining an ethical code of conduct in all it does. This book is part of this commitment. It represents tangible evidence that the Army is committed to self-examination and to making improvements when it is found wanting. Striving to be a learning organisation is never an easy path. But if the Army is to improve, become more capable, and achieve the best from its limited resources there is really no other choice.

A part of the Army's efforts to enhance its capabilities is the need to understand the human domain better in all its complexity and incorporate what it learns into its education, training and the conduct of war. If a future conference revisits the topic of ethics and war, this should not be seen as a failure to have learned the first time. Instead, it is a recognition that as a learning organisation the Army must have the wisdom to revisit what it has learned to establish a deeper understanding of its core values so that they are passed on to the next generation and continue to form the foundation of future capability. The chapters in this book are part of that journey.

NOTES

Introduction

1   David Wroe and Rory Callinan, 'Australia's elite special forces being investigated over disturbing stories of conduct and culture', *Sydney Morning Herald*, 17 April 2016.

2   Chief of Army letter OCA/OUT/2016/R27117625 dated 1 September 2016.

1   Why ethics matter

1   Geoffrey Best, *War and Law Since 1945*, Oxford University Press, 1997, p. 289.

2   Lieutenant Gabriel Bradley, 'Honor, not law', *Armed Forces*, 1 March 2012, <armedforcesjournal.com/honor-not-law/>.

3   Bradley, 'Honor, not law', 2012.

4   Tom Vanden Brook, 'Secdef Hagel's parting ethics advice to brass: Do better', *Military Times*, 17 February 2015 <www.militarytimes.com/story/military/pentagon/2015/02/17/chuck-hagel-parting-ethics-advice-to-brass-do-better/23572451/>.

5   Vanden Brook, 'Secdef Hagel's parting ethics advice to brass', 2015.

6   Jim Garamone, 'Dempsey emphasizes trust at West Point commencement', DOD News, Defense Media Activity, 23 May 2015 <www.defense.gov/News-Article-View/Article/604710/dempsey-emphasizes-trust-in-west-point-commencement-address>.

7   Brian Agnew, *Building Trust: Civil-Military Relations in Australia*, Shedden Papers, Centre for Defence and Strategic Studies Australian Defence College, December 2012 <www.defence.gov.au/ADC/Publications/Shedden/2012/AGNEW%20CM%20Relations%202.pdf>.

8   George A Mastroianni, 'Looking back: Understanding Abu Ghraib', *US Army War College Quarterly Parameters*, no. 53, 2013, p. 43.

9   Agnew, *Building Trust: Civil-Military Relations in Australia*, 2012.

10   '78% of Americans see military officer as prestigious occupation', Harris Poll, 20 May 2016 <www.theharrispoll.com/health-and-life/Military-Officer-Prestigious-Occupation.html>.

11   Harris Poll, 20 May 2016.

12   Harris Poll, 20 May 2016.

13   Jim Norman, 'Americans' Confidence in Institutions Stays Low', Gallup, 14 June 2016 <www.gallup.com/poll/192581/americans-confidence-institutions-stays-low.aspx>.

14   Commonwealth of Australia, Department of Defence, *2016 Defence White Paper*, 2016 <www.defence.gov.au/whitepaper/Docs/2016-Defence-White-Paper.pdf>.

15   'Perceptions of corruption and ethical conduct', ANU Poll, Australian National University, October 2012 <www.ibac.vic.gov.au/docs/default-source/research-documents/anu-poll-october.pdf?Sfvrsn=4.>.

16   William George Eckhardt, 'Lawyering for Uncle Sam when he draws his sword', *Chicago Journal of International Law*, vol. 4, no. 1, 2003, p. 431.

17   William Michael Reisman and Chris T Antoniou (eds), *The Laws of War: A Comprehensive Collection of Primary Documents on International Laws Governing Armed Conflict*, Vintage Books, New York, 1994, p. xxiv.

18   Lisa Beyer, 'Osama's end game', *Time*, 15 October 2001 <content.time.com/time/magazine/article/0,9171,178412-2,00.html>.

19   See Carl von Clausewitz, *On War*, edited and translated by Michael Howard and Peter Paret, Princeton University Press, Princeton, 1989.

20   Russell F Weigley, *The American Way of War: A History of United States Military Strategy and Policy*, Indiana University Press, Indiana, 1973; Robert A Pape, *Bombing to Win: Air Power and Coercion in War*, Cornell University Press, New York, 1996.

21   Seymour M Hersh, 'Torture at Abu Ghraib', *New Yorker*, 10 May 2004 <www.newyorker.com/magazine/2004/05/10/torture-at-abu-ghraib>.

22   Joseph Berger, 'US commander describes Marja battle as first salvo in campaign', *New York Times*, 21 February 2010 <www.nytimes.com/2010/02/22/world/asia/22petraeus.html?_r=0>.

23   'ISIS uses Iraqi civilians as human shields, dozens killed in US-led strike near Kirkuk', *ARA News*, 4 June 2015 <aranews.net/2015/06/isis-uses-iraqi-civilians-as-human-shields-dozens-killed-in-u-s-led-strike-near-kirkuk/>.

24   Russ Read, 'ISIS turns back Iraqi Forces from Fallujah with human shields', the *Daily Caller News Foundation*, 1 June 2016 <www.dailycaller.com/2016/06/01/isis-human-shields-stop-fallujah/>.

25   Rebecca Grant, 'In search of lawful targets', *Air Force Magazine*, February 2003 <www.airforcemag.com/magazinearchive/Documents/2003/February%20 2003/02targets03.pdf>.

26   'Law, legal diplomacy, and the counter-ISIL campaign', press release, US Department of State, 1 April 2016 <2009-2017.state.gov/s/l/releases/remarks/255493.htm>.

27   'Law, legal diplomacy, and the counter-ISIL campaign', US Department of State, 2016.

28   Richard Overy, *Why the Allies Won*, WW Norton and Company, New York, 1997.

29   Overy, *Why the Allies Won*, 1997.

30   Richard Schragger, 'Cooler heads: The difference between the president's lawyers and the military's', *Slate*, 20 September 2006 <www.slate.com/articles/news_and_politics/jurisprudence/2006/09/cooler_heads.html>.

31   Schragger, 'Cooler heads', 2006.

32   *US Manual for Courts-Martial* (2012), 14.c.(2)(a)(iv), Library of Congress website <www.loc.gov/rr/frd/Military_Law/pdf/MCM-2012.pdf>.

33   Deloitte Touche Tohmatsu Limited, *2016 Deloitte Millennial Survey* (2016) at 12, <www2.deloitte.com/content/dam/Deloitte/global/Documents/About-Deloitte/gx-millenial-survey-2016-exec-summary.pdf> accessed 2 October 2016.

34   *2016 Deloitte Millennial Survey.*

35   *2016 Deloitte Millennial Survey.*

36   Chris Sheedy, 'The moral wounds of war', UNSW Newsroom, 11 February 2016 <newsroom.unsw.edu.au/news/social-affairs/moral-wounds-war>.

37   'Inside US hub for air strikes', BBC America, 29 November 2008 <news.bbc.co.uk/2/hi/south_asia/7755969.stm>.

38   Jon Boone, 'Afghanistan civilian deaths up 31% this year, says United Nations', *Guardian*, 10 August 2010 <www.theguardian.com/world/2010/aug/10/afghanistan-civilian-deaths-up-un>.

39   Aqil Shah, 'Drone blowback in Pakistan is a myth. Here's why', *Washington Post*, 17 May 2016 <www.washingtonpost.com/news/monkey-cage/wp/2016/05/17/drone-blow-back-in-pakistan-is-a-myth-heres-why/>.

40   John Michael Loh, 'ISIS campaign is morally unjustified', *Daily Press*, 6 February

2016 <www.dailypress.com/news/opinion/local-voices/dp-nws-oped-loh-0207-20160206-story.html>.

41   Charles J Dunlap Jr, 'The moral hazard of inaction in war', *War on the Rocks*, 19 August 2016 <warontherocks.com/2016/08/the-moral-hazard-of-inaction-in-war/>.

42   David Deptula and Joseph Raskas, 'Just warfare entails risk; Movie "Eye in the Sky" perverts just war laws', *Breaking Defense*, 16 May 2016 <www.breakingdefense.com/2016/05/just-warfare-entails-risk-movie-eye-in-the-sky-perverts-just-war-laws/>.

43   Marcus Luttrell and Patrick Robinson, *Lone Survivor: The Eyewitness Account of Operation Redwing and the Lost Heroes of SEAL Team 10*, Little, Brown and Company, New York, 2007.

44   Luttrell and Robinson, *Lone Survivor*, 2007.

45   RM Schneiderman, 'Marcus Luttrell's Savior, Mohammad Gulab, Claims "Lone Survivor" Got It Wrong', *Newsweek*, 11 May 2016 <www.newsweek.com/2016/06/10/mohammad-gulab-marcus-luttrell-navy-seal-lone-survivor-operation-red-wings-458139.html>.

46   Michael Ignatieff, *The Warrior's Honor: Ethnic War and the Modern Conscience*, Henry Holt and Company, New York, 1998.

47   Ignatieff, *The Warrior's Honor*, 1998.

48   'I against my brothers' entry, Illustrated World of Proverbs website <www.worldofproverbs.com/2012/09/Bedouin-proverb-brothers-sisters.html>.

49   Andrew F March and Mara Revkin, 'Caliphate of Law', *Foreign Affairs*, April 2015 <www.foreignaffairs.com/articles/syria/2015-04-15/caliphate-law>.

50   March and Revkin, 2015.

51   Qiao Liang and Wang Xiangsui, *Unrestricted Warfare*, PLA Literature and Arts Publishing House, Beijing, 1999 <www.cryptome.org/cuw.htm> accessed 2 October 2016.

52   Liang and Xiangsui, *Unrestricted Warfare*, 1999.

53   Kimberly Dozier, 'International Red Cross chief to world: "What the hell?"', *Daily Beast*, 2 May 2016 <www.thedailybeast.com/articles/2016/05/02/international-red-cross-chief-to-world-what-the-hell.html>.

54   See Stephanie Nebehay, 'Islamic State selling, crucifying, burying children alive in Iraq – UN', Reuters 4 February 2015 <in.reuters.com/article/mideast-crisis-children-idinkbn0l828e20150204>; Edwin Mora, 'Taliban Jihadists skin man alive after ripping his eyes out', *Breitbart*, 11 June 2016 <www.breitbart.com/national-security/2016/06/11/taliban-jihadists-skin-man-alive-after-ripping-his-eyes-out/>.

55   See Charles J Dunlap, Jr, 'War-sustaining targets: Scholars can better help develop norms if they focus more on understanding the military perspective of evolving state practice', *Lawfire*, 6 July 2016 <sites.duke.edu/lawfire/2016/07/06/war-sustaining-targets-scholars-can-better-help-develop-norms-if-they-focus-more-on-understanding-the-military-perspective-of-evolving-state-practice/>.

56   Joshua Foust, 'What does a humanitarian double standard mean for civilians?', blog entry, 30 October 2015 <joshuafoust.com/what-does-a-humanitarian-double-standard-mean-for-global-security/>.

57   Lieutenant Gabriel Bradley, 'Honor, not law', *Armed Forces*, 1 March 2012 <armedforcesjournal.com/honor-not-law/>

58   Bradley, 'Honor, not law', 2012.

59   Bradley, 'Honor, not law', 2012.

2   Avoiding the descent into barbarism

1   For a detailed outline of the events at Son My, see David L Anderson (ed.), *Facing My Lai: Moving Beyond the Massacre*, Modern War Studies, University Press of Kansas, 1998, pp. 19–26.

2   Tom McDermott and Steve Hart, 'Armouring against Atrocity: Developing Ethical Strength in Small Military Units', in Peter HJ Olsthoorn (ed.), *Military Ethics and Leadership*, Brill, Leiden, 2017, Chapter 2.

3   Jim Frederick, *Black Hearts: One Platoon's Plunge into Madness in the Triangle of Death and the American Struggle in Iraq*, Harmony Books, New York, 2010, p. 71.

4   Sherene H Razack, *Dark Threats and White Knights: The Somalia Affair, Peacekeeping and the New Imperialism*, University of Toronto Press, Toronto, 2004, pp. 92–6.

5   Robert C Challman, 'The validity of the Harrower-Erickson multiple choice test as a screening device', *The Journal of Psychology*, vol. 20, no. 1, July 1945, pp. 41–8, DOI: 10.1080/00223980.1945.9712759.

6   'United States Department of Defence Instruction 1304.26: Qualification Standards for Enlistment, Appointment and Induction', United States Department of Defence, 23 March 2015 <www.dtic.mil/whs/directives/corres/pdf/130426p.pdf>.

7   Michael Boucai, 'Balancing your strengths against your felonies: Considerations for military recruitment of ex-offenders', *University of Miami Law Review*, vol. 61, No. 4, 30 May 2007, pp. 1031–2.

8   Frederick, *Black Hearts*, 2010, p. 71.

9   Zimbardo describes his experiments in detail in Phillip Zimbardo, *The Lucifer Effect: How Good People Turn Evil*, London, Rider, 2007. He also discusses his involvement in the court martial of Ivan Frederick.

10   See the Court Martial Charge Sheet (to which he pleaded guilty) for Staff Sergeant Ivan Frederick, Findlaw website <news.findlaw.com/wsj/docs/iraq/ifred32004chrg.html>.

11   Zimbardo, *The Lucifer Effect*, 2007, loc. 8784.

12   Zimbardo, *The Lucifer Effect*, 2007, loc. 8348–9673.

13   Department of Defence, *Final Report of the Independent Panel to Review DoD Detention Operations* <gwdspace.wrlc.org:8180/xmlui/bitstream/handle/2041/70989/02578_040824_001display.pdf?sequence=1>.

14   Carl von Clausewitz, Michael Howard and Peter Paret (eds.), *On War*, Princeton University Press, Princeton, 1976, p. 24.

15   Sherman is believed to have originally said this in an address to the graduating class of the Michigan Military Academy in 1879. Several conflicting versions of the speech have been published.

16   John Keegan, *The Face of Battle: A Study of Agincourt, Waterloo and the Somme*, Pimlico, London, 2004, p. 314.

17   Phillip McCormack, 'Grounding British Army values upon an ethical good', 30 March 2015, p. 11, Command and General Staff College Foundation website <www.cgscfoundation.org/wp-content/uploads/2015/04/McCormack-GroundingBritishArmyValues.pdf>.

18   Charles Horton Cooley, *Social Organization: A Study of the Larger Mind*, Social Science Classics Series, Transaction Books, New Brunswick, 1983.

19   Stanley Milgram, *An Experimental View*, Pinter & Martin, London, 2010, pp. 1–12.

20   See Solomon Asch, 'Studies of independence and conformity; a minority of one against a unanimous majority', *Psychological Monographs* (1956), edition 70, no. 9, pp. 1–70.

21   Deane-Peter Baker (ed.), *Key Concepts in Military Ethics*, UNSW Press, Sydney, 2015, pp. 23–7.

22   Michael Evans, 'Captains of the soul: Stoic philosophy and the Western profession of arms in the 21st century', *Naval War College Review*, Winter 2011, vol. 64, no. 1, pp. 31–58.

23   For more on the history of the Australian Army, and the centrality of the Anzac Legend, see the Australian Army website <www.army.gov.au/Our-history>.

24   Christopher R Browning, *Ordinary Men: Reserve Police Battalion 101 and the Final Solution in Poland*, Harper Perennial, New York, 1998.

25   Australian Army Values, Australian Army website <www.army.gov.au/Our-people/Our-values>; US Army Values, US Army website <www.army.mil/values/>; British Army Values, British Army website <www.army.mod.uk/documents/general/rmas_ADR002383-developingLeaders.pdf#search=values and standards>; Singaporean Armed Forces Values, Republic of Singapore Air Force website <www.mindef.gov.sg/imindef/mindef_websites/atozlistings/saftimi/units/cld/keyideas/corevalues.html>; PLA's Values as reported in US Marine Corps publication entitled *The Culture of the Chinese People's Liberation Army*, Public Intelligence website <info.publicintelligence.net/MCIA-ChinaPLA.pdf>.

26   For a useful fact sheet on International Humanitarian Law visit the ICRC website at <www.icrc.org/eng/assets/files/other/what_is_ihl.pdf>.

27   The Australian Army Contract can be found at the Australian Army website <www.army.gov.au/Our-people/Our-contract-with-Australia>.

28   The 'Taliban Hunting Club' emblem is prolific on the internet. For the emblem of the 1–101st Aviation Regiment see the Official Website of Fort Campbell and the 101st Airborne Division <www.campbell.army.mil/Units/Pages/101CAB.aspx>.

29   British Army, *Army Doctrine Publication: Army Doctrine Primer* (Shrivenham 2011), p. 1–1 found at <www.gov.uk/government/uploads/system/uploads/attachment_data/file/33693/20110519ADP_Army_Doctrine_Primerpdf.pdf>.

30   Quote under Chatham House Rules from a presentation to the author by a senior Australian General at the Australian Command and Staff College.

31   Anderson, *Facing My Lai*, 1998, pp. 19–26.

32   Razack, *Dark Threats and White Knights*, 2004, pp. 92–6.

33   Zimbardo, *The Lucifer Effect*, 2007, loc. 9044.

34   Shannon E French, 'Sergeant Davis's stern charge: The obligation of officers to preserve the humanity of their troops', *Journal of Military Ethics*, vol. 8, no. 2, June 2009, p. 117, DOI: 10.1080/15027570903037926.

35   See text of George Bush's speech to Congress in the aftermath of the 9/11 attacks at <georgewbush-whitehouse.archives.gov/news/releases/2001/09/20010920-8.html>

36   Phillip McCormack, *Grounding British Army Values*, 2015, p. 7.

5   Connecting research, education and training

1   Jonathan Wolff, *Ethics and Public Policy: A Philosophical Inquiry*, Routledge, London, 2011, p. 2.

2   Wolff, *Ethics and Public Policy*, 2011, p. 3.

3   Martin L Cook and Henrik Syse, 'What should we mean by "military ethics"?', *Journal of Military Ethics*, vol. 9, no. 2, 2010, p. 120.

4   Michael Walzer, *Just and Unjust Wars: A Moral Argument with Historical Illustrations*, Basic Books, New York, 1977.

5   Cook and Syse, 'What should we mean by "military ethics"?', 2010, p. 120.

6   John Locke, *An Essay Concerning Human Understanding, edited with a foreword by Peter H Nidditch*, Clarendon Press, Oxford, 1975, pp. 9–10.

7   Deane-Peter Baker, 'Making good better: A proposal for teaching ethics at the service academies', *Journal of Military Ethics*, vol. 11, no. 3, 2012, pp. 208–22.

8   Kenneth D Pimple, 'Using case studies in teaching research ethics', 2004, available at <www.nationalethicscenter.org/resources/7282/download/292.pdf>, p. 1. Quoted in Baker 'Making good better', 2012, p. 216.

9   Baker, 'Making good better', 2012, p. 217.

10   Wilbur J Scott, Damian McCabe and David R McCone, 'Teaching cultural

competencies for complex socio-cultural contexts: Evidence from a realistic decision-making simulation', *Res Militaris: European Journal of Military Studies*, vol. 3, no. 2, 2013, p. 7.

11   Scott et al., 'Teaching cultural competencies', 2013, p. 7.

12   Scott et al., 'Teaching cultural competencies', 2013, p. 8.

13   Scott et al., 'Teaching cultural competencies', 2013, pp. 11–12.

14   Scott et al., 'Teaching cultural competencies', 2013, p. 14.

15   Cook and Syse, 'What should we mean by "military ethics"?', 2010, p. 120.

6   Ethics in Special Operations

1   Alan Cole, Phillip Drew, Rob McLaughlin and Dennis Mandsager, *San Remo Rules of Engagement Handbook*, International Institute for Humanitarian Law, San Remo, 2009.

2   Rule-oriented ethics have also been described as 'deontological' or principle/absolutist ethics.

3   It is customary to follow all references to the Prophet with the words 'Peace be upon Him'.

4   Aristotle, *Nicomachaen Ethics*, trans. Martin Ostwald, Bobbs-Merrill, Indianapolis, 1962, bk. 1, p. 4.

5   Jeremy Bentham, 'An introduction to the principles of morals and legislation', in *The English Philosophers from Bacon to Mill*, Edwin A Burt (ed.), Modern Library, New York, 1939, p. 791.

6   John Stuart Mill, 'Utilitarianism', in *The English Philosophers*, p. 908.

7   Joseph Fletcher, *Situation Ethics: The New Morality*, Westminister Press, Philadelphia, 1966, p. 55.

8   For more, see Ian Langford, Australian Army, *Special Operations: Principles and Considerations*, 2014, <army.gov.au/~/media/Army/Our%20future/Publications/Papers/ARP%204/AustralianSpecialOperations_B5_web.pdf>.

9   See Carl von Clausewitz, *On War*, Michael Howard and Peter Paret (eds.), Princeton University Press, Princeton, 1976.

10   Langford, *Special Operations: Principles and Considerations*, 2014.

11   von Clausewitz, *On War*, 1976.

12   RE Nisbett, GT Fong, DR Lehman and PW Cheng, 'Teaching reasoning', *Science Magazine*, no. 238 (4827), 30 October 1978, pp. 625–31.

13   Elizabeth A Minton and Lynn R Khale, *Belief Systems, Religion, and Behavioral Economics*, New York, Business Expert Press, 2014.

14   Jonathan Glover, 'Philosophy bites', *Systems of Beliefs*, 2011 <philosophybites.com/2011/10/jonathan-glover-on-systems-of-belief.html>.

15   Richard Meyers and Albert C Pierce, 'On strategic leadership', *Joint Forces Quarterly*, National Defense University, Washington DC, 2009, p. 12.

16   Daniel M Bell Jnr, 'The ethics of vicarious warfare: Debating drones', lecture given at the Fort Leavenworth Ethics Symposium, Fort Leavenworth, Kansas, 4 December 2012.

17   Bell, 'The ethics of vicarious warfare', 2012.

18   Bell, 'The ethics of vicarious warfare', 2012.

19   Bell, 'The ethics of vicarious warfare', 2012.

20   Bell, 'The ethics of vicarious warfare', 2012.

21   Bell, 'The ethics of vicarious warfare', 2012.

22   Bell, 'The ethics of vicarious warfare', 2012.

23   Bell, 'The ethics of vicarious warfare', 2012.

24   Bell, 'The ethics of vicarious warfare', 2012.

25   Matthew Beard, Jai Galliott and Sandra Lynch, 'Soldier enhancement: Ethical risks and opportunities' *Australian Army Journal* vol. 13, no. 1, 2016, pp. 5–20.

26   Beard, Galliot and Lynch, 'Soldier enhancement', 2016.

7 Moral objection and political dissent

1   Malcolm Brown, Deborah Snow and Mark Coultan, 'Doctor jailed for following his conscience', *Sydney Morning Herald*, 15 April 2006.

2   For a general outline of conscription legislation see Francis James in Forward and Reece (eds.), *Conscription in Australia*, University of Queensland Press, St Lucia, 1966. I considered the operational difficulties of recognising selective objection in Tom Frame, *Living by the Sword: The Ethics of Armed Intervention*, UNSW Press, Sydney, 2004.

3   It is difficult to assess the extent to which Australians have supported conscription because most opinion polls refer to compulsory military training or national service. Other than during the closing stages of the Vietnam War, more than 60 per cent of the adult population of Australia has purportedly supported either the introduction or continuation of national service. See Peter Sekuless, 'A comparison of RSL policies on major national issues with prevailing public opinion', Australian War Memorial history conference, 13 February 1985, p. 6. It is noteworthy that Sekuless makes no mention of any poll canvassing opinion on the recognition of conscientious objection. For a broader discussion of the politics of conscription see Henry S Albinski, *Politics and Foreign Policy in Australia: The Impact of Vietnam and Conscription*, Duke University Press, Durham, 1970, pp. 193–202. See also Peter Pierce, Jeff Grey and Jeff Doyle (eds.), *Vietnam Days: Australia and the Impact of Vietnam*, Penguin, Melbourne, 1991.

4   Compulsory military training during peacetime was conducted in the periods 1911–29 and 1950–60.

5   *Commonwealth Parlimentary Debates (CPD)* (Reps), 21 November 1950, pp. 2723–4, 2728.

6   *CPD* (Reps), 26 November 1959, pp. 3185–6. In 1957, the scheme was reduced with the introduction of a ballot which would restrict the number of young Australian men 'selected' to undergo compulsory training, *CPD* (Reps), 1 May 1957, pp. 950–2.

7   *CPD* (Reps), 10 November 1964, p. 2715, pp. 2717–8.

8   DLNS to Secretary, Prime Minister's Department, 11 December 1968, DLNS file 72/557.

9   The most recent discussion of selective conscientious objection is Andrea Ellner, Paul Robinson and David Wetham (eds.), *When Soldiers Say No*, Routledge, London, 2014. A progressive Australian view is offered by Lieutenant Colonel Ian Wing, 'Selective Conscientious Objection and the Australian Defence Force', *Australian Defence Force Journal*, no. 137, July–August 1999, pp. 31–41.

10 Conscription could also take place under section 60 of the *Defence Act* (1903) which allows the Governor General, by means of a proclamation, to call upon certain male persons to serve in the Defence Force at a time when there is a real or apprehended attack on or invasion of Australia. This version of the *Act* does not recognise any right of conscientious objection.

11 *CPD* (Senate), 23 August 1978.

12 For an interpretation of the Jones case see Kellie Tranter, 'Selective conscientious objection', *National Times*, 1 September 2010.

13 Naval Support Command (NSC) letter, Annex C, 'Human rights aspects of conscientious objection', to Assistant Chief of Defence Force (Personnel), October 1990, NSC file N90/32170, folio 56.

14 NSC letter, Annex C, 'Human rights aspects of conscientious objection'.

8 Humanitarian values and military objectives

1   Oxford Institute for Ethics, Law and Armed Conflict website <www.elac.ox.ac.uk>.
2   *Global Humanitarian Assistance Report 2016*, p. 11, Global Humanitarian Assistance website <www.globalhumanitarianassistance.org/report/gha2016/>.
3   *State of the Humanitarian System Report 2015*, State of the Humanitarian System website <sohs.alnap.org>.
4   UN-CMCoord definition, UN Office for the Coordination of Humanitarian Affairs website <docs.unocha.org/sites/dms/Documents/v.2.%20website%20overview%20tab%20link%201%20United%20Nations%20Humanitarian%20Civil-Military%20coordination%20(UN-CMCoord).pdf>.
5   *UN-Civil-Military Coordination Field Handbook 2015* p. 15, UN Office for the Coordination of Humanitarian Affairs website <docs.unocha.org/sites/dms/Documents/CMCoord%20Field%20Handbook%20v1.0_Sept2015.pdf>.
6   *The Montreux Document*, International Committee of the Red Cross website <www.icrc.org/eng/assets/files/other/icrc_002_0996.pdf>.

9 Operating within an NGO: A uniformed perspective

1   William Easterly, *The White Man's Burden*, Penguin Press, New York, 2006, p. 5.
2   Over 46 per cent of girls in Zambia are married before their eighteenth birthday. See the statistics page of the United Nations Girl's Education Initiative website <www.ungei.org/infobycountry/zambia.html>.
3   The national life expectancy was 52. World Health Organization website, Country Cooperation Strategy and Briefs page <www.who.int/countryfocus/cooperation_strategy/briefs/en/>.
4   Volunteer tourism is an industry estimated to be worth over US$2 billion worldwide. Concerns include the false impression that a one-month stint and donation can make a significant difference (a quick fix for serious problems), unskilled volunteers crowding out local workers and the exploitation of the local population, particularly children.
5   It is beyond the scope of this chapter to explore whether a change in priorities would make a difference to any of the issues that Zambia is attempting to address.
6   Senegal is a predominantly Muslim country. Those who were able would provide support to those in need. In my experience, the *Talibe* were generally assured of one meal a day. It was understood that if a child came to your door in the evening begging for food you would provide a meal. Most *Talibe* had at least one family whose door they would knock on around the time of the evening meal.
7   Female Engagement Teams were a program started by the United States Marine Corps. They were established to develop trust-based and enduring relationships with women they encountered on patrol. See Christopher McCullough, 'Female engagement teams: who they are and why they do it', US Army website, 2 October 2012 <www.army.mil/article/88366>.
8   'Female Engagement Teams in Afghanistan', Australian Army website <www.army.gov.au/Our-work/News-and-media/News-and-media-2012/News-and-media-March-2012/Female-Engagement-Teams-in-Afghanistan>; McCullough, 'Female engagement teams', 2012; Gabrielle Cook, 'Counterinsurgency and female engagement teams in the war in Afghanistan', E-International Relations Students website, 16 August 2015 <www.e-ir.info/2015/08/16/counterinsurgency-and-female-engagement-teams-in-the-war-in-afghanistan/>.
9   Cook, 'Counterinsurgency and female engagement teams in the war in Afghanistan', 2015.
10 United Nations Development Program, *Human Development Report*, 'Gender inequality index', 2015 <hdr.undp.org/en/composite/GII>.

11   Martin Luther King, 'Letter from a Birmingham jail', African Studies Centre, University of Pennsylvania website <www.africa.upenn.edu/Articles_Gen/Letter_Birmingham.html>.

12   'Women, peace and security', United Nations website <www.un.org/en/peacekeeping/issues/women/wps.shtml>.

13   The Australian National Action Plan on Women, Peace and Security 2012–2018, Australian Government Department of Social Services website <www.dss.gov.au/our-responsibilities/women/publications-articles/government-international/australian-national-action-plan-on-women-peace-and-security-2012-2018>.

14   The Australian National Action Plan on Women, Peace and Security, 2012–2018.

15   The Australian National Action Plan on Women, Peace and Security, 2012–2018.

16   Aniruddha Mitra, James T Bang, James and Arnab Biswas, 'Gender equality and economic growth: Is it equality of opportunity or equality of outcomes?', *Feminist Economics*, vol. 21, no. 1, January 2015.

17   *2004 report of the Secretary-General on Women, Peace and Security*, Office of the Special Adviser on Gender Issues and the Advancement of Women website <www.un.org/womenwatch/osagi/wps/sg2004.htm>.

18   *UN Development Program Report 2010*, United Nations Development Programme website <hdr.undp.org/en/content/human-development-report-2010>.

19   Jacqui True, *The Political Economy of Violence Against Women*, Oxford University Press, Oxford, 2012, pp. 118–19.

10   The individualisation of modern conflict

1   Fritz Allhoff, Adam Henschke and Bradley Jay Strawser, *Binary Bullets: The Ethics of Cyber Warfare*, Oxford University Press, New York, 2016; Ronald Arkin, *Governing Lethal Behavior in Autonomous Robots*, CRC Press, Boca Raton, 2009; Christian Enemark, *Armed Drones and the Ethics of War*, Routledge, London, 2013; Claire Finkelstein, Jens Ohlin and Andrew Altman, *Targeted Killings: Law and Morality in an Asymmetrical World*, Oxford University Press, New York, 2012; Jai Galliott, *Military Robots: Mapping the Moral Landscape*, Ashgate, Surrey, 2015; Armin Krishnan, *Killer Robots: Legality and Ethicality*, Ashgate, Surrey, 2009; Peter Warren Singer, *Wired for War*, Penguin, New York, 2009.

2   Anne-Marie Slaughter, 'War and law in the 21st century: Adapting to the changing face of conflict', *Europe's World*, Autumn, 2011, pp. 32–7; Gabriella Blum, 'The individualization of war: From war to policing in the regulation of armed conflicts', in Austin Sarat, Lawrence Douglas and Martha Merrill Umphrey (eds.), *Law and War*, Stanford University Press, Stanford, 2013; Glenn Voelz, *The Rise of iWar: Identity, Information, and the Individualization of Modern Warfare*, Strategic Studies Institute, Carlisle, 2015.

3   The latter's work is often considered the reference point; see Zygmunt Bauman, *The Individualized Society*, Cambridge University Press, London, 2001.

4   See similar arguments made in relation to developments in the drone and commercial space exploration scene: Jai Galliott, 'Uninhabited systems in the civilian realm', *IEEE Technology and Society*, vol. 32, no. 2, 2012, pp. 13–16; and Jai Galliott, 'Introduction' in Jai Galliott (ed.), *Commercial Space Exploration: Ethics, Policy and Governance*, Surrey, Ashgate, 2015, pp. 1–6.

5   Charles Dunlap, 'The hyper-personalization of war: Cyber, big data, and the changing face of conflict', *Georgetown Journal of International Affairs*, vol. 15, 2014, pp. 108–18.

6   Blum, 'The individualization of war', 2013.

7   The one exception here is humanitarian intervention. If individualising technologies overcome some kind of casualty adverseness, this might be a positive thing in that

states are made to live up to moral responsibilities and expectations to protect
vulnerable groups that they may have otherwise failed to meet.

8   David Rodin, *War and Self-Defense*, Oxford University Press, Oxford, 2002; and Jeff
     McMahan, *Killing in War*, Oxford University Press, New York, 2009.

9   This term was coined by Dennis Thompson, writing on the topic of the moral
     responsibilities of political office holders within large bureaucracies. For more, see
     Dennis Thompson, *Political Ethics and Public Office*, Harvard University Press,
     Cambridge, 1990; and Dennis Thompson, 'Moral responsibility and public officials:
     The problem of many hands', *American Political Science Review*, no. 74, no. 4, 1980.

10   Jai Galliott, 'Closing with completeness: The asymmetric drone warfare debate',
     Journal of Military Ethics, vol. 11, no. 4, 2012, p. 356.

11   The ethics of enhanced human performance

1   Eric Juengst, 'The meaning of enhancement' in Erik Parens (ed.), *Enhancing Human
     Traits: Ethical and Social Implications*, Georgetown University Press, Washington, 1998.

2   Brian Orend, *The Morality of War*, Broadview Press, Toronto, 2006.

3   Dennis M Giangreco, *Hell to Pay: Operation Downfall and the Invasion of Japan,
     1945–1947*, Naval Institute Press, Annapolis, 2009.

4   Another political deterrent is high non-combatant casualties, which enhancement may
     also help to address.

5   Michael Walzer, *Just and Unjust Wars*, 4th edition, Perseus, New York, 2006.

6   Jeff McMahan, *Killing in War*, Clarendon Press, Oxford, 2009.

7   See An Officer, 'A combatant's view', in Tom Frame (ed.), *Moral Injury: Unseen
     Wounds in an Age of Barbarism*, UNSW Press, Sydney, 2015.

8   Jonathan D Moreno, 'Mind wars: Brain science and the military', *Monash Bioethics
     Review*, vol. 31, no. 2, 2013, p. 90.

9   See Matthew Beard, 'Virtuous soldiers: A role for the liberal arts?', *Journal of Military
     Ethics*, vol. 13, no. 3, 2014, pp. 274–94.

10   Thomas Douglas, 'Moral enhancement via direct emotion modulation: A reply to
     John Harris', *Bioethics*, vol. 27, no. 3, 2013, p. 161.

11   Nancy Sherman, *The Untold War: Inside the Hearts and Minds of Our Soldiers*,
     WW Norton, New York, 2010, p. 76.

12   Jonathan Shay, *Achilles in Vietnam: Combat Trauma and the Undoing of Character*,
     Simon & Schuster, New York, 1995.

13   Immanuel Kant, *Groundwork of the Metaphysics of Morals*, Mary Gregor (trans.),
     Cambridge University Press, Cambridge, 1997, p. 399.

14   Nancy Sherman, *Making a Necessity of Virtue: Aristotle and Kant on Virtue*, Cambridge
     University Press, Cambridge, 1997, p. 57.

15   Matthew Beard, 'Will super soldiers be the heroes we deserve?', the Ethics Centre
     website, 12 September 2016 <www.ethics.org.au/on-ethics/blog/september-2016/will-
     soldiers-with-super-powers-be-the-heroes-we-d>.

16   Patrick Mileham, 'Unlimited liability and the military covenant', *Journal of Military
     Ethics*, vol. 9, no. 1, 2010, pp. 23–40.

17   Michael Gross, 'Military medical ethics: A review of the literature and a call to arms',
     Cambridge Quarterly of Healthcare Ethics, vol. 22, 2013, p. 92.

18   Maxwell J Mehlman, 'Captain America and Iron Man', in George Lucas (ed.),
     Routledge Handbook of Military Ethics, Routledge, London, 2015.

19   Michael J Selgelid, 'Freedom and moral enhancement', *Journal of Medical Ethics*,
     vol. 40, no. 4, 2014, p. 215.

20   Australian Army, 'Our values', Australian Army website <www.army.gov.au/Our-
     people/Our-values>.

21 Shannon E French, *The Code of the Warrior: Exploring Warrior Values Past and Present*, Rowman & Littlefield, Lanham, 2003, pp. 1–19.

22 Christian Enemark, *Armed Drones and the Ethics of War: Military Virtue in a Post-heroic Age*, Routledge, London, 2014.

23 See Nancy Sherman, *The Untold War*, WW Norton, New York, 2010; Jonathan Shay, *Odysseus in America: Combat Trauma and the Trials of Homecoming*, Scribner, Sydney, 2002; Nolen Gertz, *The Philosophy of War and Exile: From the Humanity of War to the Inhumanity of Peace*, Palgrave MacMillan, Hampshire, 2014; and Matthew Beard, 'Conceptual distinctions between types of moral injuries and different ways of seeing them' in Frame (ed.), *Moral Injury*, 2015.

24 See Brett T Litz et al., 'Moral injury and moral repair in war veterans: A preliminary model and intervention strategy', *Clinical Psychology Review*, vol. 29, 2009, pp. 695–706.

25 Nicholas G Evans and Jonathan D Moreno, 'Yesterday's war; tomorrow's technology: Peer commentary on "Ethical, legal, social and policy issues in the use of genomic technologies by the US military"', *Journal of Law and the Biosciences*, Advance Access Publication, 2014, pp. 1–6.

12   The ethics of emerging tactics

1 Martin van Creveld, *The Transformation of War: The Most Radical Reinterpretation of Armed Conflict since Clausewitz*, The Free Press, New York, 2001; Elinor C Sloan, *The Revolution in Military Affairs*, McGill-Queen's University Press, Montreal and Kingston, 2002.

2 Peter W Singer, *Wired For War: The Robotics Revolution and Conflict in the 21st Century*, Penguin Press, New York, 2009.

3 Patrick Hew, 'The blind spot in robot-enabled warfare: Deeper implications of the IED challenge', *Australian Army Journal*, vol. 7, no. 2, Winter 2010, pp. 45–56.

4 Gary D Solis, *The Law of Armed Conflict: International Humanitarian Law in War*, Cambridge University Press, Cambridge, 2010; Yoram Dinstein, *The Conduct of Hostilities Under The Law of International Armed Conflict*, Cambridge University Press, Cambridge, 2010.

5 Thomas W Smith, 'The new law of war: Legitimizing hi-tech and infrastructure violence', *International Studies Quarterly*, vol. 46, no. 3, 2012, pp. 355–74.

6 Maja Zehfuss, 'Targeting: Precision and the production of ethics', *European Journal of International Affairs*, vol. 17, no. 3, 2010, pp. 559–61.

7 J Marshall Beier, 'Discriminating tastes: "Smart" bombs, non-combatants, and notions of legitimacy in warfare', *Security Dialogue*, vol. 34, no. 4, 2003, pp. 411–25.

8 David R Mets, *The Long Search For a Surgical Strike: Precision Munitions and the Revolution in Military Affairs*, Research and Education Paper No. 12, College of Aerospace Doctrine, Maxwell Air Force Base, AL, 2001; Agnieszka Jachec-Neale, *The Concept of Military Objectives in International Law and Targeting Practice*, Routledge, London and New York, 2015; Horace B Robertson, 'The principle of the military objective in the law of armed conflict', *Journal of Legal Studies*, no. 8, 1997, pp. 35–70.

9 Geoffrey S Corn and Gary P Corn, 'The law of operational targeting: Viewing the LOAC through an operational lens', *Texas International Law Journal*, vol. 47, no. 2, 2012, p. 362.

10 Nicholas J Wheeler, 'Dying for "enduring freedom": Accepting responsibility for civilian casualties in the war against terrorism', *International Relations*, vol. 16 no. 2, 2002, pp. 210–12.

11 Gregor Noll, 'Analogy at war: Proportionality, equality and the law of targeting', in Janne Elisabeth Nijman and Wouter G Werner (eds.), *Netherlands Yearbook of*

International Law 2012: Legal Equality and the International Rule of Law – Essays in Honour of PH Kooijmans, vol. 43, TMC Asser Press, The Hague, Netherlands, 2012, pp. 215–16.

12 Ward Thomas, *The Ethics of Destruction: Norms and Force in International Relations*, Cornell University Press, Ithaca, NY, 2001, p. 170.

13 Bradley Jay Strawser, 'Moral predators: The duty to employ uninhabited aerial vehicles', *Journal of Military Ethics*, vol. 9, no. 4, 2010, pp. 342–68.

14 Paul M Salmon, Neville A Stanton, Guy H Walker and Daniel P Jenkins, *Distributed Situational Awareness: Theory, Measurement and Application to Teamwork*, Ashgate, Farnham, 2009.

15 Tyler Wall and Torin Monahan, 'Surveillance and violence from afar: The politics of drones and liminal security-scapes', *Theoretical Criminology*, vol. 15, no. 3, 2011, pp. 239–54; Fernando R Teson, 'Targeted killing in war and peace: A philosophical analysis', in Claire Finkelstein, Jens David Ohlin and Andrew Altman (eds.), *Targeted Killings: Law and Morality in an Asymmetric World*, Oxford University Press, Oxford, 2012, pp. 403–33.

16 John A Hardy, 'Reframing the drone debate', in *Proceedings of the Sixth Oceanic Conference on International Studies*, University of Melbourne, Melbourne, 2014; Avery Plaw and Mathew S Fricker, 'Tracking the predators: Evaluating the US drone campaign in Pakistan', *International Studies Perspectives*, vol. 13, no. 4, 2012, pp. 344–65.

17 Christian Enemark, *Armed Drones and the Ethics of War: Military Virtue in a Post-Heroic Age*, Routledge, London and New York, 2014.

18 James Turner Johnson, *Can Modern War Be Just?* Yale University Press, New Haven, 1986.

19 Robert Sparrow, 'Drones, courage, and military culture', George R Lucas (ed.) *Routledge Handbook of Military Ethics*, Routledge, Oxford, 2015.

20 Medea Benjamin, *Drone Warfare: Killing by Remote Control*, OR Books, New York and London, 2012.

21 Strawser, 'Moral predators', 2010.

22 Joseph A Ouma, Wayne L Chappelle and Amber Salinas, *Facets of Occupational Burnout Among US Air Force Active Duty and National Guard/Reserve MQ-1 Predator and MQ-9 Reaper Operators*, Air Force Research Laboratory, Wright-Patterson AFB, 2011.

23 Enemark, *Armed Drones and the Ethics of War*, 2014.

24 Paul M Salmon, Neville A Stanton, Guy H Walker and Daniel P Jenkins, *Command and Control: The Sociotechnical Perspective*, Ashgate, Farnham, 2009.

25 Michael T Flynn, Rich Juergens and Thomas L Cantrell, 'Employing ISR: SOF best practices', *Joint Forces Quarterly*, no. 50, July 2008, pp. 56–61.

26 Corn and Corn, 'The law of operational targeting', 2012.

13 Weaponising social media

1 Charlie Winter and Haroro J Ingram, 'How ISIS weaponised the media after Orlando', *The Atlantic*, 17 June 2016 <www.theatlantic.com/international/archive/2016/06/isis-orlando-shooting/487574/>.

2 Winter and Ingram, 'How ISIS weaponised the media after Orlando', 2016.

3 Winter and Ingram, 'How ISIS weaponised the media after Orlando', 2016.

4 Thomas E Nissen, 'The weaponisation of social media', Royal Danish Defense College, Copenhagen, 2015, p. 97.

5 Nissen, 'The weaponisation of social media', 2015, p. 103.

6 Nissen, 'The weaponisation of social media', 2015, p. 96.

7   Thomas Rid and Peter McBurney, 'Cyber-weapons', *RUSI Journal* vol. 157, no. 1, 2012, p. 6.

8   Rid and McBurney, 'Cyber-weapons', 2012, p. 7.

9   Randall R Dipert, 'Other-than-internet (Oti) cyberwarfare: Challenges for ethics, law, and policy', *Journal of Military Ethics*, vol. 12, no. 1, 2013, p. 42.

10   Nissen, 'The weaponisation of social media', 2015, p. 112.

11   Nissen, 'The weaponisation of social media', 2015, p. 112.

12   Andrew J Bacevich, *The New American Militarism: How Americans Are Seduced by War*, Oxford University Press, Oxford, 2013, p. 239.

13   Joseph Margolis, 'Terrorism and the new forms of war', *Metaphilosophy*, vol. 35, no. 3, 2004.

14   Jessica Wolfendale, '"New wars", terrorism, and just war theory', in Paolo Tripodi and Jessica Wolfendale (eds.), *New Wars and New Soldiers: Military Ethics in the Contemporary World*, Ashgate, London, 2011, p. 13.

15   Mary Kaldor, *New & Old Wars*, Stanford University Press, Palo Alto, 2007; Herfried Münkler, *The New Wars*, Polity Press, Cambridge, 2005.

16   Paul Gilbert, *New Terror, New Wars*, Edinburgh University Press, Edinburgh, 2003.

17   Michael L Gross, *Moral Dilemmas of Modern War: Torture, Assassination, and Blackmail in an Age of Asymmetric Conflict*, Cambridge University Press, New York, 2010, p. 4.

18   Simon Bronitt, Miriam Gani and Saskia Hufnagel, *Shooting to Kill: Socio-Legal Perspectives on the Use of Lethal Force*, Hart Publishing, Oxford and Portland, 2012, pp. xiii–xiv.

19   Christopher Kutz, 'The difference uniforms make: Collective violence in criminal law and war', *Philosophy & Public Affairs*, vol. 33, no. 2, 2005, pp. 154–5.

20   Rod Thornton, *Asymmetric Warfare: Threat and Response in the 21st Century*, Polity Press, Cambridge, 2007, pp. 1–2.

21   David McCraw, 'The defence debate in Australia and New Zealand', *Defence Studies*, vol. 7, no. 1, 2007, p. 107.

22   Gross, *Moral Dilemmas of Modern War*, 2010, p. 12.

23   See Mary Ellen O'Connell, 'Unlawful killing with combat drones: A case study of Pakistan, 2004–2009', in Bronitt et al. (eds.) *Shooting to Kill*, 2012; Bradley Jay Strawser, 'More heat than light: The vexing complexities of the drone debate', *3 Quarks Daily* website <www.3quarksdaily.com/3quarksdaily/2013/02/more-heat-than-light-the-vexing-complexities-of-the-drone-debate.html>; Bradley J Strawser, *Killing by Remote Control: The Ethics of an Unmanned Military*, Oxford University Press, New York, 2013; Claire Finkelstein, Jens David Ohlin, and Andrew Altman, *Targeted Killings: Law and Morality in an Asymmetrical World*, Oxford University Press, Oxford, 2012.

24   Patrick Lin and S Brandt Ford, 'I, spy robot: The ethics of robots in national intelligence activities', in Jai Galliott and Warren Reed (eds.), *Ethics and and the Future of Spying: Technology, National Security and Intelligence Collection*, Routledge, London and New York, 2016, p. 14.

25   Siobhan Gorman and Julian E Barnes, 'Cyber combat: Act of war', *Wall Street Journal*, 31 May 2011 <online.wsj.com/articles/SB100014240527023045631045763556 23135782718>; George R Lucas Jr, 'Jus in silico: Moral restrictions on the use of cyberwarfare', in Fritz Allhoff, Nicholas Evans and Adam Henschke (eds.), *Routledge Handbook of Ethics and War: Just War Theory in the 21st Century*, Taylor & Francis, 2013.

26   See Ned Dobos, *Insurrection and Intervention: The Two Faces of Sovereignty*, Cambridge University Press, Cambridge, 2011, p. 21; Alan J Kuperman, 'A model humanitarian intervention? Reassessing Nato's Libya campaign', *International Security*, vol. 38, no. 1,

2013; Alex J Bellamy, *The Responsibility to Protect: A Defense*, Oxford University Press, Oxford 2014; Thomas G Weiss, *Humanitarian Intervention*, Polity Press, Cambridge, 2012; Martha Finnemore, 'Constructing norms of humanitarian intervention', in Peter J Katzenstein (ed.), *The Culture of National Security: Norms and Identity in World Politics*, Columbia University Press, New York, 1996; Nicholas J Wheeler, *Saving Strangers: Humanitarian Intervention in International Society*, Oxford University Press, Oxford, 2000; Chris Brown, *Sovereignty, Rights and Justice: International Political Theory Today*, Polity Press, Oxford, 2002.

27   Simon Chesterman, '"Leading from behind": The responsibility to protect, the Obama Doctrine, and humanitarian intervention after Libya', *Ethics & International Affairs*, vol. 25, no. 3, 2011, p. 279.

28   Barry M Blechman and Stephen S Kaplan, *Force without War: US Armed Forces as a Political Instrument*, The Brookings Institution, Washington DC, 1978.

29   Blechman and Kaplan, *Force without War*, 1978, p. 12.

30   Shannon Brandt Ford, '*Jus Ad Vim* and the just use of lethal force-short-of-war', in Fritz Allhoff, Nicholas Evans and Adam Henschke (eds.), *Routledge Handbook of Ethics and War: Just War Theory in the 21st Century*, Routledge, Oxford, 2014.

31   Rosa Brooks, *How Everything Became War and the Military Became Everything: Tales from the Pentagon*, Simon & Schuster, New York, 2016.

32   Thomas Hobbes, 'Leviathan', in Richard Tuck (ed.), *Hobbes: Leviathan: Revised Student Edition*, Cambridge University Press, Cambridge, 1996, p. 88.

33   Alex J Bellamy, *Just Wars: From Cicero to Iraq*, Polity Press, Cambridge, 2006, p. 69.

34   Tom Sorell, *Emergencies and Politics: A Sober Hobbesian Approach*, Cambridge University Press, Cambridge, 2013, p. 25.

35   Sorell, *Emergencies and Politics*, 2013, p. 26.

36   Tom Sorell, 'Hobbes, Locke and the state of nature', in *Studies on Locke: Sources, Contemporaries, and Legacy*, Springer, Dordrecht, 2008, p. 27.

37   Bellamy, *Just Wars*, 2006, p. 69.

38   John Stone, 'Cyber war will take place!', *Journal of Strategic Studies*, vol. 36, no. 1, 2013.

39   Randall R Dipert, 'The ethics of cyberwarfare', *Journal of Military Ethics*, vol. 9, no. 4, 2010, p. 384.

40   Michael Quinlan, 'Just intelligence: Prolegomena to an ethical theory', *Intelligence and National Security*, vol. 22, no. 1, 2007.

41   In these cases, the authors are seeking to apply principles of conflict to competitive activity rather than develop an understanding of the ethics of war as such.

42   To be fair, McNeilly does make clear that 'business people should not follow the philosophy of the destruction created by total war'. *Mark R McNeilly, Sun Tzu and the Art of Business: Six Strategic Principles for Managers*, Oxford University Press, New York, 1996, pp. 5 and 8.

43   Andrew Holmes, *Carl Von Clausewitz's On War: A Modern-Day Interpretation of a Strategy Classic*, Infinite Ideas, Oxford, 2010.

44   Cited in Matt Ford, 'The West Point professor who contemplated a coup', *The Atlantic*, 31 August 2015 <www.theatlantic.com/politics/archive/2015/08/west-point-william-bradford/403009/>

45   Michael Walzer, 'Response to McMahan's paper', *Philosophia*, vol. 34, no. 1, 2006, p. 45.

46   Shannon E French, *The Code of the Warrior: Exploring Warrior Values Past and Present*, Rowman & Littlefield Publishers, Lanham, 2004, p. 3.

47   David Luban, 'The war on terrorism and the end of human rights', *Philosophy and Public Policy Quarterly*, vol. 22, 2002, p. 9.

48   Luban, 'The war on terrorism'.

49 Stephen C Neff, *War and the Law of Nations: A General History*, Cambridge University Press, Cambridge, 2005, p. 15.

50 Neff, *War and the Law of Nations*, 2005.

51 Geoffrey S Corn, Laurie R Blank, Chris Jenks and Eric Talbot Jensen, 'Belligerent targeting and the invalidity of a least harmful means rule', *International Law Studies*, no. 89, 2013, p. 537.

52 David Whetham, *Ethics, Law and Military Operations*, Palgrave Macmillan, Basingstoke, 2011, pp. 84–5.

53 James Turner Johnson, *Sovereignty: Moral and Historical Perspectives*, Georgetown University Press, Washington DC, 2014, p. 19.

14 What cyberweapons tell us about our just war

1 Many of these issues are covered in detail elsewhere. Peter W Singer and Allan Friedman's *Cybersecurity and Cyberwar: What Everyone Needs To Know*, Oxford University Press, Oxford, 2014 is a good introduction to the issues, and for more detail, see Fritz Allhoff, Adam Henschke and Bradley Jay Strawser (eds.), *Binary Bullets: The Ethics of Cyberwarfare*, Oxford University Press, Melbourne, 2016.

2 I recognise that this distinction between *jus in bello* and *jus ad bellum* is currently the focus of extensive academic debate. However, I maintain the traditional distinction here. For more on this, see Jeff McMahan, *Killing in War*, Clarendon Press, Oxford, 2009.

3 My emphases. See CAJ Coady, *Morality and Political Violence*, Cambridge University Press, Melbourne, 2008, p. 16.

4 Brian Orend, *The Ethics of War*, 2nd edition, University of Alberta, Vancouver, 2013, pp. 112–13.

5 Orend, *The Ethics of War*, 2013, p. 113.

6 For example, some put forward the argument that cyber-attacks which do not cause physical harm warrant moral attention due to the psychological harm that they can cause (see Daphna Canetti, Michael L Gross and Israel Manor-Waismel, 'Immune from cyberfire? the psychological and physiological effects of cyberwarfare', in Fritz Allhoff, Adam Henschke and Bradley Jay Strawser (eds.), *Binary Bullets: The Ethics of Cyberwarfare*, Oxford University Press, Melbourne, 2016, pp. 157–76). The point is, even limiting the direct impacts of cyber-attacks to the cyber-realm, non-physical impacts may still need to be considered in our assessment of the moral importance of such attacks.

7 Stephen Coleman, 'Possible ethical problems with military use of non-lethal weapons', *Case Western Reserve Journal of International Law*, vol. 47, Spring, 2015, pp. 185–99.

8 Stephen Coleman, 'Possible ethical problems', 2015.

9 My emphases. See Thomas Hurka, 'Proportionality in the morality of war', *Philosophy and Public Affairs*, vol. 33, no. 1, 2005, pp. 38–9.

10 Michael Walzer, *Just and Unjust Wars*, 4th edition, Basic Books, New York, 2006, p. 3.

11 Walzer, *Just and Unjust Wars*, pp. 3–20.

12 Thomas Hurka, 'Proportionality in the morality of war', p. 38.

13 Anthony Joseph Coates, *The Ethics of War*, Manchester University Press, Manchester, 1997, p. 214.

14 Bradley Jay Strawser, 'Moral predators: The duty to employ uninhabited aerial vehicles', *Journal of Military Ethics*, vol. 9, no. 4, 2010, p. 344.

15 Michael N Schmitt (ed.), *Tallinn Manual on the International Law Applicable to Cyber Warfare*, Cambridge University Press, Cambridge, 2013, p. 114.

16 Schmitt, *Tallinn Manual*, 2013, p. 113.

17   Schmitt, *Tallinn Manual*, 2013, p. 109.

18   Schmitt, *Tallinn Manual*, 2013, p. 109.

19   Schmitt, *Tallinn Manual*, 2013, p. 109.

20   Schmitt, *Tallinn Manual*, 2013, p. 110.

21   Furthermore, some critics might consider that my general theoretical position of moral pluralism is problematic. A consequentialist, for instance, would disagree with the position that the basic respect for human rights is inimical to consequentialism, see Philip Pettit, 'The consequentialist can recognise rights', *The Philosophical Quarterly*, vol. 38, no. 150, 1988, pp. 42–55. Likewise, a deontologist would disagree with the position that consequences should outweigh or 'trump' certain moral rules, see Ronald Dworkin, *Taking Rights Seriously*, Harvard University Press, Cambridge, 1978. These arguments and discussions about normative theory cannot be covered, much less resolved, here. Some good texts on moral pluralism and applied ethics are Tom L Beauchamp and James F Childress, *Principles of Biomedical Ethics*, 5th edition, Oxford University Press, Oxford, 2001; Albert R Jonsen and Stephen Edelston Toulmin, *The Abuse of Casuistry: A History of Moral Reasoning*, University of California Press, Berkeley, 1988; and James Sterba, *The Triumph of Practice Over Theory in Ethics*, Oxford University Press, Oxford, 2005. On the theoretical arguments surrounding them see Shelly Kagan, *Normative Ethics, Dimensions of Philosophy*, Westview Press, Boulder, 1998 and Derek Parfit, *On What Matters*, vol. 1, Oxford University Press, Oxford, 2011.

22   Seth Lazar, 'War' entry, *Stanford Encyclopedia of Philosophy* website, 2016 <plato.stanford.edu/archives/sum2016/entries/war/>

15   The Australian Defence Force and military ethics

1   Nick Jans, 'Academy cadets should be taught behavioural science', *Australian Defence Force Journal*, no. 59, July–August 1986.

2   Major General Craig Orme, *Beyond Compliance: Professionalism, Trust and Capability in the Australian Profession of Arms*, Report of the ADF Personal Conduct Review, Department of Defence, §25, 2011, p. 16.

3   *Pathway to Change: Evolving Defence Culture*, Department of Defence, 2012, p. 1. This report was itself a synthesis of six more specific inquiries into ADF culture, including *Beyond Compliance*.

4   See Stephen Coleman, 'The problem of duty and loyalty', *Journal of Military Ethics*, vol. 8, no. 2, 2009.

5   Orme, *Beyond Compliance*, §30, 2011, p. 17.

6   Orme, *Beyond Compliance*, §15, 2011, p. 14.

7   *Pathway to Change*, 2012, p. 3; *Beyond Compliance* sets out the arguments for this higher standard, §76–77, 2011, pp. 28–9.

8   Orme, *Beyond Compliance*, §14, 2011, p. 14.

9   See Richard Adams, 'Moral autonomy in Australian legislation and military doctrine', *Ethics & Global Politics*, vol. 6, no. 3, 2013 and Jessica Wolfendale, 'Professional integrity and disobedience in the military', *Journal of Military Ethics*, vol. 8, no. 2, 2009.

10   Prior to the 2003 Iraqi war the British Chief of Defence Staff sought a statement from his government justifying the approaching hostilities on the grounds that soldiers and their families ought to be reassured about the legal and moral rightness of risking their lives and taking those of others.

11   Tom McDermott, *Soldiers, Squadrons and Strategists*, Occasional Paper no. 1, Australian Centre for the Study of Armed Conflict and Society, UNSW Canberra, n.d., p. 10.

12	HR McMaster in Don Carrick, James Connelly, Paul Robinson (eds.), *Ethics Education for Irregular Warfare*, 2009, Ashgate, Aldershot, p. 15.

13	Carl von Clausewitz, *On War*, Princeton University Press, Princeton, 1976, p. 140.

14	See Tom Frame (ed.), *Moral Injury: Unseen Wounds in an Age of Barbarism*, UNSW Press, Sydney, 2015; Peter Marin, 'Living with moral pain', *Psychology Today*, November 1981.

15	See, for example, RC Smith, *Ethics and Informal War*, Vantage Press, New York, 1991 and Carrick et al. (eds.), *Ethics Education for Irregular Warfare*.

16	James Burk, 'Strategic assumptions and moral implications of the constabulary force', *Journal of Military Ethics*, vol. 4, no. 3, 2005.

17	Richard Adams, 'Moral autonomy', 2013, p. 150.

18	Alvin Toffler argues that in the information age the dominant source of wealth is not an individual's possessions but his knowledge, *The Third Wave*, Bantam Books, New York, 1981.

19	For a critical discussion see David Schmidtchen, 'Developing creativity and innovation through the practice of mission command', *Australian Defence Force Journal*, no. 146, January–February 2001.

20	Peter Olsthoorn, 'The ethics curriculum at the Netherlands Defence Academy, and some problems with its theoretical underpinnings' in Paul Robinson, Nigel de Lee and Don Carrick (eds.), *Ethics Education in the Military*, Ashgate, Aldershot, 2008, p. 125.

21	Paul Robinson, 'Introduction: Ethics education in the military' in Robinson et al. (eds.), *Ethics Education in the Military*, 2008, pp. 6–7. He points out that the Israeli Defence Force is perhaps unique in including 'respect for human life' as a value.

22	Orme, *Beyond Compliance*, §96–7, 2011, p. 34.

23	Orme, *Beyond Compliance*, §21, 2011, p. 15.

24	Jessica Wolfendale, 'What is the point of teaching ethics in the military?' in Robinson et al. (eds.), *Ethics Education in the Military*, 2008, p. 161.

25	Paul Robinson, 'Introduction: Ethics education in the military', in Robinson et al. (eds.), *Ethics Education in the Military*, 2008, p. 5.

26	Don Carrick, 'The future of ethics education in the military: A comparative analysis' in Robinson et al. (eds.), *Ethics Education in the Military*, 2008, p. 188.

27	See Jeffrey Wilson, 'An ethics curriculum for an evolving army' in Robinson et al. (eds.), *Ethics Education in the Military*, 2008, p. 32.

28	See Hugh Smith and Anthony Bergin, *Educating for the Profession of Arms in Australia*, Special Report no. 48, Australian Strategic Policy Institute, Canberra, August 2012, pp. 29–31.

29	Wolfendale, 'What is the point of teaching ethics in the military?', 2008, p. 169.

30	McDermott, *Soldiers, Squadrons and Strategists*, n.d., p. 6.

31	Paul Robinson, 'Introduction: Ethics Education in the Military', 2008, p. 9, referring to the British Army.

32	Colonel Yvon Desjardins, 'Canada's defence ethics program and ethics training' in Robinson et al. (eds.), *Ethics Education in the Military*, 2008, p. 75.

33	Martin Cook, 'Ethics education, ethics training, and character development: Who "owns" ethics in the US Air Force Academy?' in Robinson et al. (eds.), *Ethics Education in the Military*, 2008, p. 65.

34	Major General Maurie McNarn, presentation at 'Ethics Under Fire' conference, Australian Centre for the Study of Armed Conflict and Society, UNSW Canberra, 21 June 2016 (author's notes).

35	I can cite one example where my 'Legal and Moral Problems' course proved of practical value: an ADF officer who was assigned to United States headquarters in

the First Gulf War told me that my teaching about necessity, discrimination and
proportionality had greatly helped his contribution to targeting discussions.

36 Orme, *Beyond Compliance*, Annex A, 2011, p. 46.
37 Patrick Mileham, 'Teaching military ethics in the British Armed Forces' in Robinson
    et al. (eds.), *Ethics Education in the Military*, 2008, p. 47.
38 Nick Jans, 'The sorry state of military sociology in Australia', *Australian Defence Force
    Journal*, no. 175, January–February 2008.
39 Major General Craig Orme, *Beyond Compliance*, § 82, 2011, p. 30.
40 McDermott, *Soldiers, Squadrons and Strategists*, n.d., p. 6.

16 Military ethics education in the Army: An Achilles heel?

1   Dr Michael Ignatieff, address to the United States Naval Academy, Annapolis, 2001.
2   For example Australian Army Land Warfare Doctrine, LWD 0-2-2 Character, 2005.
3   Major General Stephen Day, 'Thoughts on generalship: Lessons from two wars', Army
    Research Papers, June 2015.
4   ADDP 00.7, Doctrine and Training, 2006, pp. 2–8.
5   Paul Robinson, Nigel de Lee and Don Carrick (eds.) *Ethics Education in the Military*,
    Ashgate, Aldershot, 2008.
6   Dr Hugh Smith, discussion with author, 2006.
7   James Toner, 'Mistakes in teaching ethics', *Aerospace Power Journal*, Summer, 1998,
    pp. 1–7.
8   Simon Longstaff, 'Ethical intelligence and fitness for command', Australian Defence
    College, 2004.
9   Nick Jans, 'Ethical dilemmas survey', Australian Defence College, 2008–2009.
10 Dr Bob Hall and Dr Andrew Ross, 'Confronting moral dilemmas in combat: Vietnam
    1966–1971', CDLE Papers, 1/2010.
11 Army officer interviewed by the author, 2008.
12 Special Forces officer interviewed by the author, 2014.
13 CDLE survey, Australian Defence College, 2011.
14 CDLE, Project Achilles, 2009–2012.
15 Dr Stephen Mugford, correspondence with the author, 31 July 2014.
16 Dean Ludwig and Clinton Longenecker, 'The Bathsheba syndrome: The ethical
    failure of successful leaders', *Journal of Business Ethics*, no. 12, 1993. The paper argues
    that many ethical violations by senior leaders are a by-product of success. This is an
    appropriate theme for reflection by the Army's senior ranks.
17 Defence Abuse Response Taskforce (DART), *Final Report*, March 2016.
18 *DART Report*, 2016, p. 6.

17 The practicalities of ethical accountability

1   Commonwealth of Australia, Australian Army, *Land Warfare Doctrine – 1, The
    Fundamentals of Land Power*, Canberra, 2014, p. 48.
2   Oxford Living Dictionaries, definition of 'ethics', Oxford Living Dictionaries website,
    2016 <www.oxforddictionaries.com/definition/english/ethics> Ethics are defined as:
    1. [usually treated as plural] Moral principles that govern a person's behaviour or the
    conducting of an activity: 'medical ethics also enter into the question'. 2. [usually
    treated as singular] The branch of knowledge that deals with moral principles: 'neither
    metaphysics nor ethics is the home of religion'.
3   *Land Warfare Doctrine – 1*, 2014, p. 52, my emphasis.
4   *Land Warfare Doctrine – 1*, 2014, p. 53, my emphasis.
5   *Land Warfare Doctrine – 1*, 2014, p. 53, my emphasis.
6   Oxford Living Dictionaries, definition of 'ethics', Oxford Living Dictionaries website,

2016 <www.oxforddictionaries.com/definition/english/ethics>.
7   Carl von Clausewitz, *On War*, Michael Howard and Peter Paret (eds.), Princeton University Press, Princeton, 1982, p. 120.
8   *Land Warfare Doctrine – 1*, 2014, p. 14.
9   *Land Warfare Doctrine – 1*, 2014, p. 14.
10   *Land Warfare Doctrine – 1*, 2014, p. 23.
11   *Land Warfare Doctrine – 1*, 2014, p. 51.
12   Eliot A Cohen, *Supreme Command: Soldiers, Statesmen, and Leadership in Wartime*, Free Press, New York, 2002, p. 241.
13   Cohen, *Supreme Command*, 2002, pp. 241–42.
14   Cohen, *Supreme Command*, 2002, p. 243.
15   Cohen, *Supreme Command*, 2002, p. 246.
16   Cohen, *Supreme Command*, 2002, p. 246.
17   *Land Warfare Doctrine – 1*, 2014, pp. 51–2.
18   *Land Warfare Doctrine – 1*, 2014, p. 7.
19   3rd Brigade, *100 Day Assessment*, Commonwealth of Australia, May 2016, pp. 10–11.
20   3rd Brigade, *100 Day Assessment*, p. 11.

18 Postscript

1   Lieutenant General Angus Campbell, 'Chief of Army address to the Army Logistic Training Centre Birthday and Banner Parade', Australian Army website, 3 December 2016 <www.army.gov.au/sites/g/files/net1846/f/speeches/20161203_ca_address_to_altc_parade_3_dec_16_final.pdf>.
2   Carl von Clausewitz, *On War*, Princeton University Press, Princeton, 1989, p. 87.
3   Seymour Hersh, 'Torture at Abu Ghraib', the *New Yorker*, 10 May 2004 <www.newyorker.com/magazine/2004/05/10/torture-at-abu-ghraib>.
4   Australian Army, 'Our values', Australian Army website <www.army.gov.au/our-people/our-values>.
5   Australian Army, 'Our contract with the Australian people', Australian Army website <www.army.gov.au/our-people/our-contract-with-australia>.
6   Chief of Army Address to the Lowy Institute, Australian Army website, 4 October 2016 <www.army.gov.au/sites/g/files/net1846/f/speeches/20161004_ca_address_lowy_institute_4_oct_16_edited_1500_4_oct.pdf> accessed 12 February 2016.
7   Brigadier Mick Ryan, *The Ryan Review: A Study of Army's Education, Training and Doctrine Needs for the Future*, April 2016 <www.army.gov.au/sites/g/files/net1846/f/2016_05_dgt_theryanreview_web.pdf>.

INDEX

248, 251 *see also jus in bello* (right
conduct in war)
    education in 278
    ethics alongside 30–31, 110
    national army values 46
international law
    applicability to non-Western nations
      30
    ethics that aligns with 26
    interference in the affairs of sovereign
      nations 8–9
    not applicable to cyberwar 222–223
international NGOs *see* Non-Government
Organisations
International Rescue Committee 142
International Security Assistance Force
    (ISAF) 140
internet *see* social media
intra-state warfare 14
Iraq 42
    Baghdad, entry to 65
    distortion effect 67
    ethics in invasion of 34–35, 40–41
    selective conscientious objection 122–
      123, 126–128, 130
    use of 'mother of all bombs' ('MOAB')
      proposed 65–66
ISIS (Islamic State in Iraq and Syria) 24, 28
    individualisation of conflict 179
    non-adherence to international codes
      30
    social media and 215
Islam *see* Muslim ethics
Islamic State in Iraq and Syria *see* ISIS

J

al-Janabi, Abeer Qasim Hamza 37
Jans, Nick 245
Jewish ethics 107
Johnson, James 202, 225
Jonathan Church ethical soldier award 277
Jones, LS Terence 126–127, 130
Journal of Military Ethics 92–93
journalists *see* media
judicial function of war 225
Juengst, Eric 183
jus ad bellum (right to wage war) 172, 180,
    199, 224, 229, 252
jus in bello (right conduct in war) 172,
    199, 224, 227, 229–230, 234, 252
    see also discrimination; International

Humanitarian Law of Armed Conflict;
    proportionality
    cyberwarfare 230–238
    incommensurable values 239
Just and Unjust Wars (Walzer) 92, 234
just war theory 14, 25–26, 28, 46, 172, 234
    annual roundtable on proposed
      132–133
    cyberweapons and 227–230
    enhanced human performance and
      184–185
    'good' versus 'bad' wars 57
    individualisation of conflict and
      176–177
    non-conventional challenges 222–225
    pluralistic doctrine 240–241
    rule-oriented ethics 110
    six principles from 57, 59, 63
    symmetry status 177, 219
    unjust peace to just war 186–187

K

Kagame, Paul 73, 79
Kaldor, Mary 218
Kant, Immanuel 191, 281–282, 287
Kaplan, Stephen 221
Keating, MAJ GEN Michael 55–56
Keegan, John 40
Kendall-Smith, FLT LT Malcolm 122–123
killing, reflecting on 273
knowledge, belief systems and 115
Kohlberg, Lawrence 268
Kutz, Christopher 219
Kuwait, waiting for war in 34–35, 40–41

L

*Land Warfare Doctrine – 1, The
    Fundamentals of Land Power, 2014*
    281–282
language of ethics and values 132, 270, 278
law, relationship to ethics 7, 30–31, 248
law enforcement operations 256
Law of Armed Conflict *see* International
    Humanitarian Law of Armed Conflict
The Laws of War (Reisman and Antoniou)
    23
lawyers 26, 95
Lazar, Seth 240
leadership 15–16, 267
    ethical behaviour 116–117, 258, 269,
      272

www.ingramcontent.com/pod-product-compliance
Ingram Content Group UK Ltd.
Pitfield, Milton Keynes, MK11 3LW, UK
UKHW020852250126
467228UK00007B/376